ASE Guide to Primary Science Education

New Edition

Edited by Wynne Harlen

The Association for Science Education
Promoting Excellence in Science Teaching and Learning

Published by:
The Association for Science Education, College Lane, Hatfield, Herts AL10 9AA

© The Association for Science Education 2011
Reprinted 2013

All rights reserved. The Association for Science Education is pleased to allow purchasing institutions to copy pages from this book for their own use provided that copyright of the Association for Science Education is acknowledged. Permission in writing from the Association for Science Education is required for any other form of reproduction.

ISBN: 978 0 86357 427 6

Design and page layout: Commercial Campaigns

Printed by: Ashford Colour Press, Gosport, Hampshire

Contents

About the authors v

Introduction – *Wynne Harlen* ix

Section 1 Learning in science at the primary level

1. Why is learning science important in primary schools?
   – *Wynne Harlen* 2
2. How are children learning? – *Sally Howard* 10
3. Progression in learning science – *Terry Russell* 17
4. Learning in the Early Years – *Jane Johnston* 25
5. Learning and the brain: insights from neuroscience – *Wynne Harlen* ...34

Section 2 Teaching primary science

6. Planning: elements of an effective lesson plan – *Rosemary Feasey* 44
7. Science within cross-curricular approaches
   – *Lynne Bianchi and Penny Thompson* 53
8. Using ICT in teaching and learning science – *Anne Qualter* 61
9. Effective questions – *Anne Goldsworthy* 69
10. Promoting understanding through dialogue
    – *Debbie Eccles and Simon Taylor* 77
11. Formative feedback and self-assessment – *Kathy Schofield* 85
12. Developing interest in science through emotional engagement
    – *Paul McCrory* 94
13. Creativity in teaching science – *Brenda Keogh and Stuart Naylor* 102
14. Using and serving the environment – *Carolyn Yates* 111
15. Assessing Pupils' Learning – *David Brodie* 119

Section 3 Provision for science at the school level

16 School-level planning – *David Simon* 126
17 The science subject leader – *Liz Lawrence* 133
18 Continuing professional development and the role of
    Science Learning Centres – *Jane Turner* 141
19 Points of transfer – *Martin Braund* and *Kathy Schofield* 149
20 Human resources to support primary science – *Joy Parvin* 157

Section 4 The national and international context

21 What are we teaching? Science curricula across the UK
    – *Wynne Harlen, Peter McAlister, Barbara Harrison,
    Philippa Minto* and *Nancy Bilderbeck* 166
22 How good is our science teaching? – *Wynne Harlen* 178
23 What are children achieving? – *Wynne Harlen* 186
24 What happens in other countries? – *Wynne Harlen and Tina Jarvis* ...195

Index 204

About the authors

Lynne Bianchi is a Senior Research Fellow at the Centre for Science Education, Sheffield Hallam University. Her work focuses on curriculum development in primary and secondary science, specialising in enhancing children's personal capabilities. She regularly works with schools on innovative projects and is inspired by the creative responses of teachers and their pupils.

Nancy Bilderbeck is a primary teacher and a member of the Primary Science, Publications and London Committees of the ASE. She was a winner of the AstraZeneca Science Teaching Trust/TES Primary Science Teacher of the Year award in 2004.

Martin Braund is Honorary Fellow at the University of York and Adjunct Professor at the Cape Peninsula University of Technology in South Africa. He has been a classroom teacher, advisory teacher, researcher and teacher trainer. He has published several research papers and a book (*Starting Science ... Again,* 2008) about primary–secondary transfer in science.

David Brodie is former Head of Science in a Midlands comprehensive school and a senior examiner. He has worked with bodies such as the British Science Association to popularise science and has published several books. He is currently a Royal Literary Fund Writing Fellow at Aberystwyth University, and a consultant in training and assessment with a special interest in visual communication skills.

Debbie Eccles works as an independent consultant in primary science and is a founder member of *Primarily Science.*

Rosemary Feasey is a freelance primary science consultant. She was the first person from a primary background to become Chair of the ASE. Rosemary has written numerous books on primary science and is also a BAFTA nominee for her work on the BBC2 *Just So Darwin* series.

Anne Goldsworthy taught for 13 years in a variety of primary schools and has run her own science education consultancy business since 1995. She was a leading member of the AKSIS research project and has written numerous articles and books including *Science Enquiry Games* (2007) and *New Star Science* (2001).

During a long career in education, **Wynne Harlen** has been a teacher, researcher and professor of science education. She was editor of *Primary Science Review* from 1999 to 2004 and President of the ASE in 2009. She is involved in many international projects and was awarded the Purkwa International Prize in 2008.

Barbara Harrison taught for 12 years in a middle school in Leeds before moving to West Scotland as a primary classroom teacher. She now teaches science throughout the school. Over the last few years she has become increasingly involved within the work of ASE, both north and south of the border.

Sally Howard was a primary headteacher and is now a senior lecturer at Nottingham Trent University and an independent educational consultant. She co-authored the Assessment for Learning book *Inside the Primary Black Box* (2008) with Christine Harrison and has a keen interest in the development of teaching and learning.

Tina Jarvis is a Professor at the University of Leicester. She is an experienced teacher trainer, publisher of articles, books and teacher support material. She was the coordinator of the UK centre in Leicester of the EU project, *Pollen: Seed cities for science* and is now a coordinator of the *Fibonacci* Project, which aims to develop and implement a process of dissemination in Europe of enquiry-based teaching and learning methods in science and mathematics.

Jane Johnston is a Reader in Education and Academic Coordinator for the MA in Education at Bishop Grosseteste College. Her passion for Early Years science and the belief that effective research is that which impacts on practice and provision are reflected in her publications and her status of Chartered Science Teacher.

Brenda Keogh started her career as a primary teacher. She has also worked as a lab technician, advisory teacher and National Curriculum consultant. **Stuart Naylor** started his career as a secondary teacher. He has also worked as a laboratory technician and advisory teacher and has taught in the USA. Brenda and Stuart both have extensive experience in teacher education and as researchers, writers, publishers, consultants and INSET providers. Now working as Millgate House Education, they have a reputation for innovative publications, thought-provoking CPD and creative ways of enhancing teaching, learning and assessment.

Liz Lawrence spent 14 years as a primary teacher, subject coordinator and senior leader before becoming an advisory teacher for primary science and technology in Barking and Dagenham. She is an active local ASE member and Chair of ASE Primary Science Committee.

Peter McAlister was a primary teacher for 14 years before taking up the post of Science Adviser for the South Eastern Education and Library Board (SEELB). He is a member of the ASE Primary Science Committee and is treasurer of the local Northern Ireland ASE Committee.

Paul McCrory is a science education consultant. He manages *Think Differently*, an education consultancy, and provides training for science teachers and informal educators. His current research is exploring how teachers can emotionally engage pupils in the science classroom.

Having completed a degree and PhD in Chemistry, **Philippa Minto** worked as a research chemist before becoming a primary teacher. She is currently a member of the ASE Primary Science Committee.

Joy Parvin is the director of the Chemical Industry Education Centre. She has worked for over 20 years in primary science education as a teacher and author of teaching and learning resources and CPD. Much of her work focuses on contextualising scientific enquiry, and supporting teachers to develop confidence, think creatively, and have fun teaching primary science.

Anne Qualter is Head of Educational Development at the University of Liverpool. She has been active in researching, writing and teaching about primary science for almost 30 years, focusing on assessment, children's learning and how good teachers support and promote excitement for science learning in young children.

Terry Russell is an education professor and Director of the Centre for Research in Primary Science and Technology in the Centre for Life-long Learning at the University of Liverpool. His particular interest is in cognitive developmental psychology applied to design-based research in curriculum and assessment.

Kathy Schofield taught in primary schools for many years before becoming Senior Lecturer for Primary Science at Manchester Metropolitan University. Her role includes providing primary professional development at the Science Learning Centre North West. She is currently Chair of ASE NW committee, a member of Primary Science Committee and of the Primary Science Editorial Board.

David Simon is Headteacher of Ditchling (St Margaret's) CE Primary School in East Sussex. He is a long-standing member of the Surrey and Sussex committee and has just completed six years as their Council representative. He has served on the Registration Board since its inception, trying to ensure that Chartered Status is available and relevant to primary teachers.

Simon Taylor is an Education Change Partner in Knowsley MBC.

Penny Thompson taught in Sheffield primary schools for ten years before becoming a Primary Professional Development Leader at the Centre for Science Education, Sheffield Hallam University.

Jane Turner is Associate Director at the Science Learning Centre East of England where she leads the Primary Science Quality Mark project. She is also an author and consultant with Millgate House Education. A commitment to exciting and enriching science teaching and learning in primary schools underpins her work as a teacher, CPD provider, researcher, curriculum developer and author.

Originally trained as a biologist, **Carolyn Yates** has been a teacher in primary and secondary schools, a teacher trainer, an education researcher, author and curriculum developer. She is currently a Literature Development Officer. With Professors Shayer and Adey, she developed the Cognitive Acceleration model. Through the Department for International Development (DFID), she has supported education reform and teacher development in the Middle East and Pakistan.

Introduction

In the five years since the publication of the last Association for Science Education (ASE) Guide to Primary Science Education there have been changes and challenges across the landscape of primary education, which have had particular consequences for science. The primary curriculum has been under review in all four countries of the UK, each identifying the content and position of science in the curriculum in a different way. Changes are in the process of being implemented in Northern Ireland, Scotland and Wales but after the change in government in May 2010 the proposals in the Rose Review in England were rejected by the new Department for Education. Decisions have been taken to end testing in science in Wales and England, leaving some uncertainty as to how the functions that these tests served are to be undertaken in the future. There has also been a comprehensive review of primary education in England in the form of the Cambridge Primary Review (CPR), going beyond the curriculum, which is likely to have implications in other countries and for many years to come.

In the classroom, change has been a regular feature of education, as reflected in this book, and looks set to continue. To mention just a few areas: the use of interactive whiteboards by teachers and pupils has become almost routine, with tablets and hand-held computers and computer-based sensors no longer a novelty; formative assessment has been widely accepted and many aspects such as sharing goals, feedback and pupil self-assessment are seen as valuable aspects of practice even if circumstances sometimes inhibit their implementation; the value of dialogue and argumentation is also endorsed; the nature of enquiry in science is beginning to be seen more in terms of what children are learning and not just what they are doing. Many of these changes have a firm basis in research, even though this may not always be recognised.

Change provides opportunities for improving science education, but also presents challenges and a need for professional development that is genuinely 'continuing'. Broader, less prescriptive national curricula and guidelines, as in the changes taking place in Northern Ireland, Scotland and Wales, although to be welcomed, place greater responsibility on schools' long- and medium-term planning and teachers' subject knowledge is an ongoing area where help is needed. The CPR acknowledges that *'in terms of the range and depth of knowledge required by a modern curriculum it may demand more than many teachers can give'* and proposes a full review of ways of staffing primary schools, including how subject specialists are used (CPR, 2010, p3). So we are in no way likely to see less turbulence in the near future than there has been in the recent past.

About this Guide

The ASE is publishing two other Guides as companions to this book. They are:

- a further edition of the *ASE Guide to Secondary Science Education*
- a new publication, the *ASE Guide to Research in Science Education*.

All three guides are written for everyone concerned with the practice of science education: teachers, teaching assistants, Early Years practitioners, student teachers, teacher educators and those with responsibility for science in the school. This book is concerned particularly with learning and teaching, planning and programme development at the class and school level in primary schools. It focuses on critical discussion of a range of professional ideas and practices that have a firm evidential base, although without the more detailed review of research that is to be found in the parallel Guide on research. It is not expected that this book be read from cover to cover at any one time. It is meant as a resource to dip into at appropriate times. To help this process, each chapter begins with an introduction indicating its content and ends with a conclusion summarising some main points.

All the material here has been written for this new edition of the guide. Four chapters here have close parallels in the *ASE Guide to Secondary Science Education*, with appropriate differences in examples and references to the school context. The authors are members of the ASE and have wide experience in and commitment to the development of primary science education, as can be seen from the notes about the authors on pages v–vii. I am immensely grateful to them for their willingness to add to the demands on their time by sharing their expertise in these chapters.

As in the last edition of the Guide, the chapters are arranged in four sections, beginning in this edition with the process of learning. The section opens with a chapter that repeats what is already known to those in education but seems to have been forgotten by those with responsibility for its governance. The gradual downgrading of the importance of science at the primary level has to be halted by reinforcing the case for its key role. This is followed by chapters that describe the process of learning science, particularly through enquiry, and the course of progression in ideas and skills. The growing attention to children's learning through interaction with everyday scientific phenomena in the Early Years is included here. The section ends with a brief view into another area of growing interest in relation to learning – the insights that neuroscience can offer.

The second and largest section is about teaching. Chapters here are concerned with aspects of lesson planning, including the use of ICT, the pros and cons of cross-curricular topics and how to make use of the school environment and develop children's ideas about it. Key elements of teaching for engagement of children, through questioning and promoting talk and dialogue are discussed. Rather than dealing with Assessment for Learning as a separate approach, there is a chapter on how its key components of feedback and self-assessment can be integrated into teaching. Two chapters look at how to teach to develop an affective response to science: whether – and, if so, how – to 'make science fun', and how to be creative in teaching. Finally, there is a chapter on assessment of pupils' learning by teachers using the Assessing Pupils' Progress approach developed in England.

In the third section, the focus moves to the school level: the consideration of the policy for science and planning for continuity and progress in the school programme. Much of this work falls upon the school science subject leader but the involvement of all teachers has added importance in the context of the new curricula in Northern Ireland, Scotland and Wales, which leave decisions about content to schools to decide, particularly for the early primary years. Schools in England, while continuing to use the National Curriculum revised in 1999, have become less dependent on the scheme of work devised by the QCA. The implications for CPD are discussed in a chapter describing the opportunities available and how to ensure maximum benefit from them. Preparing pupils to move into secondary school is a continuing challenge but this is only one point of transition in primary children's progress that is discussed in a chapter on transfer. The final chapter in this section discusses the role of various adults in providing enrichment for pupils and help for teachers in supporting learning in science.

The fourth section looks at primary science from the perspective of national policy and international practice. It begins with a review of the curricula in the four countries of the UK, showing how divergent these have become in several respects, although all emphasise the development of numeracy, literacy and ICT and other skills across the curriculum. There is discussion of how schools can evaluate and give an account of their work and how they are improving it. Other chapters review the trends in attainment of pupils as measured by national tests and what is known about how attitudes to science change in the primary years. The final chapter takes a more global perspective, reflecting the intense interest in primary school science across the world and various approaches to solving shared problems of implementation. International cooperation is a feature of developments in Europe and in many parts of the world, opening up alternatives and showing how to support teachers and schools in different contexts, from which we in the UK can only benefit.

Wynne Harlen
2010

Reference

CPR (Cambridge Primary Review) (2010) *Policy Priorities for Primary Education.* Cambridge Review Briefings. Cambridge: University of Cambridge.

Section 1

Learning in science at the primary level

Chapter 1

Why is learning science important in primary schools?

Wynne Harlen

A UNESCO document published 20 years ago was able to claim that the 'the case for beginning science in the pre-secondary years has been accepted universally for some years' (Morris, 1990). Yet in 2010 it appears that primary science has been demoted in status, largely by the increased emphasis on numeracy and literacy, and is no longer regarded as a core subject of the primary curriculum.

The Cambridge Primary Review, noting the impact on science of the national strategies in England, concluded that '*Science is far too important to both a balanced education and the nation's future to be allowed to decline in this way*' (Alexander, 2010, p493). Ironically, the ending of the Key Stage 2 national testing in science in England, although long criticised for distorting science teaching and learning in the final year(s) of the primary school, is also seen as a symptom of science being devalued.

All this suggests that we may have lost sight of the reasons for children learning science throughout the primary school and the implications for the way in which it is taught. So it seems appropriate to begin this section of the book, on learning science, by reminding ourselves of the answer to the question in the title of this chapter. The starting point is the prior question, of why learning science is important at *any* stage, before turning to the reasons for beginning in the primary years. This concerns the importance of laying the foundations for the development of scientific ideas, enquiry skills, attitudes and learning how to learn. The final section of the chapter faces some obstacles to teaching in the way that will achieve these firm foundations.

Why learn science at all?

Reasons fall under two main headings: value to the individual and value to society. For learners as individuals, science education helps them to:

- understand aspects of the world around them, both the natural environment and that created through application of science – not only does this serve to satisfy and at the same time to stimulate curiosity, but it helps in personal choices affecting their health and enjoyment of the environment as well as their choice of career
- develop learning skills that they will need throughout life in order to continue learning and operate effectively in a world that changes rapidly (Box 1)
- develop attitudes towards science and towards the use of evidence in making decisions as informed citizens, to reject quackery and to recognise when evidence is being used selectively to support arguments in favour of particular actions.

Box 1   Skills for learning throughout life

> *'Students cannot learn in school everything they will need to know in adult life. What they must acquire is the prerequisites for successful learning in future life. These prerequisites are of both a cognitive and a motivational nature. Students must become able to organise and regulate their own learning, to learn independently and in groups, and to overcome difficulties in the learning process. This requires them to be aware of their own thinking processes and learning strategies and methods.'*
>
> OECD (1999, p9)

For society, the benefits of education in science of all citizens follow from:

- individuals and groups making more informed choices in relation to avoiding, for instance, waste of energy and resources, pollution, and the consequences of poor diet, lack of exercise and use of drugs
- citizens being scientifically literate, understanding the factors that need to be taken into account in decisions about, for example, food and energy supply, and reducing greenhouse gases
- ensuring that there is a sufficient supply of future scientists and technologists.

Only the last of these requires the specialised deep knowledge of the practising scientist or technologist. For the other benefits – for individuals and society – the understanding needed is the grasp of some basic ideas of and about science, which are wrapped up in the concept of scientific literacy. In this context, 'literacy' means being able to engage effectively with different aspects of modern life, having the knowledge and skills that are needed by everyone, not just those who will be specialists or make a career using knowledge in some area of science. It requires a general understanding of the main or key ideas of science, the nature and limitations of science and the processes of science, and the capacity to use these ideas in making decisions as an informed and concerned citizen.

Achieving such outcomes requires considerable changes in the pupils' learning experiences, away from accumulating large amounts of factual knowledge and towards experiences that develop skills, attitudes and understanding. For example, much content knowledge can now be readily found from information sources through the use of computers; learners need the skills to access these sources with discrimination, to select what is relevant and make sense of it.

Learning in science at the primary level

Why start in the primary school?

The reasons for learning science and for changing the way it is taught leave open the question of why science education should start at the primary school. The answers that used to be given included claims, for example, that it promoted 'intellectual development' and can be 'real fun' (UNESCO, 1983), based on aspirations and a few inspirational projects. These claims were too insubstantial (everyone wants science to be 'fun', but is that enough justification?) to resist the strong moves that regularly sweep across primary education behind a 'back to basics' banner. In contrast, we now have firm research evidence that learning science in the primary years has a significant role in the development of scientific understanding, enquiry skills, attitudes and skills of learning. We now look briefly at this evidence.

Developing scientific ideas

The evidence that children are arriving at their own ideas in the early years, whether or not there is science in the curriculum, is a powerful argument for ensuring that they explore and enquire in a way that promotes the development of reliable knowledge and basic science concepts. We are now in no doubt that children develop ideas about the scientific aspects of the world around them whether or not they are taught science (Osborne and Freyberg, 1985; SPACE, 1990–98). Children's own ideas are often in conflict with scientific ones and, if taken into the secondary school, they can inhibit effective learning (Driver, 1983). For example, children's reasoning and experience alone often lead to the following view, expressed by a nine-year-old, of the function of the leaves and roots of plants:

> 'The plant will need leaves to get air. It will need roots to collect food and water from the soil and the stem to carry the food to the flower.'
>
> SPACE Report, *Growth* (1990, p22)

Although this is an advance on a common idea that the soil is no more than an anchor for the plant, there is no suggestion here that the leaves have a role in nutrition. Thus, study of photosynthesis in secondary science is likely to be seen as confusing and not related to how the child makes sense of plants. This is not an argument for introducing photosynthesis in the primary school – rather for the more systematic exploration of a range of plants growing in different conditions, leading to a more discriminating view of the functions of roots, leaves and stems. Realising that light and air as well as water are needed for healthy plants raises questions about how these help a plant to grow – questions to which children will find answers in their later studies in the secondary school. In this way, the exploratory approach opens minds for later study.

A key aim of scientific literacy for all is the development of 'big' ideas, meaning ones that are widely applicable and enable a grasp of situations where they apply. Examples are that '*all material is made of very small particles*' and that '*energy is needed to make things happen*'. Although such ideas seem remote from primary children's grasp, nevertheless the foundation for later development can be laid in their early experiences. These 'big' ideas cannot be taught directly; they are necessarily highly abstract and indeed meaningless if they do not evoke the many real situations that they link together. For example, if children develop, through investigation and observation, an understanding that there is interdependence among plants and animals in their own environment – their back garden, the park, the stream or the hedgerow – they may eventually understand the reasons for protecting the rain forests. But if the big issues relating to conservation are the starting points, they may be understood at no greater depth than slogans and the relationships never more than superficially grasped. So the 'big' ideas (so called because they explain a range of related phenomena) have to be created from 'small' ones, developed through understanding specific events familiar to the children. The role of science at the primary level is therefore to lay a foundation of experiences, and ideas about them, that can later be built into the broader understandings characterising scientific literacy.

Developing enquiry skills

The importance of the development of enquiry skills follows from the way children develop understanding. When children are developing their ideas through their own thinking, the outcome will depend on the nature of the thinking. The first reaction of anyone encountering a new phenomenon is to use ideas from earlier related experience to try to explain what is observed (that is, developing a hypothesis). There may be several ideas that come to mind and could provide an explanation. Some ideas may be eliminated through discussion with others who bring different previous experience to bear; other ideas will require new information to be sought in order to test whether they really provide an explanation. An idea is tested by using it to make a prediction ('*if this is the reason, then it follows that …*'). New information can be sought in various ways – for instance, though a practical investigation involving the manipulation of objects or through consulting appropriate sources such as books, people, the internet and other reference material.

The new evidence may not agree with the prediction and so not support the initial hypothesis, in which case an alternative explanation needs to be sought. This is an important learning experience, since without the new evidence, learners would continue to think that their earlier ideas would apply. When new evidence does support the initial idea then that idea becomes strengthened because it then explains the new phenomenon as well as earlier experience. In this way ideas move from being 'small' (explaining just a particular event) to being 'bigger' since they explain a greater number of events. Understanding is built through this activity, which depends crucially on the enquiry skills used, how predictions are made, what evidence is collected and how it is interpreted.

If the ways of thinking are non-scientific, then it can be expected that non-scientific ideas will be formed. Indeed, this is the case when children bring to the classroom ideas formed as result of 'everyday' reasoning. When children observe events they may focus on certain aspects that confirm their ideas, leaving out of account evidence that might challenge them. They sometimes make 'predictions' that they already know to be true and so are not a test of an idea. In setting up a test they may not control variables that should be kept constant. In other words, the way in which these processes are carried out crucially influences the ideas that emerge – hence the importance of developing enquiry skills.

Developing attitudes

Attitudes are usually taken as describing a person's state of being prepared or predisposed to act in a certain way in relation to particular objects or situations. In the context of science education it is useful to distinguish between two kinds:

- attitudes *towards* science – made evident in the liking for, interest in and confidence in learning science (Chapter 12)
- attitudes *of* science, part of engaging in scientific activity – made evident in open-mindedness and willingness to consider evidence as well as to change ideas in the light of new evidence.

Learning in science at the primary level

Attitudes towards science are usually measured by asking people to say how much they agree or disagree with statements about liking or disliking specific activities, rather than through observation of behaviours that indicate certain dispositions. Often the statements are in written form, as in the international survey of science and mathematics (TIMSS) in 2007, where responses to three statements ('*I enjoy learning science*', '*Science is boring*' and '*I like science*') were used to assign pupils to levels of positive feelings towards science (Mullis et al., 2008). Attitudes measured in this way for children at different ages appear to show that feelings about science form early but gradually decline with age (Murphy and Beggs, 2003). Some of this decline may be due to a general pattern for pupils' attitude towards most school subjects to become less positive with age (Tymms et al., 2008) but it will also be due to their experience of science at school and influenced by myths and hearsay about science.

Surprisingly, the relationship between attitudes and achievement is, at most, weak (Chapter 23). Nevertheless attitudes to science are important because they influence the way in which the study of the natural world is approached and, very likely, pupils' decisions about continued study of the subject. To develop positive attitudes towards science, it is important for pupils to experience scientific activity, to develop and use enquiry skills in answering some of their own questions about things around them (Rocard et al., 2007). Through this essential starting experience they can begin to reflect on the questions that can and cannot be answered by scientific investigation and the kinds of conclusions that can and cannot be drawn from certain kinds of evidence.

Scientific attitudes, or attitudes *of* science, describe willingness to act in a scientific way, particularly towards the use of evidence. They are generalised aspects of behaviour and are developed through a range of experiences in which respect for evidence is shown (Box 2).

Box 2 Developing scientific attitudes

'An attitude of willingness to take account of evidence does not result from a single activity or even several activities around a topic. Instead it may result from extended experience in which the value of using evidence has been clear or from the example over a period of time of someone who showed this attitude in their behaviour. In other words ... they are 'caught' rather than 'taught', particularly from influential adults. Thus showing an example of the behaviour in practice is a key action that teachers can take. Others are: providing opportunity for children to make the choices that enable them to develop attitudes; reinforcing positive attitudes; and discussing attitude-related behaviour.'

Harlen and Qualter (2009, p138)

Learning how to learn

The skills involved in learning how to learn are different from those used in learning subject matter. They are more like attitudes, in that they result from a range of experiences, with the addition of reflection on how learning took place in these experiences. Those with these skills will be able to take responsibility for their learning and become autonomous learners, a key aim of education in a rapidly changing world. The notion of being autonomous and reflective may seem rather distant from the concerns of primary education but, as for all complex goals, there is an essential foundation to be laid at this stage. What is needed for this foundation is close to the aims of formative assessment – for instance, children being aware of the goals of learning, receiving feedback that shows them how to move forward and being able to assess their progress towards their learning goals (Chapter 11). Science makes a valuable contribution to this learning, since children can be helped to recognise the ideas they have at a particular time and how these ideas may have changed. The skills of enquiry used in bring about the change can be identified and discussed. Realising the kind of thinking needed for this learning is an important contribution to realising that different kinds of thinking are required in other domains of knowledge.

Experiences for learning science

Putting together the various points made above about development of understanding, enquiry skills, attitudes and the skills of learning at the primary level, suggests that pupils should have, over a period of time but not necessarily in every activity, the kinds of the experiences listed in Box 3.

Box 3 Pupils' experiences and activities for learning science

- engaging in observation and, where possible, handling and manipulating real objects
- expressing their ideas and considering what evidence is needed to test them
- working collaboratively with others, communicating their own ideas and considering others' ideas
- expressing themselves using appropriate scientific terms and representations in writing and talk
- pursuing questions that they have identified as their own, even if introduced by the teacher
- taking part in planning investigations with appropriate controls to answer specific questions
- using and developing skills of gathering data directly by observation or measurement and by using secondary sources
- using and developing skills of interpreting data, reasoning, proposing explanations, making predictions based on what they think or find out
- applying their learning in real-life contexts
- reflecting self-critically about the processes and outcomes of their enquiries.

adapted from IAP (2006)

Obstacles to learning science in the primary school

There is a growing body of research evidence to support the value of the activities in Box 3 and the importance of learning in this way is supported worldwide by organisations such as the OECD, The InterAcademies Panel (IAP), the European Commission and the National Research Council in the USA. So why do we find children learning in a much more passive way and teachers frustrated by circumstances that prevent them teaching in the way many know would better serve children's scientific development and which they would prefer?

Surveys of teachers have been conducted in many different countries to reveal primary teachers' perceptions of the obstacles to teaching science through enquiry and investigations.

Learning in science at the primary level

They consistently find the main factors to be:
- teachers' confidence in their grasp of the subject matter
- external tests that require only factual knowledge
- inadequate space and resources
- shortage of time
- an overcrowded curriculum, lacking progression in the development of ideas and skills
- large classes
- lack of teaching assistants.

There is a striking recurrence of these problems in all countries. Wherever teachers are expected to teach all subjects, many feel the need for more resources and support in the classroom if they are to do more than give text-based instruction. Wherever there are high stakes tests, there is direct teaching to the content of what is tested and enquiry-based teaching is rare. Wherever teachers have large classes, they may be overwhelmed by the difficulties of managing practical and group work and resort to whole-class teaching and demonstrations. Wherever teachers lack a personal understanding of enquiry, they focus on the 'doing' rather than the thinking that is needed to develop understanding. These problems combine to reduce children's role to that of passive receivers and not active agents in their learning. Hopefully, by being aware of these problems and sharing solutions, as in the chapters of this book, the value of learning science will become so obvious that the question posed in the title of this chapter becomes redundant.

In conclusion

Reviewing the case for science in the primary school highlights its importance for the development of scientific understanding, attitudes and skills. Although there is firm evidence and widespread agreement as to the activities and experiences children need in order to realise the benefits of primary science, there are obstacles to implementation. To overcome these obstacles and derive the full benefit of science education in the primary school there needs to be greater priority given to:

- the provision of continuing professional development to support teachers' confidence and increase their subject knowledge
- ensuring help within the school
- guidance on progression in the curriculum
- removing the negative pressure of high stakes testing.

References

Alexander, R. (2010) *Children, their World, their Education*. London: Routledge.

Driver, R. (1983) *The Pupil as Scientist?* Milton Keynes: Open University Press.

Harlen, W. and Qualter, A. (2009) *The Teaching of Science in Primary Schools*. London: David Fulton.

IAP (2006) *Report of the Working Group on International Collaboration in the Evaluation of IBSE Programs*. Santiago, Chile: Fundación para Estudios Biomédicos Avanzados de la Facultad de Medicina, University of Santiago.

Morris, R. (1990) *Science Education Worldwide*. Paris: UNESCO.

Mullis, I.V.S., Martin, M.O. and Foy, P. (with Olson, J.F., Preuschoff, C., Erberber, E., Arora, A. and Galia, J.) (2008) *TIMSS 2007 International Science Report: Findings from IEA's Trends in International Mathematics and Science Study at the Fourth and Eighth Grades*. Chestnut Hill, MA: TIMSS and PIRLS International Study Center, Boston College.

Murphy, C. and Beggs, J. (2003) Pupils' attitudes towards school science. *School Science Review*, **84**(308), 109–116.

OECD (1999) *Measuring Student Knowledge and Skills*. OECD Programme for International Student Assessment (PISA). Paris: OECD.

Osborne, R. and Freyberg, P. (1985) *Learning in Science: the Implications of 'Children's Science'*. Auckland: Heinemann.

Rocard, M., Csermely, P., Jorde, D., Lenzen, D. and Walberg-Henriksson, V. (2007) *Science Education Now: A Renewed Pedagogy for the Future of Europe*. Brussels: EC Directorate for Research (Science, Economy and Society).

SPACE Reports (1990–1998) Titles include: *Evaporation and condensation* (1990), *Light* (1990), *Growth* (1990), *Electricity* (1991), *Materials* (1991), *Processes of life* (1992), *Rocks, soil and weather* (1993), *Earth in space* (1996), *Forces* (1998). Liverpool: University of Liverpool Press.

Tymms, P., Bolden, D. and Merrell, C. (2008) Science in English primary schools: trends in attainment, attitudes and approaches. *Perspectives on Education 1* (primary science), 19–42. Available online at www.wellcome.ac.uk/perspectives

UNESCO (1983) *New Trends in Primary Science Education*. Paris: UNESCO.

Chapter 2

How are children learning?

Sally Howard

How teachers choose to teach is influenced by their understanding of how children learn. Current views of learning favour an enquiry-based approach to science education in which children construct their understanding through a variety of experiences including first-hand exploration and investigation of objects and phenomena, using information sources and dialogue with others. This chapter expands on these ideas about learning, how it can be facilitated and the implications for teaching, providing an overview of these factors, which are taken further in later chapters of this Guide.

Why teachers need to understand how children learn

Understanding how children learn is a fundamental aspect of creating the right environment for learning and the construction of appropriate experiences. It provides the rationale for why teachers make decisions about various aspects of the classroom environment and the kinds of interaction among pupils and between pupils and teachers that are encouraged. For the most part, teachers teach in the way that they believe helps children to learn in a particular way.

Teachers are well aware that, in spite of their best efforts, it has to be recognised that children do not learn everything they are taught and it is a painful realisation that on many occasions' children actually construct something totally different from the intended learning. This is in part due to children developing their ideas through their daily encounters with misunderstood science explanations from parents and friends as well as their unchallenged thinking about experiences. These alternative ideas are often strongly held because they make sense to the children and are very hard to challenge especially when the science explanation seems to be in direct conflict with reality. For example, the idea that the temperature of a metal bike handle is the same as the temperature of the surrounding air just does not seem right when it clearly feels colder! These encounters are at the root of many misconceptions and the reason why teachers need insight into the children's perspective and their thinking, so they can help children to see where they need to use different, more scientific, ideas. This has to be an ongoing process since children's ideas make perfect sense to them and the longer alternative ideas are held the harder it is to change them even in the light of counter-evidence.

By better understanding how the brain works and considering the big ideas behind current pedagogy, teachers can build on children's current understanding and interest, bearing in mind factors such as the individual's emotional responses to learning. While myths might still exist – such as individuals being *either* visual *or* kinaesthetic *or* auditory learners, and requiring lessons to be adapted to one preferred learning style (Coffield *et al.*, 2009) – the evidence developing through collaboration of educationalist and cognitive neuroscientists would strongly indicate that good learning is a whole-brain process, and not a left- or right-brain activity. This means that good teaching encourages the use of all available senses, not just because it is more interesting but because it reduces the cognitive demand on the working memory (Chapter 5). So hands-on tactile experiences, discussing what is seen, listening to each other and responding to adults' mediating questions, significantly enhance a child's ability to ask questions and make better sense of their world (de Jong *et al.*, 2009).

Ideas about how children learn

There is plenty of research evidence (for example, SPACE Reports 1990–1998) that when children encounter something new to them, they attempt to make sense of it using ideas formed from earlier experiences. These ideas become modified through being used in trying to explain new experience. In this process, an idea is used to make a prediction and then tested by seeing if the evidence from the new experience agrees with what was predicted. If it does, then the idea becomes just a little 'bigger' because it then explains a wider range of phenomena. Even if it doesn't 'work' – and an alternative idea has to be tried – the experience has helped to refine the idea. Through these processes there is not only a change in the range of events and phenomena that can be understood, but there is also a qualitative change in the ideas. Scientific ideas that are widely applicable are necessarily context-independent – for example, the idea of what makes things float can be used for all objects and all fluids. To move from an idea of why a particular object floats in water to the big idea of 'floating' is a large step, which involves making connections between observations in very different situations (Harlen, 2010 p26). Such ideas are only understood if they make sense to children because they are the product of their own thinking.

Generally speaking, teachers have moved away from the early behaviourist view that a mind is hard-wired from birth and learning is about reinforcing behaviours through sanctions and rewards. Instead, a constructivist approach underpins most classroom practice and builds on the Piagetian principles that knowledge is actively constructed through practical interaction and play with objects (Piaget, 1959). These approaches enable children to explore their world and make more sense of it, first at a concrete physical level and then at a more abstract reasoned level. The teacher's role in this process is to start with the premise that children come to science with ideas of their own, and by accepting this and using their ideas and interests the teacher can challenge and develop their thinking and use children's own questions to lead further investigative work.

There is much evidence to support the view that successful learning does not occur in isolation and there is a strong interaction between social and environmental factors as well as physical and emotional factors, which contribute to high self-esteem and strong self-efficacy. Together they influence an individual's motivation and willingness to persevere or take the risks necessary to learn. Accepting that all brains have the same potential if they are physically sound, it would indicate that the experiences a child has before and during the primary school years are hugely important in developing that individual's potential as well as fostering an enjoyment of science well before the start of secondary school.

Over time and through a range of experiences, teachers are well placed to mediate the learning of even very young children so that peer interactions include asking 'why' and giving answers that are supported by 'because', which are not a natural part of a young child's repertoire. Working in mixed attainment groups means there are opportunities for joint learning as described by Vygotsky. His premise was that what a child can do on his or her own can be enhanced when working with guidance from a more 'expert' other in a collaborative manner, and this enhances understanding. This working in advance of what a child can already achieve is termed working in the 'zone of proximal development' (Vygotsky, 1978, p86) and contributes to the maturation of thinking. By emphasising the role of dialogue and collaboration with others in a social and cultural context, children can make better sense of the world as they are challenged to reframe their ideas and develop their immature notions of science into more complex ones.

Teachers under pressure to 'cover the curriculum' quickly often feel impelled to use a didactic approach as opposed to quality time being spent on practical exploration with plenty of opportunities for dialogic exchanges (Alexander, 2008). It is well documented (EPPE, 2004) that an environment that is rich with opportunities for structured and unstructured play, exploration and investigation helps children to develop an enquiring mind and, over time and with guidance, they will also learn the skills necessary to review and evaluate critically the many sources of information they will encounter throughout their lives.

Experiences that help children's learning

Good science is about observing, sorting and classifying, exploring, raising questions, predicting, checking predictions through investigation, communication and reflection.

In the Early Years the focus is on handling things and looking for physical properties and how things can be used or changed (Figure 1 and Chapter 4). In later years this is extended to include characteristics such as magnetic and non-magnetic properties, reversible and irreversible changes.

Figure 1 Providing opportunities for observation, touch and talk in a Y1 classroom.

Encouraging questions

Encouraging children of all ages to ask questions requires coaching and modelling by the teacher so that children can learn to sift and sort questions into those that can be explored, those that have an answer and those that remain unknown. Take, for example, a common topic in science such as 'ourselves'. Questions like *'Does the length of your legs have an effect on how fast you can run?'* can be explored by carrying out a range of measurements and tests, whereas the child-initiated question *'Why can't we tickle ourselves?'*, while very intriguing, can only be confirmed but not explained. At first this might seem a 'silly question' yet it is a valuable part of learning in science and reinforces the notion that we cannot answer all questions through scientific investigation.

Context

The development of deep learning takes time to plan and the teacher has to consider not just a range of related experiences but the inclusion of appropriate higher-order questions that will challenge and explore the child's current thinking (Harrison and Howard, 2009). When science learning is set in an appropriate context it will capture children's natural curiosity and help sustain their interest over the tricky or confusing bits. Many teachers already recognise this and actively take account of what the child already knows and build on this through challenge and problem solving approaches rather than instruction. It requires skill on the part of the teacher not only to capture the children's current interests, but to teach them how to question their own tentative thinking and help them to engage in exploratory talk with their peers so that they can 'think about their thinking'. Thinking about their thinking is termed metacognition and is thought to be a uniquely human capacity. This process can be greatly enhanced by thinking aloud and in this way not only do children consolidate their thinking by putting it into words, but they also make it available for others to consider it and comment on it in relation to their own inner thoughts.

Talk

It is well documented that language plays a crucial role in the thinking process (Mercer, 2004; Alexander, 2008). By acquiring scientific vocabulary as a means to communicate with others, even young children can enhance their learning. However, they need to be able to compare their understanding with that of others by communicating using a shared vocabulary. This language is more than the authorised science terminology such as 'dissolving', 'melting' or 'condensation'; it is about having shared understanding and a means to compare and contrast individual thinking with that of others who have had similar experiences.

It is often hard for adults to empathise with that stage of not knowing, once knowing has been achieved, yet through peer interaction children can co-construct meaning in a way that adult intervention cannot. The success of this collaborative thinking process also helps the teacher to resist intervening too quickly, taking a minor yet crucial role in mediation and guiding the group back on track using a range of questioning strategies. With good subject knowledge and a sound grasp of how learners learn at different stages of development this timely intervention becomes easier as the early indicators of alternative constructs become more apparent through listening to the children's discourse during their engagement with 'real science'.

Promoting talk and encouraging children to predict is a good precursor to hypothesising, which is an essential part of scientific thinking. This can be developed by giving time for children to think imaginatively and offer a range of predictions about what might happen, followed by an opportunity to talk about their reasoning. In this manner, their thinking process can evolve over time and practice into 'educated guesses' and ultimately reasoned hypothesising.

Analogies

Analogies, metaphors and models are useful mechanisms for the teacher and the child to get a shared understanding (Asoko and de Boo, 2001). They provide the means for abstract ideas to take a concrete form enabling the child to articulate their understanding in relation to known shared experiences such as *'it's like an ice cream melting'*. Even complex ideas can be clearly articulated by children using analogies from their own experiences, such as an 11-year-old saying:

> 'Gases move around like the balls in the kiddies' play area at the pub when there are loads of children playing … the balls go all over the place. They can't get out because of the net … but solids, they are like the balls lying still on the floor before the kids get in. When the balls are just moving around but not flying around, that's like liquid.'

However, analogies are not without risk and can inadvertently lead to misconceptions. For example, describing the flow of electricity in a circuit as being like water flowing in a pipe might imply that when an electric wire is cut the electricity leaks out in the same manner as water would leak from a pipe.

Formative assessment

Sometimes a science experience makes too great a demand on both the working memory capacity and understanding, or does not build neatly on previous understanding so confusion and frustration occur. The teacher has to respond quickly, perhaps by guidance that helps the children to fill in the crucial missing pieces so they can make the appropriate links between experiences and modified understanding and move on again. This is where formative assessment plays a significant role in teachers being able to respond rapidly to the learning as it takes place, as well as develop the individual's ability to cope with the frustrations of learning. Where assessment focuses on the learners' behaviour and talk as they engage in science activities, instead of what they know, the teacher can judge when to intervene, or not, to enhance learning. Knowing when to observe from afar and when to mediate with a well-considered question or activity that challenges the child to think beyond their first thoughts comes with conscious effort and practice.

Implications for teaching

With an ever-increasing use of technology such as the internet and live television transmissions, youngsters today experience a much larger world and wider range of experiences than any of us did at their age. Seeing outer space, having real-time news from distant places or engaging in fantasy through asynchronous communication, including computer games or Second Life, provide the backdrop to children's school work.

Some have argued that today's child expects instant gratification and as a result their ability to sustain mindful engagement or imaginative empathetic thought is being undermined by over-use of, and prolonged exposure to, such things as computer stimulation. Some neuroscientists are going so far as to say that young brains may be adapting to these experiences in a manner that could impede problem solving capabilities and increase the likelihood of attention deficit disorders and reckless behaviour. Whether or not this is the case, there is a need to be alert to the potentially unknown impact of new communication technologies as well as recognising their worth as tools to aid learning.

Exploration and enquiry involves being physical – for example, handling, looking, smelling and tasting – as well as mental engagement such as the articulation of amazement, wonder, imagination and confusion. At a physical level, children can be helped to make sense of things by organising their thoughts using simple tools like sorting, grouping, drawing or writing, which not only create a permanent feature they can return to at a later stage to help recall things, but also act as a means to slow down the thinking process, which aids the process of understanding and helps to make connections between things.

Science learning through practical hands-on experiences and enquiry approaches provides the greatest opportunities to enhance understanding and challenge current beliefs, as long as these experiences are context bound and act as links in the chain rather than an isolated activity. Where an experience is too exciting or not mediated correctly a child will recall the experience for ages afterwards but this is likely to be to the detriment of the science being encountered. For example, understanding irreversible changes by observing a firework display may be lost in the excitement of the moment.

Enquiry plays a central role in the Early Years and primary school science lesson, and is far more than a mere 'experiment' with the identification and controlling of variables. Although this is a valuable aspect of the necessary skills that children need in order to explore in a systematic way, what they need is plenty of opportunity to explore and question and talk so that they can check out their ideas about the world of which they are part. It is through a process of comparing one thing to another and actively looking for similarities and noticing differences that prompts child-initiated questions. Meanwhile, the teacher's role is to try to get a glimpse into their thinking process by encouraging the children to talk about it as they work.

Science knowledge is not something that is imparted or is innate. It needs to be constructed slowly over many years and teachers play a crucial role in providing supportive yet stimulating environments suitable for the stage of cognitive growth and interest. The only thing that is certain about the future is the uncertainty of it and for this reason primary school science needs to foster critically reflective practice, and opportunities to think creatively and imaginatively from as early an age as possible. It is this ability that will enable our future generation of citizens to actively seek patterns and make connections between things to solve new problems or reframe old ones.

In conclusion

The goal of effective teaching from the earliest ages is to identify individual needs and develop more autonomous and independent learners who are able to take an ever-increasing and proactive role in seeking clarification and exploration of a range of questions and queries in order to make sense of the world they interact with and know. Understanding how children learn and what they need in order to develop ideas about the scientific aspects of the natural world is the basis of good primary science education. Schools that focus on creating the right conditions for young minds to explore their environments and utilise child-initiated enquiries will help produce a critically reflective generation that will not passively accept all they read, see and hear, but think about it in relation to their own ideas and experiences, and question it.

References

Alexander, R. (2008) *Towards Dialogic Teaching: Rethinking Classroom Talk* (fourth edition). Cambridge: Dialogos.

Asoko, H. and de Boo, M. (2001) *Representing Ideas in Science Through Analogies and Illustrations.* Hatfield: Association of Science Education.

Coffield, F., Moseley, D., Hall, E. and Ecclestone, K. (2009) *Learning Style and Pedagogy in Post-16 Learning: A Systematic and Critical Review.* London: Learning and Skills Development Agency (LSDA).

de Jong, T., van Gog, T., Jenks, K., Manlove, S., van Hell, J., Jolles, J., van Merrienboer, J., van Leeuwen, T. and Bosschloo, A. (2009) *Explorations in Learning and the Brain.* Dordrecht: Springer Science and Business Media, LLC.

EPPE (2004) *Effective Provision of Pre-school Education: Final Report.* Available online at www.dcsf.gov.uk/everychildmatters/publications/0/1160/

Harlen, W. (Ed) (2010) *Principles and Big Ideas of Science Education.* www.ase.org.uk

Harrison, C. and Howard, S. (2009) *Inside the Primary Black Box. Assessment for Learning in Primary and Early Years Classrooms.* London: GL Assessment.

Mercer, N. (reprint 2004 with corrections) *The Guided Construction of Knowledge: Talk Amongst Teachers and Learners.* Clevedon: Multilingual Matters.

Piaget, J. (1959) *The Language and Thought of the Child.* London: Routledge.

SPACE Reports (1990–1998) Titles include: *Evaporation and condensation* (1990), *Light* (1990), *Growth* (1990), *Electricity* (1991), *Materials* (1991), *Processes of life* (1992), *Rocks, soil and weather* (1993), *Earth in space* (1996), *Forces* (1998). Liverpool: University of Liverpool Press.

Vygotsky. L.S. (1978) *Mind in Society: The Development of Higher Psychological Processes.* Cambridge, MA: Harvard University Press.

Chapter 3

Progression in learning science

Terry Russell

This chapter is concerned with the benefits to be gained by the considered ordering of learners' experiences in a way that takes account of what we know about development. In teaching science, it helps to know the science content; being able to tune one's teaching (pedagogy) to the way learners' thinking progresses over time is equally invaluable. When the two are put together, we arrive at knowing what and how to teach particular concepts – 'pedagogical content knowledge', as Shulman (2004) refers to this kind of professional knowledge (or 'PCK' for short). The chapter begins with a brief overview of aims and of how progression in science is set within the context of early experiences across the curriculum, indicating how science draws upon work particularly in language, mathematics and art. Against this background, the focus on progression in science is taken forward under three headings: conceptual understanding, ideas and evidence, and procedural understanding.

The whole learner in a life-long learning context

The teacher's intention should be to arrive at a regulated exposure of challenges within the range of curricular expectations that apply in the UK. The broader context is a view of the primary science experience as part of a continuum, building on experiences in the Early Years and preparing the ground for the secondary phase. While children's primary school experiences must, of course, be tailored to the particular needs of that phase, taking the long view is more likely to result in continuity and progression in learning experiences, so helping to avoid the setbacks associated with phase transfers. The long view provides a rationale to guide the fitting of local and daily details of learning and teaching into the wider endeavour of nurturing prospective scientists and a scientifically literate population.

Why and how do children engage with learning science? The response could be that they have no option, but of course they do, and many decide to turn off and opt out. The implication is that our fundamental concern must be to sustain motivation (for it is surely present at the outset) by nurturing curiosity and a questioning attitude about any and all phenomena. Equally fundamental is to promote a frame of mind that expects reasons and justifications for assertions, one's own and those of others. These two assumptions must be the constants that hold good for any age, stage and phase of learning science. Attempting to transmit facts without first ensuring that curiosity (and so a sense of the relevance of the information) and without learners being intellectually satisfied with the supporting evidence, will result in transactions devoid of affective and cognitive value. The result will be rote learning that would be at odds with an overriding concern of education systems in the UK to produce independent, 'self-regulated' learners.

Cross-curricular and Early Years contributions to science progression

Primary education in the UK tends to favour holistic, integrated and cross-curricular approaches. Artwork that takes the form of accurate drawn observations offers ways of checking the correspondences between what is observed and what is recorded – the non-verbal equivalent of setting out an argument with supporting evidence. In early language work, children explore forms and functions of writing including making lists – a linear precursor of what is required to label a bar chart. Work on oracy supports progression in presenting and arguing a cogent case for a point of view. In mathematics, pupils will have experienced classifying and ordering, using non-standard and standard measures – skills fundamental to handling variables. Science tends to draw on mathematics in the sense that quantification assumes increasing importance, with extensions beyond everyday scale in every conceivable dimension. Scientists relish crossing the boundaries into the other worlds of the gigantic and the microscopic as explorers of previously unseen and unimagined worlds. It will take pupils some years to establish the confidence to share this enthusiasm for 'other worldly' scales as they progress from labelling variables qualitatively, then using whole numbers, moving to decimals and more complex scales. In a similar way, science ideas tend to be presented initially using the everyday scale observable to humans – the 'macroscopic' or large view – and only when concepts are established at the everyday scale is a different level of interpretation introduced. For example, evaporation will be discussed in terms of puddles 'disappearing' long before a particle model is introduced as an explanatory framework.

A teacher who is better informed about developmental progression will have a larger PCK repertoire to call upon to scaffold children's learning. Knowledge of progression will also help a teacher's formative assessment practice in helping to identify current understandings and enabling the next steps in learning. This is not to assume linear development with every child following the exact conceptual route as all who have gone before. The metaphor of migration routes is a better analogy: swallows generally return to the UK in early April, but precise routes and dates of arrival are not entirely predictable and many may be blown off course. Teachers' knowledge of conceptual progression will sensitise them to certain possibilities and suggest fruitful routes forward while avoiding conceptual pitfalls and blind alleys.

Science-specific progression

With a general orientation established, we can consider some of the more science-specific aspects. These are classified under three headings with the caution that, in effective teaching, they are inseparable:

1 **conceptual understanding** of the 'subject matter content', as specified to some extent in national curriculum documents
2 **ideas and evidence**, considering the procedures used for checking learners' own claims as well as assertions made by others
3 **procedural understanding** as it relates to practical enquiry in investigative science, including in particular the 'variables handling' aspects.

These three areas are each intrinsically important, but also significant in the manner in which they complement one another. Science content and processes have always been strongly linked in best practice.

Progression in conceptual understanding

Through the 1980s to the present, a stream of research has been published, motivated by constructivist developmental psychology, into the development of learners' science ideas (for example, the SPACE approach – see *Websites*). Whether thought of as preconceptions, misconceptions or alternative conceptions, more important is the fact that these ideas certainly occur, differ consistently from orthodox science and need to be taken seriously as starting points for 'conceptual change' strategies. There is far more published material than can be summarised here. Fortunately, there are also some excellent overviews. (A rich source is the American Association for the Advancement of Science publications relating to Project 2061: AAAS, 2001, 2007). Figure 1 offers a more direct experience of qualitative progression in learners' understanding. Given an illustration of a torch aimed at a patterned mug, 8 to 14-year-olds were invited to draw the cast shadow they anticipated.

Figure 1   Conceptions of shadow formation, from Russell and McGuigan (2005) INSET Toolkit for KS3, Module 4, p28.

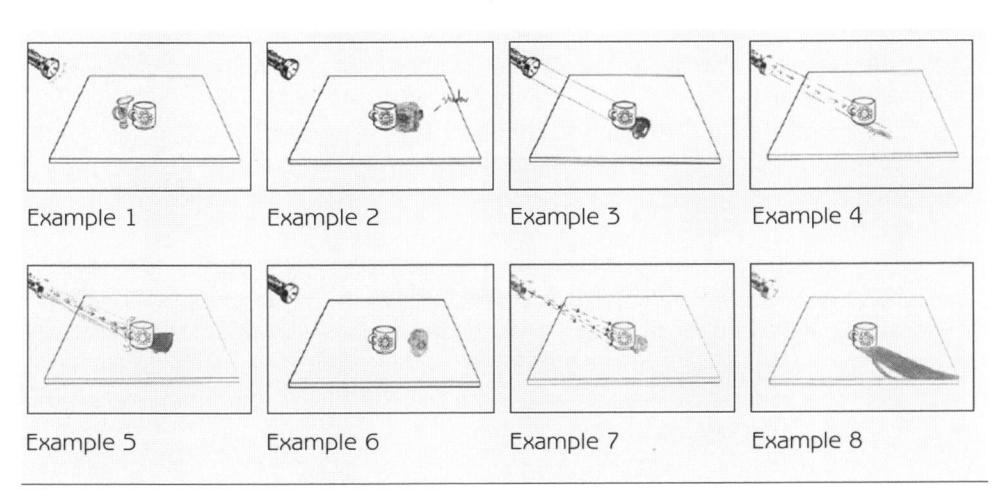

Example 1   Example 2   Example 3   Example 4

Example 5   Example 6   Example 7   Example 8

Learning in science at the primary level

The illustrations are the products of eight different pupils. The data collected are not 'longitudinal' (from one individual over time) but 'cross-sectional', from a number of pupils of different ages. The predictions are in random order, but it is possible to discern the use of increasingly complex (and scientifically more accurate) assumptions – for example, whether the shadow reproduces the pattern on the mug; whether it would appear attached to the mug; position relative to the light source, and so on. Readers are invited to speculate on the ordering of this conceptual progression for themselves and consider conceptual change strategies such as, for example, encouraging pupils to reflect on their drawn assumptions, followed by self-assessment informed by practical experimentation.

Ideas and evidence

With the digital information, technical and social revolution, educationalists have seen the advantages of information stored in online servers rather than overloading the capacity of learners' memories. One consequence has been that curricular prescriptions for the science to be covered have been reduced, in favour of establishing information search and evaluation skills. There is a progression to be nurtured in learners' development of these ICT skills (Chapter 8). The second area to be discussed in this chapter – ideas and evidence – is in some sense the least science-specific of the three, but arguably the most important due to its life-long learning and cross-curricular relevance.

Up to the age of about four (perhaps beyond), children find it difficult to entertain the idea that others do not understand the world as they do, or do not know what they themselves know, as the scenario in Box 1 illustrates.

Box 1

A young child (Child One) is shown chocolates being removed from a chocolate box and replaced with pencils. When invited to predict what Child Two (who has not witnessed the switch) will answer when asked to say what he thinks is in the box, Child One will predict 'pencils'. Child One knows that there are pencils in the box and cannot entertain the idea of any other person holding a different idea, one that is different from the 'reality' they know to be correct. They find it difficult or impossible to accept 'false beliefs'. Child One's mode of thinking is 'realist', characterised by an assumption that there is only one way of knowing the world, and that is how they themselves (and everyone else, so they would have it) assume it 'really is'. The study of the process of knowledge construction ('epistemology' is the name of the discipline) can offer invaluable insights to teachers. In order to accommodate the possibility that others may have a different view of reality than one's own, Child One has to envisage Child Two having his or her own mental state.

We are likely to assume, as adults, that we have always had self-awareness, a consciousness of both our own mind and of others as likewise having minds. In fact, enquiries reveal that the emergence of a 'theory of mind' (or ToM, for short) is a significant event, developmentally. (This capability is related to empathy, tending to be more developed in females than males on average, and one with which persons diagnosed on the autistic spectrum may have life-long difficulties.) ToM is an important development because, once others are understood to have their own minds, alternative points of view can be accepted, albeit initially in a restricted 'absolutist' sense, as will be explained.

Progression in learning science

While the appreciation that others are likely to have constructed their own versions of events is a significant advance in thinking, limitations remain to be resolved. The most important restriction is that the alternative ideas that have now come to be accepted are not treated as equally possible alternatives, but as absolutes. Others may have different ideas, but they are thought of as either right or wrong. This is why this mode of thinking (or knowing about knowing) is named 'absolutist'.

With increasing experience, and corresponding with children's maturation in age in years through single to double digits, the nature of knowing progresses to a 'relativist' quality: when alternative perspectives in beliefs and knowledge are encountered, they are accepted as genuine options. The downside is that certainty of belief is elusive, with every idea entertained as a possible and everyone assumed to be entitled to their own point of view. This state of mind can only be resolved with the development of value systems that allow different possibilities (claims, beliefs or arguments) to be weighed up and decided between. With the capability to appraise alternatives by reference to some form of judgement system, learners' thinking enters the 'evaluativist' stage. Kuhn's (2005) evidence is that the evaluativist phase is unlikely to emerge before the age of about 14, under advantageous circumstances.

Means of accelerating progression through the realist, absolutist and relativist states may be facilitated, for example, by encouraging young children to articulate what is in their heads. Providing opportunities for the expression of ideas will help them to clarify their own beliefs and appreciate what others think. This process of thinking about thinking (or 'metacognition') is receiving increasing attention as a significant area of enquiry linking developmental neuropsychology research and education. Classroom strategies might include role playing, encouraging children to step out of their own persona to adopt that of someone having different beliefs and ways of behaving that can be 'tried on for size'. Puppets (Chapter 13), having bodies and heads but no minds (until populated with such by the puppet operator), will encourage children to project their thinking, as will other strategies for shifting experience from the everyday habitual to the focused and self-consciously reflective. The use of video to record and debate learners' expressed ideas has proved highly encouraging in this respect, and podcasting offers a variation on this theme.

When thinking is regarded as a 3D high-definition recording and expression of the way things are, shared by all, some important consequences are apparent:

1. what 'is' does not require confirmatory evidence
2. since beliefs exactly mirror reality, there can be no 'false belief'
3. everyone is assumed to hold the same version of reality, so the possibility of different versions of reality (opposing opinions or points of view) does not reach consciousness.

Kuhn's *'coordination of subjective with objective elements'* (Kuhn, 2005) will entail discriminating among divergent claims on the basis of evidence. At the subjective end of the scale, we want learners to show imagination in their questions and hypotheses; at the objective end, we must require them to provide well-considered reasons (with empirical data especially valued) to support their ideas.

Procedural understanding

The previous sections have introduced the ideas of progression in knowledge construction and the importance of evidence in supporting claims. 'Argumentation' (Box 2) procedures offer a way of analysing and debating all kinds of claims, whether logically based, rhetorical

Learning in science at the primary level

or even aesthetic, across the curriculum. Practical science investigations offer something additional: a particular sub-set of practical evidence-collecting and hypothesis-testing procedures to which children can be gradually introduced.

Box 2 The meaning and value of argumentation

> 'Stop arguing!' is a familiar adult reprimand to curb unruly 'argumentative' behaviour, so we need to specify the classroom behaviours advocated in the name of 'argumentation'. The simplest form of 'argument' in the context of science education is i) a 'claim' with ii) supporting evidence. 'What I believe' and 'Why I think so' need to be thought of as the two essential and inseparable elements. Of course, many claims are made without support, simply as assertions. For a person at any age, thinking through why a particular belief is held may require a period of reflection, perhaps reference to direct observation or some other representation of the idea under consideration. In the science classroom, 'That activity really made them think!' is possibly the highest accolade and warrants attempts to understand the processes of coming to hold (or modify) beliefs. How can such thinking activities be stimulated and nurtured by teachers as habits of mind in learners? One way of looking analytically at the processes involved is to take a developmental perspective. 'Argumentation' (Toulmin, 2003) is the technical term used to describe the process of coordinating 'claims' (that is, expressed ideas or assertions) with evidence. For the teacher, the form of intervention that encourages such linking of ideas and evidence may take the form of modelling questioning behaviours, requiring justifications and encouraging counter arguments (Osborne et al., 2004).

Starting in the Foundation years, children are encouraged to observe real-world phenomena, to comment, to record (possibly using drawing), to make predictions and to speculate about causes and effects by raising questions that are capable of being tested. Teachers can help children to move their thinking forward both by sustaining or stimulating curiosity and imagination (the subjective dimension) and by encouraging systematic procedures (the objective dimension).

With increased attention to 'thinking skills' in UK curricula, 'thinking tools' intended to support learners' reasoning have been identified. These might be defined as re-usable cultural constructions: language, the number system, musical notation and perspective drawing are pre-eminent examples. Science also has its set of 'thinking tools', many of which are shared with technology and mathematics. A table, bar chart or line graph, each with their two axes, can be thought of as 'thinking tools': a concrete–symbolic device where one thing (each axis) stands for another thing (for example, length of shadow and time of day). As adults, teachers and science educators, we assume that there is order in the world that can be understood better by using observation, measurement and recording, rather than assuming random events or resorting to superstition.

Children can be gradually introduced to ways of handling information systematically – for example:

- in the Foundation Phase, making lists, perhaps in order of magnitude
- putting lists into tables
- adding columns to their tables for comments on conditions or outcomes associated with each item (defining x and y variables)

Progression in learning science

- transferring discontinuous data (for example, colour of car, type of seed) from their tables into bar charts
- using continuous (quantitative) data on one variable (for example, length in mm, mass in g) in graphs
- using continuous data on both variables.

Figure 2 Progression in handling information, from Russell and McGuigan (2005) INSET Toolkit for KS1, Module 2, p20).

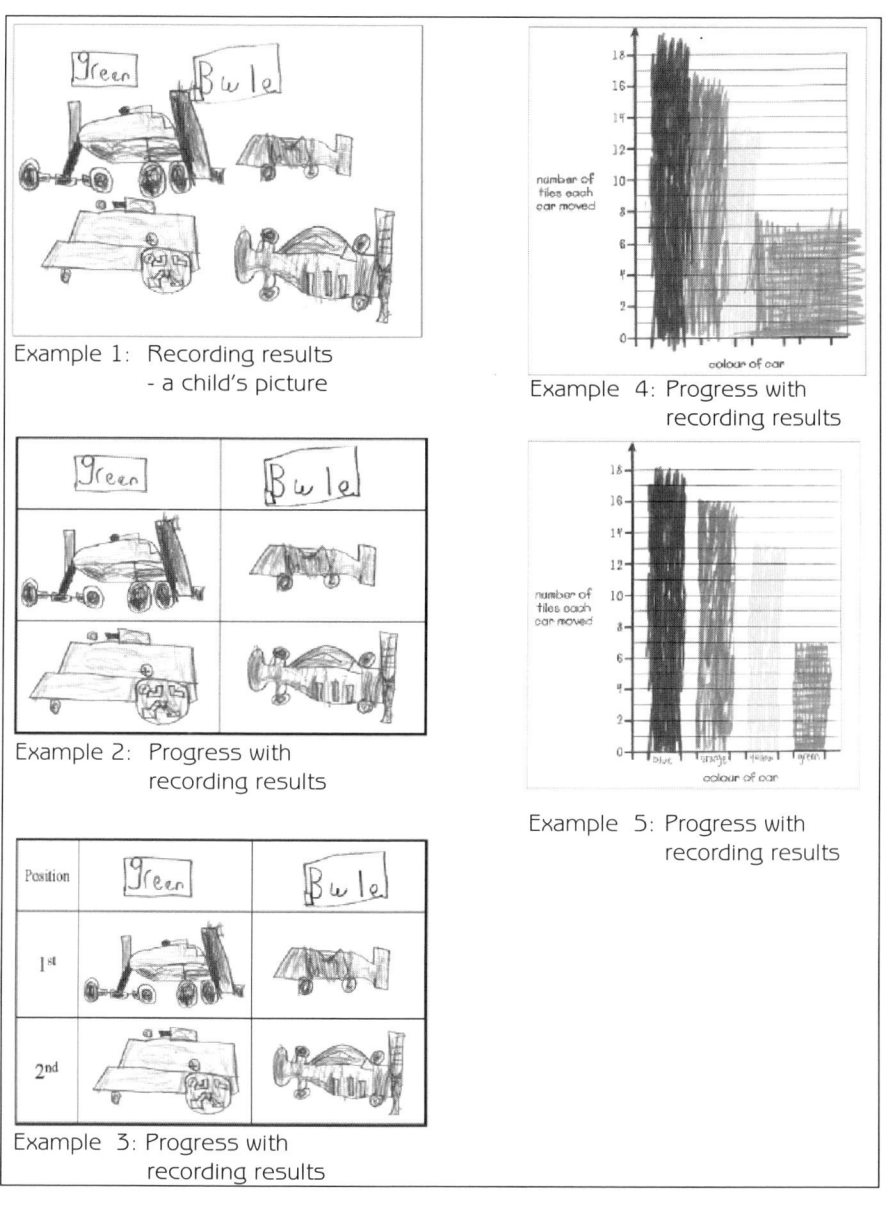

Example 1: Recording results - a child's picture

Example 2: Progress with recording results

Example 3: Progress with recording results

Example 4: Progress with recording results

Example 5: Progress with recording results

Figure 2 illustrates this kind of progression, starting with drawings of an informal investigation into rolling cars, gradually having structure imposed following a teacher's suggestion to use a table and introduce measurements. The subtlety and precision in the use of such tools as tables, bar charts and graphs for defining and recording variables can be encouraged to progress steadily throughout the primary phase. The labelling of the axes with the name of the variable and units of measurement will be handled with increasing facility, as will the measurement scales. A significant proportion of learners will be capable of investigating and recording two continuous variables (for example, shadow length over time) by the end of their primary education as the result of the systematic steps suggested above. (The bar graph in Figure 2 could shift to a line graph if the pushing force were to be quantified, making both variables continuous.) The process will continue into secondary education with children appreciating the distinction between the independent variable (the cause, such as angle of the Sun in the sky) and the dependent variable (the effect, such as shadow length).

In conclusion

While sceptics may wish to argue that progression in science learning does not happen as neatly as the theoreticians set it out, the important point to hold on to is that the development is painted with a broad brush and has practical PCK value. Any attempt to peg age norms to such progression is a risky business. (We can all think of individuals in middle age whose views may be realist or absolutist!) Within science and between scientists there will be controversy and strongly divergent views. The important element that science brings to the debate is a formal, rigorous and systematic manner of dealing with ideas and evidence that learners can be inducted into and encouraged to apply when deciding between competing claims. In this manner, discriminations can be made between different interpretations (the subjective view) of the same data (the objective aspect).

References

AAAS (2001) *Atlas of Science Literacy: Volume 1*. Washington: American Association for the Advancement of Science and National Science Teachers Association, Project 2061.

AAAS (2007) *Atlas of Science Literacy: Volume 2*. American Association for the Advancement of Science and National Science Teachers Association, Project 2061.

Kuhn, D. (2005) *Education for Thinking*. Harvard: Harvard University Press.

Osborne, J., Erduran, S. and Simon, S. (2004) Enhancing the quality of argumentation in school science. *Journal of Research in Science Teaching*, **41**(10) 994–1020.

Russell, T. and McGuigan, L. (2005) *Assessing Progress in Science. INSET Toolkits for KS1; KS2; KS3*. London: Qualifications and Curriculum Authority.

Shulman, L.S. (2004) *The Wisdom of Practice. Collected Essays of Lee Shulman*, Volume 1. Stanford: Carnegie Foundation for the Advancement of Teaching.

Toulmin, S.E. (2003) *The Uses of Argument* (updated from 1958 first edition). Cambridge: Cambridge University Press.

Websites

SPACE reports and some hard copies are available via www.cripsat.org.uk/previous/space.htm. Some approaches to primary science are illustrated at the National Grid for Learning Wales: www.ngflcymru.org.uk/eng/vtc-home/vtc-ks2-home/vtc-ks2-science(2) – enter search term 'CRIPSAT'.

Chapter 4

Learning in the Early Years

Jane Johnston

Early Years science is science for our youngest children. Using the international definition of Early Years this means science for children aged between birth and eight years of age. Everyone concerned with science education at every stage of development ought to have an understanding of Early Years science and how scientific understanding, skills and attitudes develop in young children, so that teachers and others know not just what we want children to learn in the future, but the journey they have taken already in their learning. Young children's scientific abilities are often misunderstood and underestimated, resulting in a top-down approach and a mismatch between children's abilities and the experiences we provide for them and the support we give them.

This chapter considers how young children's scientific development (understanding, skills and attitudes) occurs in harmony with language development and is supported by adults and the pedagogical approaches employed. Case studies illustrate the importance of adult support and the benefit of different approaches. The chapter finishes with a discussion of how the issues of transition and progression affect early years scientific development.

Supported experiential learning

Early Years science should be practical and motivating, with children interacting with everyday scientific phenomena in social contexts. Experiential learning has long been recognised as important in the Early Years (Rousseau, 1911, for example). It is represented in discovery and play approaches advocated in England in the Early Years Foundation Stage (EYFS) (DCSF, 2008) and thematic approaches that set science in the real world in which they live and are appropriate for children at Key Stage 1 and beyond (Bruce, 2009). These approaches involve children in experiencing familiar scientific phenomena and being supported and challenged through social interaction with peers and knowledgeable adults. This social interaction should support scientific development, through challenge, questioning and modelling, rather than providing knowledge that children will quickly forget, or leaving children to make connections between the experiences and scientific concepts for themselves. For example, an Early Years professional can set up experiences for a child, but without some social interaction to question the children about what they are experiencing or challenge them to look more closely or think differently (as in Box 1), the learning will be incidental and ad hoc.

Box 1

> A collection of natural objects, such as shells, leaves, seeds or stones, can be set out for children to explore. Children will be challenged by adults who ask questions such as 'What do you notice ...?', 'How can you ...?' and other children who will identify differing views and understandings about the objects.
> When baking cakes, the children will not focus on the changes in state of the ingredients when mixed, heated or cooled unless they are guided with questions such as, 'What do you think will happen when ...?', 'What do you notice?' or 'How has the mixture changed?'

Early skills

Early skills are identified in outline in the English National Curriculum EYFS (DCSF, 2008) and schemes of work for Key Stage 1 (QCA, 2000). In Table 1 these skills have been mapped out for both stages so that some progression of each skill can be seen. The skills have been grouped as exploring, planning, recording, interpreting and communicating skills, but only exploring and interpreting skills are really appropriate for the youngest children – from birth to five years of age. This does not mean that the youngest children do not plan or record, but their skills are developing rather than being more finely tuned.

Table 1 Scientific skill development in the Early Years (under five years of age in italics and five to eight years of age in roman).

Observation is an important skill in both science and the Early Years. For young children early

Group	Skill	Examples
exploring skills	observing	• *observing and describing simple features and events* • *examining objects and living things to find out more about them* • noticing patterns • identifying similarities and differences • identifying patterns in and between objects and scientific phenomena • interpreting observations
	raising questions	• *asking questions about why things happen and how things work* • raising questions about scientific observation and phenomena • exploration and investigation and non-productive questions • beginning to plan how questions can be answered through exploration and investigation

Learning in the Early Years

Group	Skill	Examples
planning skills	planning (deciding what can be explored or investigated, by what method, using what resources, and keeping what records)	<ul><li>*oral planning to try out ideas (deciding what to do, what to use)*</li><li>identifying opportunities for exploration and investigation</li><li>planning explorations and investigations with structured support (planning boards, ladders etc.)</li></ul>
	predicting	<ul><li>*making sensible 'guesses' about what they think will happen*</li><li>making predictions about observable scientific phenomena/events</li><li>making sensible predictions based on evidence</li></ul>
	handling variables	<ul><li>*beginning to identify if what they are doing is 'fair'*</li><li>identifying key variables (what you are changing/independent variable and what you are finding out/dependent variable)</li><li>identifying control variables (what is needed to make investigation fair)</li></ul>
	hypothesising	<ul><li>explaining an event or phenomenon (not necessarily scientifically correctly and not obviously based on evidence or experience)</li><li>using limited, everyday evidence to explain events or phenomena</li></ul>
	measuring (e.g. length, mass, force, sound, light, electricity, temperature)	<ul><li>beginning to measure using non-standard measures</li><li>measuring using non-standard measures (measuring qualitatively)</li><li>recognising the need for standard measures</li><li>using simple standard measures with simple measuring devices (e.g. temperature strips, probes), with support/decreasing support</li><li>using more complex measuring equipment, with support/without support</li></ul>
recording skills	preparing graphs, charts, tables	<ul><li>constructing simple pictograms, Venn diagrams etc.</li><li>constructing more complex charts and graphs (bar charts to line graphs)</li></ul>
	writing reports (question/what trying to do, resources/what used, method/what did, results/what found out, interpretation/what does this mean?)	<ul><li>describing in own words what was done and what happened</li><li>using a simple writing structure to support ideas</li></ul>

Learning in science at the primary level

Group	Skill	Examples
	drawing pictures and diagrams	• drawing simple observational pictures • labelling pictures • drawing a sequenced cartoon of exploration/investigation • constructing group/pictorial concept maps
interpreting skills	interpreting	• *talking about what is seen and happening* • recognising different ways to present data/record data to support interpretation • interrogating graphs, charts, tables (simple to more complex), with support
	analysing	• describing what has happened in an exploration or investigation • using more scientific language in their descriptions/analyses • providing own ideas for why something has/may have occurred • using previous knowledge
	concluding	• identifying what results of explorations or investigations mean • identifying what has been learned • posing new questions for exploration or investigation • making specific or generalised conclusions
communicating skills	displaying ideas and results	
	presenting ideas and results	
	explaining ideas and conclusions	

observation involves using all their senses to explore the familiar world around them and beginning to look for similarities and differences, patterns and change. They can compare objects, initially focusing on differences, which are easier for young children to observe and later focusing on similarities. They can look for patterns in the world around them, such as daily and seasonal pattern, patterns in growth and events, as well as patterns in nature. They can focus on changes in the natural world: daily and seasonal changes in animals and plants; changes in the material world when you put them in water, mix them, heat them and cool them; changes in the physical world, between light and dark, shadows, sounds and moving objects. As the children develop through the Early Years, their observations will move from the familiar to the slightly less familiar so that their experiences will expand with their understandings.

Observation also leads to the development and use of other early scientific skills, especially where there is effective and supportive social interaction. Children's ability to raise questions and show curiosity will be encouraged by adult curiosity and modelling of questions. They can be encouraged to make predictions based on their observations and as they experience scientific phenomena and events they can also be supported and encouraged in making simple hypotheses (explanations for why something has happened or will happen). For example, children can identify why they think some objects sink and others float, or why slugs like wetter environments. We need to remember that predictions and hypotheses do not have to be scientifically correct and neither should they be corrected. It is more important that they are based on evidence from the child's experiences. Professional decisions need to be made to ensure that other experiences are provided if and when appropriate to the child and the context.

In the early years most scientific experiences will be exploratory and children will move from these directly to make sense of their observations and experiences; that is to interpret them. Some children (especially as they move into the first years of formal school) will begin to plan further explorations, with support from adults, or some simple investigations (especially as they move through the early school years). They will also begin to handle simple variables, take measurements and more regularly record their findings in a variety of forms. The skill of interpreting is almost as important as observation, as without the time and support to make sense of scientific experiences, children will not make progress in science. Children need the opportunity to interpret experiences from a personal perspective, explaining what they have observed or found out in their own words, and once again supported by social interaction. It is at this part in the Early Years scientific process that children's conceptual development is consolidated and new ideas can be explored.

Early understandings

Early understandings are different from the ideas of older children and adults. What very young children see is absolute and they have far fewer experiences to draw upon. Early understandings develop as a result of early experiences (Mayall, 2007) and this, combined with the way young children see and make sense of the world, means that their ideas are more intuitive than logical. They develop simple theories about the world around them, based on their observations and experiences, and these often lead them to alternative conceptions, such as '*heavy things sink and light things float when put in water*', or '*all moving objects are living*'. They will hold onto these ideas even when faced with contradictory evidence: '*you change the weight of something by changing its shape and this causes objects that previously sank to float*'. Indeed, adult intervention does not always move thinking forward, but combines with children's tacit ideas to create more complex alternative conceptions. For example, children soon learn about different animals they encounter in their everyday world or in books (pets, insects, farm or wild animals) and they notice similarities and differences between them. When they are taught about animal groups, although they are able to distinguish between animals, they may become confused about whether a bee is an animal or a minibeast or an insect, or whether a whale is a fish or a mammal, and so it may appear that their understanding about the animal kingdom is less sophisticated than when they were younger.

Scientific thinking can be developed through careful pedagogical approaches that ensure that teaching accelerates cognition and does not perpetuate alternative conceptions. Effective approaches are not those that impart knowledge to children. Kallery *et al.*, (2009) have found, in their research focusing on young children's understanding of floating and sinking, that such didactic approaches are unsuccessful in supporting understanding. Approaches should enable children to explore and talk about scientific phenomena with adults and other children and help them to make links between their exploratory findings and scientific ideas. It is not enough to provide experiences alone, as children will often not make these links for themselves without this support.

Language development

Early scientific development involves children in developing a wide and increasingly scientific vocabulary – labelling, naming and recognising the meanings of words they encounter and linking them to their experiences. This occurs through teaching that involves discussion and dialogue (Johnston, 2009) and so a quiet science activity is not effective in advancing children's conceptual understanding. When children talk amongst themselves they often realise that the way they view the world is not the same as others' views and this may act as a challenge to their thinking. Early Years professionals can set up opportunities for children to discuss views by introducing conflicting ideas, maybe in a type of Concept Cartoon scenario (Naylor and Keogh, 2000) or using role play areas (de Boo, 2004) and puppets to promote discussion in children who are less likely to interact with adults. A role play area of a doctor's surgery allows children to explore ideas about the human body and first aid, as well supporting language and social development. A pet shop can help children to explore ideas about similarities and differences among animals and among their physiological needs.

Early attitudes

Early years experiences form the foundation of early attitudes, such as curiosity, perseverance and objectivity, all of which are important for future scientific development. Johnston (2005) grouped attitudes into four areas:

- **motivational** – curiosity, questioning, enthusiasm
- **social** – cooperation, independence, tolerance
- **practical/behavioural** – perseverance, sensitivity, flexibility
- **reflective** – open-mindedness, objectivity, respect for evidence.

All of these are important for cognitive development.

Children need to be motivated and curious about the world around them and should have a questioning attitude. They need to be able to cooperate and discuss with others and tolerate their ideas. They need to be able persevere with tasks, to perfect their skills and repeat their explorations to help them understand scientific phenomena. They need to respect the evidence they find, even if the evidence conflicts with their intuitive ideas. In this way, attitudes support further conceptual development.

Approaches to Early Years learning and teaching

In this part of the chapter we have two case studies, which showcase different Early Years science teaching and learning (Boxes 2 and 3).

Box 2

> **Case study 1: A nursery setting with children aged two and three years old**
> A group of two- and three-year-old children are playing in the outside play area of the nursery. They are digging in the soil at the edge of the area. Dipa brings some water from the water trough in a bucket and pours it on the soil. Jack says, 'Look at this, its all gooey now'. The Early Years professional uses this as a starting point to discuss the differences between the wet and dry soil and asks the children to predict what will happen if they add more water to the soil. The responses vary from 'Go really gooey', to 'It will drain away'. The children get more water and see what happens.
> They start to make mud pies and Sonia suggests that they leave them on the side of the path to dry. The professional asks them what will happen to the pies and Sonia says, 'They will all dry up'. But Dipa says, 'Not if it rains', and so the discussion moves to what will happen to the pies in different weather conditions. The children decide to leave them on the side of the path and look at what happens to them during the rest of the week.
> Pippa then notices a worm in the wet soil and points it out. The children and the professional then start to look closely at the worm and how it is moving and discuss what it is doing there, how it lives and moves, developing their vocabulary and understandings of worms.
> In this way, the scientific learning emerges from the children's natural exploration or discovery. The professional uses each experience as an opportunity to look more closely at the scientific phenomena (how materials change and animals in the environment) and encourages the children to express their ideas orally. They develop their vocabulary by talking about mixtures, changes in materials and the movement of the worm, and increase their conceptual understanding by making links between events and ideas.

Box 3

> **Case study 2: A Reception/Year 1 class**
> The role play area in the classroom is set up as an airport and children make their own passports (identifying their personal features, such as hair and eye colour, height and so on), pack their suitcases with clothes suitable for different destinations and weather conditions, get on the plane and watch videos of different destinations, as well as looking at holiday brochures. The teacher joins the play by being a passenger, questioning the children (who are in role as airport staff) about the destination, what clothes they should take and how heavy their luggage can be. Through the role play, a range of developments can be addressed in a thematic way:
> - knowledge and understanding of the world, involving aspects of:
>   – science (exploring and investigating similarities and differences between ourselves and others, materials and their properties)

Learning in science at the primary level

> – geography (exploring places)
> – ICT (using digital cameras to take photographs to add to the passport and data handling in adding details to the passport)
> - problem solving, reasoning and numeracy (deciding weight, height and so on)
> - language, literacy and communication.
>
> In one session, a group of children were playing in the airport and the teaching assistant took the role of the passport controller. She spent a long time looking at each child's passport and questioned them about their photograph and how they knew this was their passport and not someone else's. Ellie said, 'I know it is mine 'cos I have long hair and Suzie has short'. Suzie said, 'But, we [both] have blue eyes and we're fair', to which the professional responded by asking both children to stand side by side and look in a mirror to see what their similarities and differences were. Bobbie stamped their passports and asked where they were going, to which Suzie responded, 'We are going to see Santa'. Bobbie thought for a moment and said, 'It is cold where Santa lives ... why you got these?' (pointing at some sunglasses and a sun hat). After a little more discussion the girls decided to repack the bags for colder climes.

These two case studies illustrate how exploratory, discovery and play approaches can be highly successful. The success is dependent on the supported social interaction, as in the discussion between the professional and the children in Case study 1 and the engagement of the professional in the role play in Case study 2. In both cases, the social interactions help the children to develop scientific vocabulary (for example, about worms in Case Study 1) and share ideas (for example, about physical similarities and differences in Case study 2). In each case study the children were engaged in exploration of scientific ideas in a motivating, relevant and thematic way, helping the children to make sense of their experiences and everyday life and develop positive attitudes towards science.

Issues in Early Years science

The main issues that challenge children's progression are generic rather than specific to science and revolve around transitions from home to formal care to school. The design of the National Curriculum in England and Wales (DfEE, 1999) did not build on Early Years practice and provision and so the introduction of a play- and skills-based curriculum for the youngest children in England (DCSF, 2008) made transition to Key Stage 1 and the more formal knowledge-based National Curriculum difficult for children. Even within the Early Years there are obstacles to transition because of professionals' different expertise and emphases – birth to three years of age, three to five years of age, or a focus on social care, physical well-being or education. This makes a difference in scientific development as different professionals may or may not emphasise the science in the activities.

The differences between the EYFS and primary school extend beyond the structure of the curriculum to strategies and foci for assessment and as a result professionals can find it difficult to see how scientific development progresses through the stages and beyond. Indeed, it takes good scientific knowledge on the part of the professional or teacher to understand:

- the scientific concepts and skills
- what they look like at different stages of development
- how young children develop their understandings, skills and attitudes
- the approaches that can support them on their journey.

In conclusion

So much that is good practice in primary science education is also good practice in Early Years education in general. Experience and talk are key factors and better routes to development of early understandings than didactic approaches. The case studies have illustrated how exploratory and play activity can lead to learning with the support of professionals who go with the flow of children's ideas rather than trying to direct them.

Finally, working with young children should aim to motivate them so that they want to explore the world around them, supporting them as they explore by modelling behaviours and pointing out features of scientific phenomena and involving them in discussion to encourage further exploration and the development of the foundations of understandings, skills and attitudes.

References

Bruce, T. (2009) *Early Childhood* (second edition). London: Sage.

DCSF (2008) *The Early Years Foundation Stage: Setting the Standard for Learning, Development and Care for Children from Birth to Five; Practice Guidance.* London: DCSF.

De Boo, M. (ed) (2004) *The Early Years Handbook. Support for Practitioners in the Foundation Stage.* Sheffield: Geography Association.

DfEE (1999) *The National Curriculum: Handbook for Teachers in England.* London: DfEE/QCA.

Johnston, J. (2005) *Early Explorations in Science.* Buckingham: Open University Press.

Johnston, J. (2009) What does the skill of observation look like in young children? *International Journal of Science Education.* **31**(18) 2511–2525.

Kallery, M., Psillos, D. and Tselfes, V. (2009) Typical didactical activities in the Greek early-years science classroom: do they promote science learning? *International Journal of Science Education*, **31**, 9.

Mayall, B. (2007) Children's lives outside school and their educational impact. *Primary Review Research Briefings* 8/1. Available online at: www.primaryreview.org.uk/Downloads/Int_Reps/3.Children_lives_voices/Primary_Review_8-1_briefing_Children_s_lives_outside_school_071123.pdf

Naylor, S. and Keogh, B. (2000) *Concept Cartoons in Science Education.* Cheshire: Millgate House Education

QCA (2000) *A Scheme of Work for Key Stages 1 and 2 – Science.* London: QCA.

Rousseau, J.J. (1911) *Emile.* London: Dent and Sons.

Chapter 5

Learning and the brain: insights from neuroscience

Wynne Harlen

Until the 1990s, direct knowledge of the inside of the brain was a matter of mystery to all except the few – the brain surgeons, revered for their specialist knowledge. Now, however, according to a recent OECD/CERI report:

'After two decades of pioneering work in brain research, the education community has started to realise that 'understanding the brain' can help to open new pathways to improve educational research, policies and practice.'

OECD/CERI (2007, p13)

Early work was focused on explaining and attempting to treat unusual behaviours and conditions, but interest now extends to the implications of neuroscience for regular education. In this chapter, we look at what neuroscience – the study of the brain – reveals about conditions that promote learning. Physiologically, learning is the creation of networks of connections in the brain that form as a result of response to the environment. Understanding of how the brain responds, however, depends on realising how it functions, so we begin with what research has revealed about the working of the brain and how it changes over a lifetime. We then look at what brain research can reveal about the conditions that promote learning in general and how it might apply to learning science at the primary level.

Brain basics

Needless to say, the brain is very complex and there is still a great deal to learn about its structure and functions. In the brain, there are cells are called neurons, which are concerned with the transmission of information, and glial cells, which have various functions in supporting the neurons but are not involved in dealing with information. The adult brain consists of about 100 billion neurons and something like a trillion glial cells. Each neuron comprises a cell body, to which are attached a number of thread-like structures, known as dendrites, and a longer, thinner, thread called an axon (Figure 1).

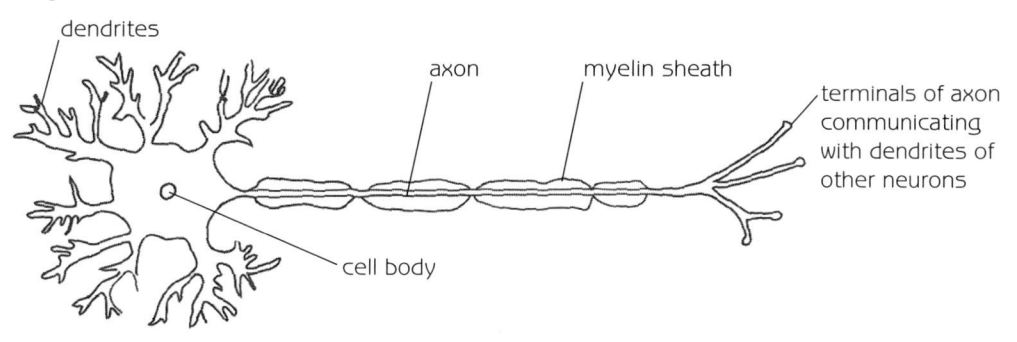

Learning and the brain: insights from neuroscience

Figure 1 A neuron.

The branches at the other end of the axon each end in a terminal, capable under certain circumstances of communicating with one of the dendrites of another cell. Given the number of cells, the possible combinations of cells with each other is truly astronomical, accounting for the power of the brain to carry out a vast range of different functions, many at the same time. Whether or not a particular connection is made depends on the signal reaching the terminal through the axon. There is a small gap between the axon terminal of one neuron and the dendrite of another, called the synapse, which is only crossed if the electric signal from the neuron sending information is strong enough. This could happen as a result of signals from several neurons arriving at the same time. Signals are transmitted more quickly if the axon is well insulated by a covering of a fatty substance called myelin. Myelin forms gradually, particularly in adolescence, and is associated with an increase in the efficiency of the brain.

Brain activity depends not on the *number* of neurons (most are present at birth) but on the *connections* between them, each one being able to link with many others. Learning and forgetting involves creating new connections, or synapses, and pruning others no longer being used. The term 'plasticity' describes the brain's ability to change in this way.

Where in the brain such changes are made depends on the type of message involved, for not every part is involved in responding to every stimulus. To map the areas of response to certain types of stimulus, each of the two halves of the brain is divided into areas. The main divisions are described as lobes: frontal at the front behind the forehead, occipital at the back, parietal in between and temporal at the side. Actually, these terms refer to the outer layer of the brain, the cortex, which is well developed in higher animals and folded to accommodate a large surface area in the skull. Inside the cortex are other structures that have important roles in learning, relating to memory and emotions. More localised areas of the cortex are found to be connected with certain stimuli and responses and so are described as the motor cortex, visual cortex, auditory cortex and so on. However, in relation to more complex activities such as language, different areas of the brain are active according to whether speaking, reading, listening or writing is involved. So Greenfield concludes that:

> '... it is misleading to think of one brain region as having one specific, autonomous function, as in the phrenologists' scenario. Instead, different brain regions combine in some way to work in parallel for different functions.'
>
> Greenfield (1997, p39)

This explains why, following a stroke or an accident that damages a particular part of the brain, the functions immediately lost are, in time, regained as other parts of the brain take over its role. A similar point applies to the two halves of the brain. It has been shown that these control different abilities, the right hemisphere being dominant in spatial abilities and face recognition and the left hemisphere in language, mathematics and logic. However, both are highly complex and contribute to overall brain activity, so:

> '… it is much too simplistic to describe any person as a 'left-brain learner' or a 'right-brain learner'.'
>
> OECD (2007, p39)

Brain changes over the lifetime

While most neurons are present at birth, learning from experience requires the creation of networks of groups of neurons. Some networks are formed before birth, as evident in a foetus' response to the mother's voice. Indeed, the environment in the womb *'can affect later cognition'* (Goswami and Bryant, 2007, p1). For instance, the result of excessive consumption of alcohol by a mother has a direct effect on the brain development of her child.

After birth the brain continues to grow in size (at the age of four it is four times its size at birth) due to the formation of connections. A newborn learns in various ways, such as noticing patterns, imitation or applying what is noticed in one simple situation to another. Growth in brain size accompanies learning at any age (Box 1) but is particularly marked in the pre-school years and underpins the importance of early childhood experience and education. Severely impoverished environments and neglect in the early years are associated with delayed cognitive development. However, there is no evidence in favour of 'hot housing' children at an early age; a normally stimulating environment is all that is needed.

Box 1 Physical change associated with learning

> *'In a study of juggling, the brain areas activated at the beginning of a three-month training period increased in size by the end of it. After three months of rest, these areas had shrunk back and were closer to their original size. This graphic example of 'if you don't use it, you lose it' demonstrates the potential importance of education in mediating brain development throughout our lives.'*
>
> Howard-Jones et al. (2007, p21)

The brain continues to grow, but more slowly during the primary school years. Nevertheless there are constant changes as new connections between neurons are made and existing ones strengthened or pruned in response to experience. So the ideas that children develop at an early stage can be changed later.

> *'The nervous system sets up a large number of connections; experience then plays on this network, selecting the appropriate connections and removing the inappropriate ones.'*
>
> Bransford et al. (1999, p104)

Learning and the brain: insights from neuroscience

The onset of adolescence is marked by growth in several parts of the brain, which can account for some of the changes in mood, behaviour, physical control and higher-level thinking. For instance, taking risks may increase as a result of changes in the parts of the brain regulating the desire for quick rewards. The release of sex hormones at adolescence affects the parts of the brain connected to emotions through the release of serotonin and other chemicals influencing mood and 'thrill-seeking behaviour', particularly in peer groups. At the same time parts of the brain relating to the exercise of judgement are still developing. The frequent effects of this combination account for the cost of car insurance for teenage drivers!

The brain continues to change in adulthood, mainly in the number of connections rather than in the number of neurons. The plasticity of the brain – the ability to prune, reinforce or create connections – enables learning to continue. The key finding in relation to brain change in older people is that synapse connections will decline, with the loss of cognitive functions, if they are not used and constantly reinforced. In addition to continuing to learn and use the mind, trials have shown that physical fitness also helps in maintaining cognitive functioning.

Brain activity and learning

The structure of the brain already provides some clues in relation to learning. For example, it seems likely that practice will help to create connections between neurons that have some permanence as long as they continue to be used, instead of everything having to be learned from scratch. But modern research, using non-invasive techniques for detecting activity in the brain (Box 2), has advanced our knowledge of what kinds of experiences lead to learning. In this section, we look at what this tells us about learning in general before turning to what can be said about particular domains of learning.

Box 2 Detecting brain activity

Finding which parts of the brain are active when a person is engaged in various activities – functional imaging – uses the fact that when neurons are activated they use more energy and this is supplied by oxygen in the blood. Thus changes in the oxygen carried by the haemoglobin provide an indirect measure of neuron activity. The amount of oxygen carried affects the magnetic field of the haemoglobin and these changes in magnetic field can be detected by Magnetic Resonance Imaging (MRI). The strong magnetic field produced in MRI results in radio signals from atoms in the haemoglobin, which vary with the activity of the brain area under examination.

Memory

In terms of changes in the brain, memory is what is left as a result of processing information. The more the same path is activated, the more easily the experience causing it is recalled. It is through memory, both short term and long term, that we are able to learn. Different systems in long-term memory are associated with different types of learning. 'Semantic' memory refers to the storing of factual knowledge, and 'episodic' memory enables and requires the conscious recall of information from past experiences. 'Implicit' or 'procedural' memory concerns actions that, once learned, become automatic, such as riding a bicycle. These types of memory develop at different rates, procedural at an earlier age than episodic

Learning in science at the primary level

memories, which require construction and so depend on how experience is interpreted (Goswami and Bryant, 2007, p8). Remembering is important in learning and life. Research shows that detailed and enduring memories are formed when the original events are accompanied by talk, especially by conversation with adults who elaborate and evaluate the experience.

Short-term or working memory holds information while it is being used, or processed into the longer-term memory. If information is not used within about 30 minutes the memory of things such as new telephone numbers will be lost. But the more it is rehearsed and recalled, the longer it lasts, and with frequent revisiting it will be held in long-term memory (as for often-used telephone numbers). Research shows that short-term memory depends on the sounds of words and is particularly important in learning to read. Investigations of the conditions that favour memorisation have shown that making notes or drawings helps in the solution of problems. It appears that putting something on paper relieves some of the heavy demand on the working memory (Howard-Jones et al., 2007).

Language

As already mentioned, language has an important role in the development of both long-term episodic and short-term memory. Brain studies tell us when language-related areas of the brain are activated during learning. As interactions leading to learning are likely to involve speaking, listening, reading and writing words, several parts of the brain are used. Words are important because they represent objects or events, while being separate from the objects or events. This detachment of the symbol, the word, from what it represents enables the mental manipulation of experience, which is then no longer dependent on direct action.

This representation is also essential to the development of metacognition – thinking about thinking – which is necessary for the development of control over mental processes, feelings and behaviour. The emergence of metacognition begins in the late primary years, according to Goswami and Bryant (2007), but mainly takes place in adolescence and adult life. It enables secondary pupils to improve their learning and memory by *'adopting effective cognitive strategies and by being aware of when they don't understand something'* (Goswami and Bryant, 2007, p14). These changes are consistent with neuroscientific findings about the nature and timing of the development of the brain (OECD/CERI, 2007, p198).

The role of emotions

Learning is not only influenced by the parts of the brain associated with cognition, but is also dependent on inner structures concerned with emotions. Most people have had some experience of intense stress or anxiety that interferes with normal functioning. Great excitement, anger or sudden danger can affect judgement. On such occasions, the release of chemicals from parts of the middle of the brain interferes with the operation of areas of the cortex, while triggering automatic reactions in the nervous system. Two of these chemicals are adrenaline, which causes a sudden release of energy affecting the heart rate and blood pressure, and dopamine, which is associated with pain and pleasure.

While excessive stress is damaging to cognitive functioning, some stress is needed in order to face the challenges involved in daily life and particularly in learning. At a level that enables energy to be directed effectively so that new ideas or skills are mastered, stress is positive, motivating learning and leading to the pleasure that comes from achieving a goal (Zull, 2004). So here is support for the importance of taking account of children's initial ideas and skills and providing, in the words of the Plowden report:

'an environment and opportunities which are sufficiently challenging for children and yet not so difficult as to be outside their reach.'

CACE (1967, paragraph 533)

In addition to these environmental factors, there are others relating to interest and importance to the learner, which derive from past experience. Engagement in learning depends on giving attention to certain stimuli, which depends on the brain's assessment of their importance to the learner's self-identify.

'Central to the unconscious selection of what to attend to and what to learn is the self, which is itself learned and developed through our interactions with others.'

Hallam (2005)

Health and well-being

The planned activities in school are one aspect of the external environment that influences learning. Everyday experiences of a good diet, sufficient physical exercise and sleep are also important. There is, for instance, evidence to support the value of eating breakfast, of avoiding caffeine and of not becoming dehydrated. There is little evidence of the value of drinking large quantities of water when not dehydrated. The effectiveness of additional omega-3 oils in the diet is not proven for the general population but there does appear to be some value in these supplements for children with ADHD (Richardson and Puri, 2002).

A variety of reasons have been proposed for the value of sleep. It may consolidate learning that has taken place when awake, but there is no evidence that learning can take place while sleeping. Sleep also gives the brain time to produce proteins and other substances needed for it to function properly, not only for learning but also in controlling the processes of the body. Greenfield explains:

'We normally use only a part of the energy derived from food and oxygen for immediate conversion to heat. The remaining energy is stored for all the other vital functions of the brain and body. If people are allowed only three hours of sleep a night, many of these functions start to decline within a week. If we are deprived of sleep, energy is not stored efficiently; more is immediately squandered, dissipated as heat. Thus, persons who are continuously and completely sleep deprived would eventually, literally be burning themselves out.'

Greenfield (1997, p75)

Physical action and concept development

It is common experience that infants and young children learn through acting on objects and observing what happens. When an action repeatedly leads to a particular result it strengthens the cognitive representations in the brain as neural connections distributed across various areas of the brain. Relationships between action and effect lead to the development of explanations in terms of what has been observed: an action followed by an event is considered to be the cause of the event. This kind of reasoning is found in infants in simple cases, but the ability to deal with more than one cause develops more slowly. In this way children build their ideas about the things around them. These ideas may conflict with the scientific view and so are often called the children's own or alternative ideas. They are likely to persist in the face of contradictory events because what the children observe is focused by their pre-existing knowledge.

Learning in science at the primary level

Pupils need to be introduced to different ways of thinking about things in order to develop scientific understanding. However, Goswami and Bryant report on the basis of brain studies that:

> 'When we learn particular science concepts, such as the Newtonian theory of motion, these concepts do not replace our misleading naïve theories. Rather than undergoing conceptual change, the brain appears to maintain both theories.'
>
> Goswami and Bryant (2007, p5)

This confirms evidence from studies at the macroscopic level of behaviour that pupils can hold conflicting ideas at the same time (for example, Driver, 1983). The teacher's role is to help pupils recognise situations in which it is appropriate to use scientific reasoning and concepts rather than their naïve ideas. Repeated use of the connections relating to scientific ideas, and neglect of naïve theories, should eventually lead the latter to fade.

Implications for learning science at the primary school

A key message for science education from neuroscience is that the development of science concepts depends on simultaneous activity in the visual, spatial, memory, deductive and kinaesthetic regions of the brain, and in both hemispheres (Goswami and Bryant, 2007). This indicates the need for a variety of different kinds of experience involving both physical and mental activity. It involves being able to touch and manipulate objects, using language, linking to previous experience, reasoning and reflection.

Perhaps not surprisingly, this evidence found at the microscopic level of brain cells confirms what is found at the macroscopic level of studying how pupils respond to educational stimuli. Both support the assertion that pupils should be provided with experiences that:

- interest and engage children – are seen by them as relevant and appealing
- build upon their previous experience, allowing some repetition to consolidate and apply learning
- provide challenge within the reach of children so that they experience pleasure in learning
- engage the emotions by making learning science exciting.

There is also support for teaching methods that:

- encourage talk, argumentation and exchange of ideas among pupils
- enable active investigation and the use of the senses
- provide practice in using skills and applying ideas
- create habits of using representations and keeping notes to aid memory
- ensure that pupils understanding their goals and how to assess achievement (formative assessment)

- encourage reflection on what they are learning and how they are learning, and awareness of what they don't understand
- promote the use of scientific ideas, once formed, in preference to intuitive naïve theories.

In conclusion

Studies of the brain show that it is changing all the time in response to the environment. The changes associated with learning involve the creation of connections between neurons and of networks of connections. After a period of considerable growth through the rapid creation of connections, in the first four or five years of life, the next big changes in the brain occur as adolescence begins. In the primary school years, brain development proceeds through creating and removing connections in response to experience – connections that are frequently used are retained while others that fall out of use may be lost.

The investigations of brain activity during learning lend support to many of the ideas about how to promote learning that derive from educational research – in particular, the importance of talk and discussion, and of starting from existing ideas, as well as many of the strategies associated with assessment for learning. Physical activity and the use of the senses lead to the development of ideas about scientific aspects of the world. Children are learning how to learn and it is important that they enjoy it. This means that the subject should interest and engage them but also that they should be aware of what they are trying to learn and know when they have achieved a particular goal. In the upper primary years, learning becomes more efficient due to increased insulation (myelination) of the parts of the neurons transmitting messages. This is also the time when pupils can be involved in thinking about how they learn, thus beginning to develop metacognition and responsibility for their learning and behaviour.

References

Bransford, J.D., Brown, A.L. and Cocking, R.R. (eds) (1999) *How People Learn: Brain, Mind, Experience and School.* Washington DC: National Academy Press.

CACE (Central Advisory Council for England) (1967) *Children and their Primary Schools.* London: HMSO.

Driver, R. (1983) *The Pupil as Scientist?* Milton Keynes: Open University Press

Goswami, U. and Bryant, P. (2007) *Children's Cognitive Development and Learning.* Primary Review Research Survey 2/1a. Cambridge: University of Cambridge Faculty of Education.

Greenfield, S. (1997) *The Human Brain: A Guided Tour.* London: Pheonix.

Hallam, S. (2005) *Enhancing Motivation and Learning Throughout the Lifespan.* London: Bedford Way Publications, Institute of Education.

Howard-Jones, P., Pollard, A., Blakemore, S-J., Rogers, P. Goswami, U., Butterworth, B., Taylor, E., Williamon, A., Morton, J. and Kaufmann, L. (2007) *Neuroscience and Education: Issues and Opportunities.* London: TLRP/ESRC.

OECD/CERI (2007) *Understanding the Brain: the Birth of a Learning Science.* Paris: OECD.

Richardson, A.J. and Puri, B.K. (2002) Omega-3 fatty acids in ADHD and related neurodevelopmental disorders. *International Review of Psychiatry,* 18 (2), 233–239.

Zull, J.E. (2004) The art of changing the brain. *Educational Leadership,* **62** (1), 68–72.

Section 2

Teaching primary science

Chapter 6

Planning: elements of an effective lesson plan

Rosemary Feasey

This chapter explores the key elements of effective planning in primary science. There is no single 'right' way to plan science lessons, hence the chapter offers a framework against which teachers can audit their science planning. It begins by putting lesson planning in the context of planning at different levels. This is followed by a short but essential reminder of the importance of creativity. The main section considers key elements of an effective lesson plan under 15 headings. These are aspects that must be considered, but not necessarily written down, in order to support flexible and creative teaching.

Levels of planning

Planning helps the teacher to think through a lesson, and identify those aspects needing particular preparation. There are three main levels of planning, which are like pieces of a jigsaw; when the pieces (levels) are put together they show the whole picture at different degrees of detail. Common to each level of planning is:

> '… the expectation that children should make progress in their learning, should build on, and integrate their knowledge so that they deepen their understanding and skills.'
>
> Pollard (1997, p183)

Long term

This level of planning provides an overview of what is taught in science in each year group across the school and should always be audited against the relevant national curriculum to ensure coverage. As well as covering the statutory curriculum, there is an important subtext; the science leader should ensure that across a child's primary science career they are given regular experience of the following:

- links with other areas of the curriculum
- development of personal competences (for example, Smart Science – see *Websites*)

Planning: elements of an effective lesson plan

- exposure to other people with science expertise, such as university scientists
- frequent use of the school grounds
- visits to different environments, science venues and organisations.

Medium term

This next level of detail provides an overview of a topic or a unit of work. This level of planning should indicate the learning in science and links to other curriculum areas such as maths, literacy and ICT. A medium-term plan indicates progression in developing children's thinking and working in science beginning with eliciting children's prior understanding, then activities to develop an idea or skill, followed by provision of opportunities for broadening and deepening children's understanding, and finally opportunities for applying their recently developed knowledge and skills in a range of new contexts. Throughout the medium-term plan opportunities for formative assessment should be identified.

Short term

Short-term planning identifies the detail of teaching and learning throughout individual lessons or sessions. Lesson planning should relate to previous and subsequent lessons, as outlined in the medium term plan to ensure progression.

Planning and creativity

It is a lot easier to write a lesson plan than to translate it into reality. The most successful lessons usually belong to those teachers who, although they may provide meticulous planning in science, are able to be flexible in how those plans work in the classroom. Kyriacou suggests that:

> '… while lesson plans are important, all teachers will need to tailor the development of the lesson to the needs of the moment.'
>
> Kyriacou (2007, p61–2)

Effective lessons are those that the teacher has carefully planned but has not forgotten to:

- be enthusiastic
- offer experiences that are relevant to the children
- share ownership with the children
- take a risk and try new approaches
- be willing and able to listen to the children
- change course in a lesson where appropriate
- change role many times (for example, manager, facilitator, challenger and so on)
- stand back and know when to observe and when to interact.

Oliver (2006, p39) reminds us that when planning science we should also be planning for creativity, which might be seem a *'paradox, in that planning is the very activity that stifles creativity'*. She also observes that creative planning in science needs *'an understanding of how a flexible framework for creative planning can be constructed, used and developed'*. She offers the following key points in relation to creative planning (Oliver, 2006, p60).

- Creative planning needs construction within a flexible framework.
- Adaptation of resources and ideas are part of a creative approach.
- Creative planning involves making interesting connections.
- Planning to use and develop children's creativity widens understanding.
- Unknown outcomes are inevitable if flexibility is valued.
- Creative planning does not limit science to a specified time slot.

Key elements of an effective lesson plan

In this section, the key elements of an effective lesson plan are considered. They are not intended as a set of headings to be ticked off, but ideas to think about in order to decide which are applicable to the lesson or series of lessons being planned. A note of caution is given here relating to the 'three-part lesson' favoured by Literacy and Numeracy Strategies (introduction, activity and plenary). In primary science, this can lead teachers to be less creative in their approach. Science lessons could have many parts – for example, teachers might begin with a game to reinforce language, then introduce children to a problem to solve over several lessons, then the children might communicate the outcomes to a specific audience. In another lesson, the children might explore magnets to remind themselves what they already know, and then decide what else they want to find out about magnets, explore and investigate answers and make a book of their new knowledge. The best lesson plans are those that are not written to an imposed formula, but are written to meet the needs of the learners in the classroom.

Learning outcomes

Learning outcomes should focus on two key areas of science learning:

- conceptual understanding of key scientific ideas (such as forces, electricity, adaptation)
- thinking and working scientifically.

Some schools base their planning on developing a set of core or key skills across the curriculum, such as asking questions, planning, evidence, analysis, drawing conclusions, using the concepts in science as the contexts for developing these skills.

Where schools are using a cross-curricular approach, the challenge in planning is to ensure the integrity of the science learning – to ensure that the science is not diluted to the extent that it becomes a literacy or history lesson rather than science. (See Chapter 7 for issues related to science in cross-curricular activities.)

While learning outcomes are useful, we should not become too focused on them to the detriment of the bigger picture. When planning at any level, we need to know where we are – as Skamp (2008, p31) suggests, we need to have some knowledge of the *'conceptual territory of the lessons.'* This fits well with Harlen and Qualter (2009, p38) who write that understanding begins with making sense of immediate experiences, which they call 'small ideas'. As children's experiences are extended over a series of lessons, it becomes possible for children to '*link events which are explained in different ways to form ideas which have wider applications and so can be described as bigger ideas*'. This offers a logical sequence to all the levels of planning, and reinforces the importance of providing children with experiences that strengthen and deepen different learning to '*secure the new ideas in their thinking*' (Harlen and Qualter, 2009, p118).

Towards the end of a lesson or a topic, giving children a challenge to apply their skills and understanding to new contexts provides a natural opportunity for formative assessment, giving the teacher '*the opportunity to see how secure the new idea really is*' (Harlen and Qualter, 2009, p118). At this point the teacher can make adjustments to the plan – for example, to go over the idea again, provide experiences that offer breadth or depth to a pupil's understanding or move the pupil onto a new idea.

Starting points

Starting points for lessons need to be hands-on and motivate the learner. They can range from a game, picture or poem to a story or a letter challenging the children to solve a problem. Science activities need a 'hook' and the more realistic the hook, the more easily children will be able to apply their personal learning to the context. It has become common in primary science to begin lessons by asking children what they remember or what they know. Interestingly, this is often met with blank faces because young children find it difficult to recall prior knowledge if there is no context or practical activity to cue them into the area of learning.

Activities

The mistake that many teachers make in primary science is to find activities first and then decide what learning outcomes fit. This is a dangerous approach and can lead to an eclectic mix of tasks that lack progression and do not meet the needs of the learner. It is best to begin planning activities with an overview of the bigger idea (main concept or skills) and how that idea might be broken down into smaller bite-size learning. Then consideration should be given to the most appropriate learning opportunities for the children in the class – for example:

- **exploration** – activities where children try something out to see what happens
- **investigation** – often a fair test activity
- **research** – finding information using books, posters, leaflets, internet and experts
- **observation** – using all the senses and collecting measurements
- **data gathering** – using secondary data, carrying out surveys
- **exemplification** – following instructions to develop a concept or a skill.

Effective questions

When planning science lessons, some teachers jot down a set of key questions as an aide-mémoire to help ask children appropriate and challenging questions during a lesson. In most lessons the teacher will include in their lesson planning opportunities for developing children as effective questioners (Chapter 9).

Teaching primary science

Key vocabulary

When planning a lesson, the easy task is making a note of both the basic and extended vocabulary that is linked to the learning outcomes. The challenge is to weave into a lesson different ways of supporting children in learning and using key scientific language. Feasey (2009) offers a range of science games to use as starters, during or at the end of lessons, to support children in learning scientific words – for example, Kim's Game, word chains and many others.

Personal capabilities

Primary science requires children to develop a range of personal capabilities such as teamwork, creativity, communication, self-management and problem solving, backed up by:

- tenacity – sticking at a task in order to meet deadlines
- positive self-image – valuing yourself and your achievements
- self-motivation – motivating yourself to do what needs to be done
- critical thinking – critically reviewing and evaluating what you do and how you do it
- social intelligence – responding appropriately to people and situations.

In primary science, we would expect to see these as learning outcomes since they require children to work cooperatively and collaboratively to solve problems and communicate outcomes to a range of audiences.

Classroom management

Planning must take into account the way in which the class and classroom is structured in order to facilitate teaching and learning.

> 'To succeed, classroom organisation must relate to the values, aims and curriculum plans as a whole and to practical circumstances.'
>
> Pollard (1997, p208)

So, what might be considered effective classroom management? First, to organise the classroom in such a way that children develop as independent learners who are able to choose appropriate equipment to use in their work. Second, to realise that the optimum size for a working group in science is probably four; with larger groups the teacher runs the risk of having children who are off task. Four is a good number for discussions, enabling children to work with 'science talk partners' and share ideas with their opposite pair. Four is also a useful number for children carrying out fair test type investigations, allowing each child to have a role – for example:

1. science resource manager (the only child allowed away from their group to get resources)
2. science fair tester
3. science measurer
4. science recorder.

Planning: elements of an effective lesson plan

These roles can be rotated ensuring that each group member develops different skills. Children enjoy wearing role badges, which can be purchased from education suppliers or made by the teacher or children.

Planning for discussion

'It is our view that the teacher and the student talk around these activities is at least as important in establishing scientific knowledge in the classroom as the activities themselves.'

Miller et al. (2000, p126)

Children prefer to engage in discussion with each other rather than with the teacher because, as one child commented, *'I learn more from talking to my friend than I do listening to my teacher'*. When children are engaged in talk with each other they share ideas, possibly change their ideas, and spend more time discussing science than they could do with a teacher who might have 30 other children needing attention in the same lesson. As with practical work, four is the optimum size where they can discuss in pairs, and then share ideas within the foursome. So lesson planning should allow sufficient time for children to engage in discussion.

The teacher's role should also be planned: certainly it will be as a listener, but it might also include joining in discussions to model ways of talking. At other points it might be to help children to clarify their thinking by asking questions, or moving children from discussing to explaining and debating ideas. Of course, the teacher will always demand that children use key scientific language, which has been identified in the planning. (See Chapter 10 for further ideas about encouraging talk in science.)

Pace and timing

Pace does matter and it is not just about timing. In primary science, we aim to develop children as autonomous individuals; the level of pupil independence can affect the pace of a lesson. A lesson can be slowed down when children are constantly requesting resources or key words, or are reliant on the teacher to tell them what to do next. Pace also requires the teacher to take cues from the children in terms of when they are ready to move on, or understand an idea. Experienced teachers divide the lesson into pockets of time and support children in working independently to maintain the flow of a lesson. Kyriacou suggests that:

'... pupils' involvement in the lesson can also be facilitated if they are given a clear idea of how much time and effort they are expected to devote to particular tasks or activities.'

Kyriacou (2007, p60)

Children recording and communicating science

An effective lesson plan identifies how children will record and communicate their science and whether the teacher will need to scaffold children in using approaches that are linked to literacy, numeracy or ICT. For example, in a fair test investigation when children have to record measurements the teacher might support them in putting data in a table, or recording observations using an Easi-Speak microphone. In an electricity lesson, the teacher might suggest that children take photographs of, or draw, their circuit or ask them to write a set of instructions for others to follow to make the same circuit.

A different group of children might be able to work independently and decide for themselves which is the most appropriate way to record for a given audience. Each approach makes different demands on children, and takes into account the language ability of the children, but does not compromise the quality of the science.

Differentiation

'It is perhaps the teacher's sensitivity to pupils' needs that is the most important of all the skills involved in effective teaching. This refers to the ability of the teacher to plan lessons and adapt and modify their delivery by taking account of how the lesson will be experienced by different pupils and foster their learning.'

Kyriacou (2007, p19)

There are some areas of scientific understanding that cannot be differentiated because the concept or the skill cannot be broken down into smaller steps. For example, the idea of a push or a pull force is so basic that it defies division. Other concepts, on the other hand, are more complex – for example, evaporation. In a class, children might be at different stages of their understanding of evaporation, from those requiring concrete examples, such a making puddles that will evaporate, to others who are ready to model the water cycle.

Differentiation must be based on the individual's ability in science, not in language. Children's ability to write is not always commensurate with their scientific ability. Many children are orally competent in explaining their science ideas, but for a range of reasons find writing in science difficult. Nevertheless developing children's ability to communicate (and that includes writing) in science is important and the lesson plan should, where appropriate, indicate how children will be supported in recording and communicating their science.

This leads to one of the most frequently asked question in relation to differentiation: whether or not to plan for ability groups. There are many arguments for and against; there is no one answer – it depends on the children, the area of learning and the type of activity. Perhaps the most convincing argument for ability groups results from asking yourself if placing the children in mixed-ability groups would help or hinder progress. For example, what would you do if some children in the class were able to carry out a fair test, in which they repeated readings, took quantitative measurements and drew a line graph – would you include a child who was not yet able to use standard measures or to read a bar graph?

Other adults

Other adults provide important support for primary science, and can vary from teaching assistants assigned to specific individuals or groups, to visitors such as scientists working alongside the children and the teacher (Chapter 20). Their role should be included in the lesson plan, and of course the plan should be shared with those adults. When planning for other adults, you should consider some of the following questions:

- Who will the adults work with, why and where?
- What activities will they support?
- Will additional resources be required?
- How can you ensure that children take the lead in practical work?

- What level of understanding do the adults have of how to support children and scaffold learning?
- Will the adults need help in sharing their expertise with children?
- Will the adults have all of the information that they need – for example, ability levels of the children, timing of the session, key ideas and vocabulary, expectations?

Assessment

Assessment for learning should be built into all short-term plans and the long-term plan should include ways in which pupils' achievement can be summarised over a period of time. So lesson plans should include how teachers will gather information about children's ideas and skills and how children will be involved in self-evaluation. Details of how to do this, and so what the plans might include, are given in Chapter 11. Assessment for Learning should be integral to planning and not an added extra, and it should be used to inform future teaching and learning. This means that planning must remain flexible to ensure that teachers can change their plans according to the developing needs of the children.

Home activities

Home activities should be an integral part of planning. They should be fun, and encourage the children to try out ideas as well as look for applications of concepts. Homework should not try to teach children ideas in science; research (Farrow *et al.*, 1999) indicates that this serves at best only to confuse children.

In conclusion

Planning is an iterative process, demanding reflection on the success of a lesson or topic. That in turn informs practice, which informs planning, and so on. The most successful planning is not formulaic but uses a flexible framework which fosters creativity so that:

> '… teachers are open to different possibilities and also to appreciate that developing creativity is not an option to be disregarded but that, as professionals, we have a duty to be creative and develop creativity in children.'

Feasey (2005, p35)

References

Farrow, S., Tymms, P. and Henderson, B. (1999) Homework and attainment in schools. *British Educational Research Journal*, **5**(3).

Feasey, R. (2005) *Creativity in Science – the WOW Factor.* London: David Fulton.

Feasey, R. (2009) *Jumpstart Science.* Abingdon: Routledge.

Harlen, W. and Qualter, A. (2009) *The Teaching of Science in Primary Schools* (fifth edition). London: David Fulton.

Kyriacou, C. (2007) *Essential Teaching Skills* (third edition). Cheltenham: Nelson Thornes.

Millar, R., Leech, J. and Osborne, J. (2000) *Improving Science Education – the Contribution of Research.* Buckingham: Open University Press.

Oliver, A. (2006) *Creative Teaching – Science in the Early Years and Primary Classroom*. London: David Fulton.

Pollard, A. (1997) *Reflective Teaching in the Primary School* (third edition). London: Cassell Education.

Skamp, K. (ed) (2008) *Teaching Primary Science Constructively* (third edition). Melbourne: Thomson.

Websites

Smart Science: www.personalcapabilities.co.uk/smartscience

Chapter 7

Science within cross-curricular approaches

Lynne Bianchi and Penny Thompson

Taking a cross-curricular approach to teaching and learning provides opportunities that have personal relevance for children and connects to their questions and their everyday lives. Approaches from infusing literacy, numeracy and ICT skills, through to using a personalised topic approach, give children the chance to see the links between science and different areas of their learning and enhances their engagement and motivation for science. For teachers, cross-curricular science challenges us to keep the integrity of science and the subjects it connects with, exploiting key opportunities for learning while maintaining progression and focus on science skills, knowledge and understanding.

Learning experiences are more relevant when children's questions and interests play a part in driving the curriculum design, and subjects and skills combine to build a series of interconnected experiences. This chapter considers the meaning and benefits of cross-curricular science and provides examples of various approaches.

What do we mean by a cross-curricular approach?

Let's first think about what is meant by a 'cross-curricular approach'. It's hard to give one definition for what can be a range of interpretations, from simply making a link between an area of science learning and another subject, to presenting a fully integrated learning programme where science is interlinked in a topic or theme. Various terminology, often used interchangeably, with regard to these approaches includes 'cross-curricular', 'interdisciplinary', 'topic based' and 'thematic curricular'. For the purposes of this chapter, we suggest using Barnes' definition of cross-curricular learning:

> *When the skills, knowledge and attitudes of a number of different disciplines are applied to a single experience, theme or idea, we are working in a cross-curricular way.'*
>
> Barnes (2007, p8)

This way of working was championed in the abandoned proposals for a new primary curriculum for England and is evident in the new Northern Ireland curriculum, each configuring the content of the curriculum in six areas of learning. The idea is that subjects will be complemented by worthwhile and challenging cross-curricular studies that provide ample opportunities for children to use and apply their subject knowledge and skills to deepen understanding. Alexander (2010) questions the ethos of simply bringing subjects together in this way by suggesting that:

> 'The motivation is to make an unmanageable curriculum of ten or twelve subjects more manageable by collapsing them into half a dozen. This may not solve the problem, and in the process much that is important may be lost.'
>
> Alexander (2010, p260)

However, there is agreement on a more flexible and personalised arrangement to the curriculum whereby numeracy, literacy and ICT are embedded in science. We must not forget that creative experiences combining the arts and science can also stimulate motivation, enjoyment and engagement in science.

Some benefits of science in cross-curricular approaches

Children communicate with adults and peers in a vast array of ways, from posing questions, recounting observations, recording evidence, writing explanations or drawing or modelling the outcomes of investigations. The links between science and literacy come from speaking, listening, reading and writing. The links between science and numeracy are just as plentiful as children gather, represent and manipulate data, and the use of ICT should be second nature when undertaking investigations in a technology-rich world.

As Lakin (2006) writes, there is a range of skills such as questioning, hypothesising, predicting, using observations, planning, conducting investigations, interpreting evidence and communicating, which are not unique to science and appear across the curriculum. Assisting children in transferring these skills from one subject area to another still remains key to successful science cross-curricular experiences. The ability to talk using appropriate vocabulary, role play, ask questions and work in a group or team are skills that can be practised during investigative and exploratory activities. The key issue for teachers is to acknowledge these opportunities and to plan actively to scaffold these areas of development. It is through these that children will acquire knowledge, develop understandings and make sense of a topic.

Science and language

The use of scientific literature, including non-fiction books, science magazines, websites and news reports are ideal stimuli for reading and discussion within a topic. Such texts can model writing accounts, instructions and explanations too. Other styles of writing offer a vast array of stories, poems and songs that are ideal for supporting science vocabulary and stimulating creative contexts for scientific investigations. Whether it is in books, via the internet, or from leaflets and papers, children engage with reading science-based texts when they want to find out about something that is new to them or that puzzles them.

Science within cross-curricular approaches

'Primary Upd8' is a published resource offered by the ASE and the Centre for Science Education at Sheffield Hallam University (see *Websites*) that actively uses 'science in the news' to engage children with a wide range of scientific skills. Such activities could be taken as stimuli for further cross-curricular writing, investigation and discussion, and provide the opportunity for literacy to be applied in real contexts.

Whether teachers choose to bring science into literacy or literacy into science, it is essential that children are clear about the learning objectives and that they are supported in the development and use of the relevant skills.

Science and mathematics

Making cross-curricular links between science and mathematics gives children the opportunity to apply mathematical skills and concepts in a real or contextualised way. Working through meaningful problems is important in mathematics; if children find their own solutions to a problem, using their own methods, then their learning will make more sense. Personal experience and engagement in investigative mathematics will help children achieve a deeper understanding. Where connections are being made it is important for children to realise such links and to acknowledge the use and application of maths skills, otherwise taught at different times. Noting clear application of strategies and techniques will also further reinforce children's understanding of the relevance of mathematics in their everyday lives.

The approaches to linking science skills, knowledge and understanding to topics are relatively well understood by teachers. However, opportunities for the design of science cross-curricular experiences go much further. The next section considers these approaches.

Cross-curricular science approaches

While it is recognised that a cross-curricular approach offers a creative way of linking subjects through a common theme that results in pupils working in a meaningful, practical and motivating context, it is also recognised that *'teachers are still struggling to decide on a planning approach'* (Jarvis, 2009, p40). This section provides examples of approaches to planning science cross-curricular experiences, sourced from contemporary projects and research activities. Further information can be sought via the references provided. The range of approaches that are currently being discussed include:

- making a link
- a topic or topic web
- an integrated topic
- a personalised topic.

Making a link

First steps towards moving to cross-curricular work would be to build some connections between learning in different subjects. Here a connection from one area of learning to another is made in a planned way. Associations between knowledge or skills from one lesson or subject and another are made explicit, and opportunities to recognise or use them are encouraged in another lesson or subject.

Teaching primary science

This could be as part of a general lesson discussion, addressed in a relatively straightforward way. For example, *'Remember when we learned about different types of materials and their properties in our science lesson? Now look at the armour that Roman soldiers wore – what were the advantages of metal armour for them and what could have been the disadvantages?'* This could be as short as a five-minute conversation.

Topic or topic web

This approach was popular before the National Curriculum was introduced in England and Wales in 1989. Much was learned from this earlier experience, especially with regard to ensuring progression and keeping links and associations authentic and relevant.

A topic name is found, based on objects (for example, Toys, Plants), an occurrence in everyday life (Summer, Christmas), a theme (Health, Light, Monsters and Giants) or a story (Little Red Riding Hood, The Iron Man). Box 1 gives other examples. These stimulate a holistic experience for the learner – however, the curriculum design remains subject-defined with many being taught as stand alone and separate from one another. Such topics enrich children's learning by presenting it within an overarching theme such that experiences build on a key idea, with subjects sitting side by side and learning remaining distinctive to subject boundaries. Links would also be made with children's experiences beyond the classroom, which would assist in illustrating the learning in real-life contexts.

In all topic approaches, subject learning that is not relevant to the topic, or would be viewed as a tenuous link, would be best taught in isolation. Typically these experiences develop into longer units of work spanning from afternoon sessions up to 4–6 weeks, and benefit from being timetabled in a flexible way.

Box 1   Examples of topic approaches

> **Monsters and Giants for 4–6-year-olds**
> This is a half term topic that covers science by looking at 'monster' plants such as the venus fly trap, animals and growth – for example, the smallest and the largest creatures and what they need to live. Literacy is served by playing with 'Jack and the Beanstalk' puppets to encourage speaking, listening and role play. Maths in included by looking at measures and ordering giant numbers, and using outdoor learning to explore footprints in a dinosaur world.
>
> **The Pollen Project (Jarvis, 2009)**
> As part of a sports day for Early Years pupils, six-year-olds were paired with and monitored by 11-year-olds, who acted as their 'trainers'. This enabled pupils to find and learn about pulse rates and for older children to calculate and record these. Such work could lead to Healthy Living posters or a campaign stretching beyond the school itself to including parents and local exercise centres.
>
> **Double Crossed Project (Brodie, 2008)**
> As a primary–secondary transition activity, teachers used cross-curricular approaches to help contextualise science. Drawing on history teaching and learning approaches, the project has helped science teachers to focus more on the development of arguments, the questioning of evidence, and the application of thinking.

Science within cross-curricular approaches

Integrated topic

Integrated topics still bring together subject learning under the umbrella of a theme or topic, but subjects no longer sit side by side. Efforts are made to link areas of knowledge that share the same or similar modes of exploration and enquiry. Knowledge and skills development would aim to appear seamless to the children rather than being compartmentalised into subjects. Box 2 gives some examples of integrated approaches.

National Curriculum 'cross-curricular themes or dimensions', such as Citizenship, Enterprise, Global and Sustainable Development and Cultural Diversity, aim to be integrated into the teaching and learning using this type of approach. For example, the ethos of citizenship would be infused across the curriculum, colouring or tinting the subjects with an added element.

Box 2 Examples of integrated approaches
See *Websites* section at the end of the chapter for links to these projects.

The SAW project (Osbourn, 2009)
Cross-curricular links are made between Science, Art and Writing. Photographs of 'science in action' are used as a strategy to stimulate creative writing and artwork. This project found that children realise the interconnectedness between science and the arts in that both require skills of curiosity, observation, imagination and communication.

Smart Science (developed from research by Bianchi, 2002)
In this work, fictional contexts are used to lead the learner through 2–3 hour science activities. Although not taking a subject-integrated approach, these experiences adopt a skills-integrated approach, where the personal learning and thinking skills of problem solving, creativity, self-management, communication and teamwork are embedded into rich scientific enquiry learning experiences. The integrated approach here relates to the linking of underpinning process skills within the subject of science, although extended opportunities between other subjects are available.

Personalised topic

This approach responds to the desire for a learner-centred approach to curriculum development. It goes beyond the teacher being the sole decider of the topic themes and focuses on the children taking increasing responsibility for the context in which they learn and the content of their learning. Box 3 describes some examples. Children are encouraged to suggest topics or choose from a selection, with the emphasis on capitalising on their personal interests by posing the questions and problems to be explored. Curriculum design becomes more flexible as subject boundaries are fluid yet opportunities for direct teaching are used when appropriate. Subject knowledge and skills are drawn upon when they are relevant, and much focus is placed on exploring with the children 'how' they will go about finding out more or solving their problems. This approach is enriched by close relationships between home life and school life.

Teaching primary science

Box 3 Examples of personalised approaches
See *Websites* section at the end of the chapter for links to these projects.

Enquiring Minds (Microsoft/Futurelab)
Although Enquiring Minds is a research and development project for lower secondary schools, its principles have relevance for practice in upper primary classes. It aims to give youngsters more freedom to choose the content, process and outcomes of their learning. This requires schools to take risks and enter into a pupil enquiry-led approach, and marks a huge shift in classroom culture, namely the relationship between teacher and pupil. Far from passing all responsibility for learning onto the children, Enquiring Minds suggests that teachers support children to develop knowledge that they did not have previously through first-hand experiences, research, discussion and debate.

The Leonardo Effect (Belfast University)
Originating as a research project funded by NESTA and involving schools across the UK, the Leonardo Effect methodology involves synchronised integration of art and science, based on identifying subject commonalities and using joint learning intentions/outcomes. It focuses on starting the planning of the curriculum with the children's own questions, which evolve through play-based opportunities. An exemplar experience is the exploration of flight, where children observe and collect large amounts of information about mechanical and biological flight from various sources, including external experts. They develop these ideas by using practical activities involving both art and science and then design and create their own imaginary flying creatures. Much emphasis is placed on children working together and developing key skills for learning. Teachers found art and science to be highly compatible and found the removal of subject titles resulted in them and the children taking advantage of opportunities for learning when and where they occurred. It also resulted in creative and meaningful literacy engagement, where motivation to read and to write soared and literacy attainment went up.

Learning in Depth Project (Imaginative Education Research Group, Egan)
The Canadian Imaginative Education Research Group is encouraging the trialling of an approach to independent cross-curricular learning that transcends primary and secondary school education. From the early beginnings of schooling, children are given a random topic, such as colour, light, dust, cars, swimming and so on, which they then take charge of learning more about. They develop a portfolio over a period of 12 years, in which time they become experts, utilising a wide range of cross-curricular skills and coming into contact with different subject areas and knowledge bases. This method is being trialled as a means of encouraging imaginative endeavour and as a means of providing the freedom and wonder of learning in a way that a school curriculum currently doesn't.

Science within cross-curricular approaches

Professional dialogue related to cross-curricular developments

It is essential that any form of curriculum development stimulates professional conversations in order to reflect on the key issues and implications of an approach and in order to build critically and creatively on professional knowledge and experience. The following are some possible conversation starters.

- At what stage in learning is this approach best used, to open or consolidate an area of learning?
- How confident are we that this approach will lead to the learning of key learning outcomes and progression as identified by the National Curriculum?
- What forms of assessment would best support this type of learning?
- What do you feel are the strengths, opportunities and risks associated with this approach?
- What are the implications for me, my job share partner, my teaching assistants, my key stage coordinator, my subject leader, SLT and whole school in taking this approach?

A checklist drawn from key messages from contemporary research that apply to cross-curricular science topics is summarised in Box 4.

Box 4 Messages from research relevant to cross-curricular topics

- Start with what promotes wonder and imagination in children's minds. Inspiration and motivation stems from when children wonder about the world – 'What if I were able to walk in Space?', 'How do fireworks bang?' (Egan, 2009, conference presentation).
- Root all practice in a firm understanding of curriculum aims. Remind yourself of what the key aim of working in a cross-curricular way is. Step back from immediate linking of concepts or skills and consider how the way of working fulfils the overarching curriculum aims (Alexander, 2010).
- Be aware that change in attitudes and gaining confidence to be creative in science takes time. Teachers should use the National Curriculum as a basis for their planning and assessment if they are to make creative cross-curricular links that support progression (Jarvis, 2009).
- Decide on the style of topic approach you wish to use – linked, web, integrated or personalised.
- Be aware to check science coverage against your country's science curriculum requirements to ensure coverage and progression.
- Maintain relevant associations between subject areas or ideas, don't force a link because you feel you have to – make sure it adds value to the overall picture.
- Be aware of the varied types of assessment that could be used, capitalising on formative forms of Assessment for Learning.

In conclusion

The opportunities for science within cross-curricular approaches are ready for all to exploit. Learning in this area has benefits for children in terms of more relevant connections between skills, knowledge and understanding from different subject areas. This type of approach needs to be considered in a creative, thoughtful way, so as to ensure that the integrity of science is maintained and connections invigorate the learning of it and other subjects.

References

Alexander, R. (ed) (2010) *Children, Their World, Their Education*: London: Routledge.
Barnes, J. (2007) *Cross-Curricular Learning 3–14*. London: Sage.
Bianchi, L. (2002) Teachers' Experiences of Teaching Personal Capabilities through the Science Curriculum. PhD Thesis, Sheffield Hallam University.
Brodie, E. (2008) Double Crossed Project: http://extra.shu.ac.uk/cse/triplecrossed/doublecrossed.php
Eagan, K. (2009) Putting imagination back into classrooms, extending horizons. Paper given at the NUT Conference, London, November 2009. Available at www.teachingtimes.com/articles/extendinghorizons.htm
Jarvis, T. (2009) Pollen Project: www.pollen-europa.net
Lakin, L. (2006) Science in the whole curriculum, in Harlen, W. (2006) *ASE Guide to Primary Science Education*. Hatfield: Association for Science Education.
Osbourn, A. (2009) The SAW project: www.sawtrust.org

Websites

A big picture of the curriculum, QCDA: www.qcda.gov.uk/resources/376.aspx
Assessing Pupil Progess: http://nationalstrategies.standards.dcsf.gov.uk/node/20005
Double Crossed Project: http://extra.shu.ac.uk/cse/triplecrossed/doublecrossed.php
Enquiring Minds: www.enquiringminds.org.uk
Learning in Depth Project: www.ierg.net/LiD
National Curriculum: http://curriculum.qcda.gov.uk
New National Curriculum: www.dcsf.gov.uk/newprimarycurriculum
Pollen Project: www.pollen-europa.net
Primary Upd8: www.primaryupd8.org.uk
Science, Art and Writing (SAW) Project: www.sawtrust.org
Smart Science: www.personalcapabilities.co.uk/smartscience
The Leonardo Effect (Hickey, Robson and Flanagan): www.leonardoeffect.com

Chapter 8

Using ICT in teaching and learning science

Anne Qualter

ICT is everywhere, such that now, when we think of communication, we cannot just think about speaking and listening, and reading and writing. To be literate these days goes beyond language and print to include a multiplicity of modes. To communicate and to learn we need to be able to 'read' print, images, sounds, visual representations, people's gestures and body language. Learning through all these means is rich and exciting. This is the world that teachers have to help children to engage with as fully as possible to gain the most from it. ICT for science learning has opened up the world to investigation. We are not confined to the classroom or to the 'here and now'. This chapter considers the many ways in which teachers use ICT in planning and preparing their work and in supporting pupils' learning. ICT has enormous potential in increasing the variety of learning experiences for children but the teacher's role remains a key one.

The teacher's role

Today we can roam the internet for answers to questions immediately. Previously such questions ('*What is petrified wood?*' '*Is there life on Mars?*') might have been forgotten in the business of the day. Now we can get a quick answer and it can be one that leads to further learning. For example, the European Space Agency site, 'ESA Kids', gives a brief overview of the debate about life on Mars, including the very recent discovery suggesting water under the surface. This not only answers a question, but also brings science to life showing how new ideas and discoveries are happening all the time. Such immediate demonstrations of aspects of the nature of science have never been so readily available.

The teacher's role here is not only to provide access to ICT, but to help children to use it for deep learning. Without the intervention of a teacher helping children to reflect on what they are reading, the answer to the question '*Is there life on Mars?*' would be a relatively unsatisfactory *'We don't really know'*. This is underlined in the findings of a survey undertaken for a review of science education by students in 2001 (*Student Review of the Science Curriculum*). The respondents, aged 16–19, reported that the least effective way of learning science was from the internet and the most effective through discussion, debate and experimentation. Primary science, they felt, should show children what's going on in science through experiencing it directly. This is not an argument for avoiding ICT but it underlines the need for the teacher to provide support, framing and a purpose for learning through ICT.

The implications for ICT and primary science are that, for teacher and pupil, it must be an integral part of the learning experience. Using ICT for communication, learning, information seeking and retrieval and for entertainment is an essential skill. To be able to use it well, we need to:

- build the knowledge and skills to use these tools
- develop information literacy to be able to understand and engage with information in whatever form it is presented
- have the language skills to communicate not only face to face but in networked environments
- have well-honed skills in critical thinking and reflection, challenging what we see and hear, questioning information and balancing evidence.

Teachers as ICT users

Modelling effective use of ICT

Just as children are encouraged to write by seeing teachers writing in their daily work – making notes, writing lists, sending emails – they will be encouraged to use ICT when they see their teacher and other adults making use of such tools. Using a computer, iPod, mobile phone or other device to make notes, check out definitions or spellings online, look up recipes or driving directions, put up new photographs of class activities on a screen, look at power usage on an energy consumption monitor or pop in on newborn seals through a webcam (see *Websites*, below) all contribute to an environment in which ICT is integral.

Accessing the huge pool of information

How did people manage before we had the internet? It is now hard to imagine life without instant access to information, ideas and resources. It's strange then how difficult it can sometimes be to find just what you want. This is why we turn to tried and trusted websites, especially those recommended by others. It is useful to keep a record of sites that school staff have found to be useful, but also to use reliable sources such as CLEAPSS (see *Websites*) to which many local authorities subscribe and which provides helpful resources and advice for primary science. 'Grids for Learning' can also be a great help (just type in 'grid for learning' into your search engine to find a local one in England) – they include useful resources, a newsletter and information about local courses for teachers. 'Teachernet' provides a wide variety of resources, ideas and advice from England, while innovative intranets have been developed to cover the whole of Scotland (GLOW) and Northern Ireland (C2KNI), offering huge potential to support schools, teachers, pupils and the wider community (see *Websites*).

Using ICT in teaching and learning science

Making best use of information

The school's collection of hardware and software providing the information management system, the school website and a Virtual Learning Environment (VLE) comprise its learning platform. Managing and communicating the wealth of information that ICT gives access to can be time-consuming. The school website and VLE provide the potential for some real interaction between school and home. Parents enjoy seeing their children's science work on screen, and are more likely to share in activities suggested for home. VLEs also allow software, provided on commercial CD-ROMs, to be loaded onto a shared drive for more flexible access. An example of such a system in use can be found on many primary school websites (for example, see Hitchams School website).

Communicating with others

While the value of schools forming networks to share best practice and to develop practice has been demonstrated, the difficulties in finding time to get together can be a major barrier. Using ICT can help – for example, in the form of video conferencing and social networks. Currently, although quite cheap and effective, these resources are not widely used. However, as schools become more and more ICT competent, the costs (financial and environmental) of teachers travelling to meetings grow, and teachers become more comfortable with social network sites such as Facebook, then the electronic substitutes should come into their own.

Preparing teaching

Most teachers use the internet for ideas and tips for teaching, for lesson plans and resources. It is, however, worth delving a little further to find exciting ways to enhance teaching. For example, articles in *Primary Science* include a description of how YouTube videos can be converted to be used on the interactive whiteboard (Toucher, 2009) and how using video recording of science work can encourage discussion and reflection in evaluating evidence, thus enhancing children's higher order thinking skills (Earle, 2009).

Expanding teachers' knowledge and skills

'Teachers TV' is a must (see *Websites*). It is a multimedia resource providing access to discussions about issues, ideas for activities, case studies, reviews of books, curriculum material and other resources. For example, there are useful videos to help teachers think about planning creatively. 'Teachers TV' is easy to use, both individually and as a group, perhaps led by the school science coordinator. AstraZeneca (see *Websites*) also provide useful primary science modules for individuals or groups.

Other sites that are not structured as professional development also offer help with good ideas and tips, often contributed by teachers across the world. For example, on 'Ideas to inspire' (see *Websites*), teachers are invited to contribute via email or Twitter, and it is possible to sign up to receive RSS feeds or email alerts when something new is added to the website.

Primary teachers often feel that their own background knowledge in science is limited, and certainly when, for example, children are inspired by an issue such as global warming, or genetic testing some preparatory work can help confidence. There are many ways to do this: read a book, search the internet or take a course. There are free Open Learn online courses (see *Websites*) that you can engage with. These include modules on global warming and genetic testing as well as a module on 'Changes in Science Education'. These courses are self-study with no assessment and no additional support. Opportunities for more interactive professional development, particularly through the Science Learning Centres and the ASE regional and national conferences, are described in Chapter 18.

Teachers supporting pupils' learning

ICT has become, more or less, a part of classroom life. In the UK, interactive whiteboards (IWB), digital cameras and digital microscopes are almost standard equipment, which can aid existing practice. The IWB is now a feature of most primary classrooms and teachers are becoming more and more familiar with the range of ways in which they can be used. Whole-class teaching has become more colourful, and it includes more moving images and sound. It is important to remember that learning in science involves children in exploring their own ideas and, through observation and investigation, developing new and more powerful ideas about the world around them. The danger of the interactive whiteboard is for the teacher to lead the questioning and to move at too rapid a pace for the children to really think about their ideas. BECTA has produced a useful booklet, *Teaching interactively with electronic whiteboards in the primary phase* (BECTA, 2006). The number and range of resources available for the IWB is increasing exponentially. This can be daunting. The trick is to learn to use a limited range of resources really well, rather than attempting to master everything.

In many classrooms new technology has become embedded to provide new ways to achieve our ends. However, ICT offers more; it promises to transform the curriculum (Rudd, 2007, p7) by helping us to overcome the barriers to teaching and learning that are created by the traditional concept of the classroom. These barriers are so ingrained and long-standing that we hardly notice them. For instance:

- the teacher is the knowledgeable one, so children need to turn to their teacher and, because there are more children than staff, they have to wait and be kept occupied while they wait

- the classroom is a confined space that limits the direct experiences that the children can have

- the class comprises a limited number of people of a similar age who live in the same general area and have similar experiences.

ICT offers access to knowledge and expertise from many sources, and the opportunity for children to communicate across the world or with the next village, with professors and round-the-world sailors, as well as parents and other members of the community. ICT has the potential to make learning something that is at once personal and expansive.

In this very short chapter there isn't space to explore these ideas in any depth. However, three very short case studies demonstrate elements of the boundary-less classroom that is possible for primary science (Boxes 1 to 3). All the examples are to be found on the internet at the time of writing (see *Websites*). Table 1 shows some other ways in which ICT can be used to enhance learning.

Using ICT in teaching and learning science

Box 1   Case study – Science Flash

Two schools in Kent collaborated on a 'Science Flash Meeting Project'. The Year 5 and 6 children in both schools worked on States of Matter, each carrying out a series of different experiments, using a range of resources, and sharing their explorations with pupils in the partner school. Starting with a Science Week and spanning two more weeks, children were able to raise and answer questions, using reference sources but also through blogging, so they could seek ideas from others in the two schools. They were also able to measure and record using data loggers, gather evidence with digital cameras and publish their findings using a 'Making the News' site (see *Websites*). Finally, a flash conference using webcams was held lasting 45 minutes where the children from the two schools discussed their projects, reflected on their learning and thoroughly enjoyed the experience of reflecting not only on what they did but what others had done.

Key points: For a video conference to work, the children need to have a lot to talk about, and need a clear agenda, to be prepared for the conference with questions for the other group. Without this preparation, video conferences tend to fail.

Box 2   Case study – Science of another world

A science coordinator in Norfolk was participating in a project looking to develop children's creativity. He chose a cross-curricular topic building on pupils' previous work on habitats and computer modelling in ICT, explanations, reports and biographies in literacy and explorers in history. The children were asked to invent their own space exploration company and imagine the space crew and the various skills they would bring. The project 'took off' with the 'discovery', and then computer modelling, of a new solar system of planets with different environments depending on their distance from the new Sun. Children developed their own ecosystems with plants and animals. The coordinator commented that 'I had just as much fun teaching this module as the pupils did taking part': The module did not focus on using ICT, but its use (through computer modelling) certainly enhanced a super project.

Key points: This project underlines the need for careful planning of the whole curriculum, so that the children have opportunities to develop the skills and knowledge of ICT tools in one part of the curriculum, and can then use them to enhance their learning in another part.

Box 3   Case study – Pond dipping

Learning in the natural environment is recognised as being uniquely valuable. Using wireless connected tablet computers (with screens that lie flat like a slate and can be drawn or written on with a stylus pen), children from Fairfield Junior School, as part of a project funded by a computer company, metaphorically took down the wall between the classroom and the school wildlife area. Some pupils visited the school grounds making notes and collecting images of living things found in the pond using a digital microscope connected to the tablet. They sent

Teaching primary science

these back to classmates who projected them onto the interactive whiteboard for identification and collation into a report. (The children could then have used a wiki over the course of the project to help them record and collectively build their understanding, but wikis were less common in 2007 (Harlen and Qualter, 2009).)

Key points: We can change the way we conduct field work such that recording and finding answers to questions about observations do not have to wait until the children get back to the classroom. If these things can be done at the time the motivation is higher, and we avoid that drop in enthusiasm that happens when a half-hour minibeast hunt requires hours of tedious writing up later.

Table 1 More ways to use ICT to enhance learning.

Function	Resource	Examples in use
a reference source	internet access through a classroom computer or a mobile device such as iPhone	• find video clip demonstrations of experiments that are too dangerous for the classroom • look up and use identification keys for plants while on a spring nature walk (perhaps using a key developed by a previous class) **Note:** safety in the use of internet is crucial – see kidSMART for advice (see *Websites*)
exploring ideas	simulations and modelling software	• test out ideas for a new solar system (Box 2) • explore '*What would happen to ...*' questions (e.g. '*What would happen to ... a rocket if we changed the firing angle; ... to the rabbits if all the birds of prey were removed*').
sharing ideas	internet phone email video conferencing blogs wiki	• talk to experts, share ideas with another class of children (Box 1) • report the events of a class residential using a blog (in diary form) • collectively develop a wiki showing flowers blooming in our school grounds and in those of a distant partner
practice and revision, and 'take home'	specialist revision websites resources produced by the class (such as a big book report of a project)	• BBC Bitesize, and other free resources (such as Crickweb), as well as subscription resources or CD-ROMs, include quizzes and interactive activities for learning and enjoyment (collated by teachers onto the school website for pupils at home) • class reports and records of events can be revisited, to show parents or the next class their exciting activities in science, or to provide the knowledge to inform a class play, artwork or song

Function	Resource	Examples in use
recording and collating	digital microscope camera data logger light sensors mobile phones/audio recorders	• get the most out of pond dipping and record organisms for later identification (Box 3) • make a time-lapsed film of a germinating seed • record the temperature of liquid in a set of insulated cups
presenting and reporting	word-processing and publisher software podcasting and video making interactive whiteboard	• develop a class science page for the school website to include video clips of experiments, audio clips of interviews with a scientist, animations and a quiz for friends and family to try out, for example • allow children to use the IWB, fill gaps in text, move objects around, add data – with or without the teacher and the rest of the class involved

In conclusion

ICT has changed our world significantly over the last 20 years. The teacher's role has changed, but is just as important to successful learning as it always was. Children entering this world need to be able to use ICT so that they are a part of the digital age and that their learning is enhanced by it. This requires teachers to be familiar with ICT so that they can help provide access to a broad range of tools and materials for learning and can offer suitable guidance and support. For primary science this means ensuring that children have the opportunity to explore ideas, to use a range of tools to help them to do this successfully, and to provide them with ways to relate what they are doing and experiencing to the wider world. This includes getting the most from learning outdoors, at home and in external environments such as museums and seashores. ICT offers a way to break down the barriers created by the classroom walls and to bring the world into the classroom, to communicate with others, to see and experience things that would otherwise be beyond us. The key to learning science is still *doing* science – and ICT makes it even more exciting.

References

BECTA (2006) *Teaching Interactively with Electronic Whiteboards in the Primary Phase.* Available online at: http://publications.becta.org.uk/display.cfm?resID=25918

Earle, S. (2009) Using video to consider and evaluate evidence. *Primary Science*, 106, 18–21.

Harlen, W. and Qualter, A. (2009) *The Teaching of Science in Primary Schools.* London: David Fulton.

Rudd, T. (2007) Interactive whiteboards in the classroom: www.futurelab.org.uk/resources/documents/other/whiteboards_report.pdf

Student Review of the Science Curriculum: Major Findings (2003) Planet Science, the Science Museum in London and the Institute of Education, University of London. Available online at: www.planet-science.com/sciteach/review/Findings.pdf

Toucher, C. (2009) How television brings science learning to life. *Primary Science*, **109**, 29–31.

Websites

AstraZeneca: www.azteachscience.co.uk/resources/cpd.aspx

BBC Bitesize: www.bbc.co.uk/schools/bitesize

BECTA: www.becta.org.uk

BECTA – Interactive whiteboards and primary science: http://schools.becta.org.uk/index.php?section=cuandcatcode=ss_cu_ac_sci_03andrid=11903

C2KNI – Northern Irelands Intranet for schools and the wider community: www.c2kni.org.uk/index.htm

CLEAPSS: www.cleapss.org.uk

Crickweb: www.crickweb.co.uk/ks1science.html

GLOW – Scotland's Intranet for schools: www.ltscotland.org.uk/glowscotland/index.asp

Hitchams School: http://www.sirroberthitcham.suffolk.sch.uk/

Ideas to Inspire: www.ideastoinspire.co.uk/index.html#1

kidSMART Safety online, advice for parents, teachers and young people: www.kidsmart.org.uk

Making the News: http://kmi4schools.e2bn.net/uk_mtn/

Open Learn: http://openlearn.open.ac.uk/course/category.php?id=10

Pond dipping case study: www.technologyalliance.co.uk/pdf/case_studies/fairfield.pdf

Science Flash Meeting Project case study: www.kented.org.uk/ngfl/projects/science/technologies.html

Science of another world case study: www.uea.ac.uk/edu/creativepartnerships/primary/alien

Seal webcam: www.seabird.org/webcam-live.asp

Teachernet: www.teachernet.gov.uk

Teachers TV: www.teachers.tv

Training and Development Agency (TDA) National database of CPD: https://cpdsearch.tda.gov.uk/default.aspx

Chapter 9

Effective questions

Anne Goldsworthy

Many things influence what happens in the classroom, but one of the most important must certainly be the quality of the questions asked by both the teacher and the children. Teachers ask a lot of questions. Over the course of a lifetime career in teaching, teachers will ask thousands of questions of their pupils. It makes sense to ensure that the questions that are asked are as effective as possible.

In the first section of this chapter we look at the different types of questions that teachers ask in the classroom with a focus on two types of question – those that help us to find out what children know and those that we use to improve their scientific knowledge and understanding and their enquiry skills. We also consider how to set up conditions in the classroom to make children feel that their responses will be valued. There is no point asking a brilliant, probing question if the children feel unable or unwilling to answer. Of course it is not just the teacher who asks questions in a classroom. The questions that children ask of their teacher and of each other will also have a significant impact on their learning. The second section of this chapter considers how we can encourage children to become effective questioners.

Teachers' questions

There are, of course, different forms of questions. The following are to do with classroom management – many questions fall in this category and are used to help classrooms to run more efficiently.

'Will you all look at the whiteboard?'
'Can you move you chair a little over that way?'
'Have you cleared away your equipment?'

However, there are other questions that are very different. These are the ones that get children thinking, such as:

'What's the same and what's different about boiling and evaporation?'
'How much can you trust the results of your investigation?'
'Is a bird an insect? How do you know?'
'What is the evidence that the world is round?'

Teaching primary science

We can further categorise those questions that make children think (Harlen, 2006). For instance, we ask some questions because we want to find out and develop their understanding about science content and about science process skills. We will ask others because we want to encourage collaboration and teamwork and/or ask children to reflect on their learning. We should be aware of all types of questions but should spend most time considering the questions that will develop scientific understanding. These questions are likely to be more effective if we think them through and make them a central part of our planning. We must also ensure that we do everything to create a safe and open classroom climate where genuine debate and conversation are valued (see also Chapter 10).

Questions to promote collaboration and encourage reflection

These questions are designed to help children interact well with each other and think about what they have learned and how they have learned it. They also support open dialogue and debate. Sometimes the children will be talking in small groups and sometimes they will be discussing things in pairs with a partner. The following are examples of this type of question.

'What do you and your partner think is the best way to tackle this?'
'Which parts do your group think will be tricky to do?'
'How many ways can your group think of to explain what happened?'
'What is the one thing that your group would like to find out more about?'
'What do you and your partner understand well and what are you not so sure about?'
'Was there anything that surprised you or your partner?'
'What have you or your partner done that helped you to understand?'

Questions to find out and develop children's ideas

The first thing the teacher needs to do in science lessons is find out the ideas that children have about the concepts being taught. Science is the study of the world around us and through their everyday experiences children will try to make sense of that world. Children very rarely come to lessons without their own ideas about sounds, pushes and pulls, materials, living things or any of the other areas studied in primary science. In order to teach effectively, teachers have to take these ideas into account, so the questions they ask to uncover children's ideas are particularly important. Teachers need to make sure that these questions are open and that there are several possible answers. They also need to make sure that they deal with specific science ideas or learning objectives.

Imagine that a teacher wanted children to learn about the effects of gravity. Table 1 shows four different questions that could be asked. The most effective for finding out children's ideas will be those that are open and also linked to the learning objective.

Effective questions

Table 1 Open and closed questions.

	Open questions	**Closed questions**
Linked to learning objective	When I let the pencil go, it falls to the ground. Are there any forces (pushes or pulls) acting on the pencil, and if so what do you think they might be?	What is the name of the force that pulls the pencil down towards the centre of the Earth?
Not linked to learning objective	What do you know about forces?	Isaac Newton was the first scientist to realise that there was a force called gravity. According to the story, what tree was he sitting under when he first had his idea about gravity?

Sometimes closed questions are necessary to refresh children's memories or to cue them in to the area of science they are about to tackle. But, in the section of a lesson where the teacher wants to find out about the children's ideas, open questions linked to the learning objective are best. It is worth teachers spending time with colleagues working out what questions will get at or develop children's ideas. The following questions were generated over just a few minutes by teachers in Lancashire working together and bouncing ideas off each other.

> 'How can we find out whether plants need soil to grow?'
> 'What is the same about salt water and sugar water and what is different?'
> 'Is it always true that animals have eyes?'
> 'What could explain the materials that a thermometer is made of?'
> 'How can we be sure that gravity is less on the Moon than on Earth?'
> 'Is it always true that light things float?'
> 'Why is wool such a warm material if it is full of holes?'
> 'Is it always true that a material with a waterproof label keeps you dry?'

All of these would provide good starting points for generating discussions in science lessons and would enable children to go on to find out answers either through investigation or through research of secondary sources.

Teachers also need to consider children's likely responses and have the next question ready to further develop their thinking. The questions in the first column of Table 2 are examples of the type that will help find out children's ideas. Some suggestions of likely responses and subsequent questions are shown in the second and third columns.

Teaching primary science

Table 2 Questions starting from children's ideas.

Initial question from teacher	A likely response from children	Follow-up question
If you go into our dark playhouse, which of these things would shine out and which would not?	All the shiny things will shine.	How could we find out?
What do you think this metal spoon was before that … and before that … and before that?	It was in a lorry and before that it came from the factory and before that the factory bought the metal bits to shape into spoons.	How do you think they made the spoon shape? Where did the metal bits come from?
Where do you think soil comes from?	People buy it in bags and put it on their gardens.	When you look at soil under the microscope, does it give you any clues? Where do you think the little bits come from?
What you think happens to make the electric light bulb light up?	The electricity comes out of both ends of the battery, meets in the bulb and when they clash it makes the bulb light up.	What would happen if you had two bulbs in a circuit – how would it work then?
How do we get day and night?	The Sun goes behind a cloud. or The Sun turns into the Moon.	Sometimes the sky is clear and there are no clouds. What do you think happens then? or Where does the Sun set and where does the Moon rise?
How can you tell whether something is a solid or a liquid?	You can pour liquids – you can't pour solids.	In what way is pouring salt different to pouring water? What does salt look like under the magnifier?
How did the smell from the perfume travel to our noses?	It went through the air.	How do you think the perfume got into the air? Why do you think we couldn't see it as it went through the air?

Effective questions

Setting the right classroom climate

A vital aspect of good questioning is setting up the right atmosphere so that children feel that their responses will be valued.

There are many things teachers can do to help children to feel safe enough to suggest answers and share their thinking with others. Nothing stops children speaking more quickly than the thought of looking stupid in front of their friends. There are techniques that every teacher can use to help children to feel safe from ridicule and to let them know that their opinions will be valued.

Classrooms can be organised so that every pupil has a 'talk partner' or a 'chat group' where they can share hesitant half-formed ideas with each other and develop them into a response before sharing them with the class. Teachers also need to make sure that they respond in the right way both non-verbally and verbally. Having set up the question and asked the children to chat with their neighbours, the teacher should drop eye contact, by either turning or looking away. If the teacher stays looking at children, they will answer directly to the teacher in a formal way rather than talking to each other informally.

It is also important, when finding out children's ideas, to offer non-committal responses. A brightly positive response to the first suggestion – for example, by saying '*That's brilliant, well done!*' – will stop any other child from offering a different suggestion. Those with different ideas will stay silently confused and the conversation will stop there. Better instead to offer a non-committal response such as '*Thanks, that's interesting – any other ideas?*'

Lastly, the way the teacher asks children to offer their thoughts will affect how they respond. It's a good idea to abandon asking for 'hands up', and instead pick groups or pairs of pupils at random to say what they have been chatting about. It should be made clear that they are not asked to give the 'right' answer but just to tell everyone where their thinking was going or what was coming up in their discussions. They may be having trouble interpreting a word or understanding an idea, which teachers need to know about in order to ask a further question to help them move forward.

Children as effective questioners

Children are always asking questions, but teachers need to encourage them to ask the kind of questions that will help their learning in science. Providing the very young with collections of various things, like toys, materials or leaves, will stimulate questions from them, especially if there is an unusual twist. For example, the teacher could provide different materials (buttons, marshmallows, pan scourers, bubble wrap) (Weavers, 2008) placed in bowls and ask the children to take off their shoes and socks, put on a blindfold and feel the materials with their feet. Or they could make a variety of ice shapes (freeze water in a plastic glove, a variety of plastic containers, a plastic bag, jelly moulds) and then just wait for the questions and comments to emerge.

Another way to help children generate questions is to use question spinners as suggested in Figure 1. In these simple spinners children place a paper clip at the centre of the spinner, put the tip of a pencil through the end of the paper clip and set it spinning round the pencil tip. When the paper clip stops spinning it acts as a pointer. The children do this on both spinners. They are then asked to come up with a question using the selected question starter and the selected object. The teacher should encourage them to come up with as many questions as they can and accept all questions at this stage – including those that make them giggle. Once the children have become used to the idea of asking questions,

Teaching primary science

the teacher can ask them to look back at their ideas and select one question they could answer by doing something practically and safely in the classroom; and one that they could answer using the internet or books.

Figure 1 Question-generating spinners.

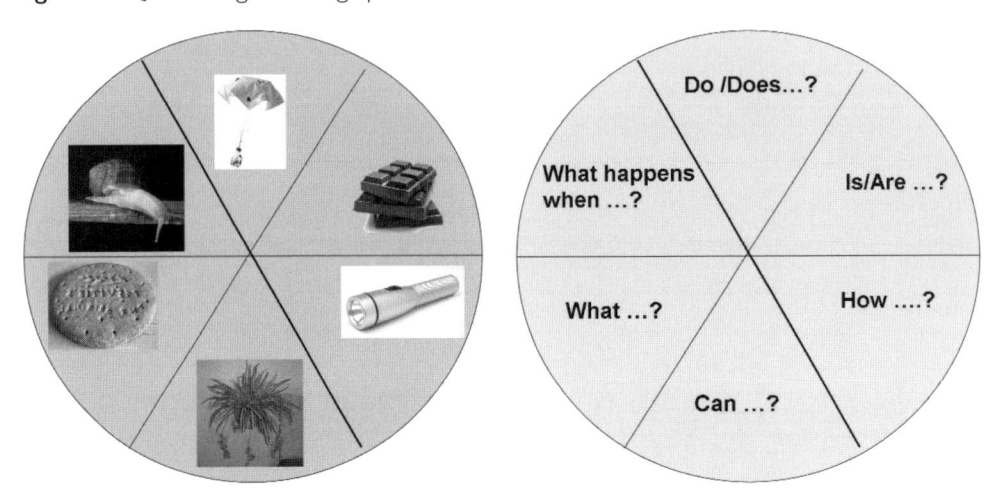

There are many other ways of encouraging children to generate questions, such as:

- a **question box**, where children post questions as they occur to them
- a **question mobile**, where questions are hung from a pair of metal coat-hangers intersected at right angles
- a **question board**, where children can display any questions that they think of (Dale, 2005).

An advantage of the question board is that blank pieces of paper can be hung under each question and the children can write their responses to each question, with other children continuing the debate with their own suggestions, comments and questions. In this way the question board turns into a debating board. Some teachers also show children how much they value their questions by having a 'Question of the week' badge and/or certificate. This is awarded each week to a child who has asked an interesting science question.

A key science skill is questioning evidence. We should encourage children to ask '*How do we know that?*', '*What is the evidence for that?*', '*How can we be sure of that?*' It can be fun to get children to do this when they are looking at factual books or watching television programmes. The following statements are taken from published nature books for children.

> 'The cabbage white butterfly has taste buds on its feet.'
> 'Marram grass leaves roll up into narrow tubes in dry weather to trap damp air inside.'
> 'A meadow that is cut every September will develop a different mix of plants and animals to a meadow that is cut in spring.'
> 'Foxgloves have dots inside each petal, which guide the bee to the inside of the flower.'
> 'The feathery feelers of the male silkworm moth can smell the scent of a female moth more than four kilometres away.'

The question for children to think about is what might scientists have done in order for those statements to be written. Teachers should encourage children to question evidence at every opportunity.

Dealing with difficult questions from children

A questioning classroom, where children feel free to ask questions of themselves and each other, will inevitably lead to them asking questions of the teacher. And there are bound to be some that the teacher will not know the answer to, such as 'Why do penguins walk in single file?', 'When you boil an egg, why does the yolk stay in the middle?', 'What is ear wax for?', 'How do they put stripes in toothpaste?' A teacher cannot possibly be expected to know all these answers. These are factual questions and the children can find an answer that satisfies them through secondary sources such as the internet.

However, there will be questions and ideas that challenge teachers as a direct result of activities linked to the primary curriculum. In this case, teachers will probably feel that they should know the answer to help guide children towards the scientific idea, as in the example in Box 1. Other ways of dealing with children's questions are suggested by Harlen and Qualter (2009).

Box 1   Answering questions through investigation

> In a school where children had been observing potato crisps and bread left out on the side for two weeks, the children wanted to know 'Why do crisps go soggy and heavier when you leave them out but bread goes harder and lighter?' The teacher replied, 'That's a really good question. I'm not sure I know the answer. What do the rest of you think?' The reaction from the class was immediate. They became really engaged. Here was a real question that even the teacher wasn't certain about. Here was something really worth discussing. And discuss they did. All sorts of suggestions were made. Was it something to do with the salt on the crisps? Was it that the crisps were thinner than the bread? Was it to do with the moisture? Was the air damper than the crisps but drier than the bread and the moisture went to the drier thing? They were keen to test out their questions. 'Let's put salt on the bread' was one sensible suggestion for testing the first question. So with the teacher acting as a chair the class worked together as scientists to think their way through the problem.

In conclusion

In this chapter we have looked at why it is so important for teachers to ask good questions. Teachers ask different types of questions for different purposes, and the questions that help teachers to uncover children's ideas and to develop their scientific concepts and skills are particularly important and worthy of careful planning. We have noted how important it is to set the right classroom climate so that children feel confident enough to respond to questions.

We also looked at how to develop children into effective scientific questioners so that they can ask questions of themselves, each other, other resources and the teacher. Finally we considered how teachers should deal with awkward questions raised by the effective science questioners in their class.

References

Dale, C. (2005) *Science on Display*, London: Folens.
Harlen, W. (2006) *Teaching, Learning and Assessing Science 5–12*. London: Sage.
Harlen, W. and Qualter, A. (2009) *The Teaching of Science in Primary Schools* (fifth edition). London: David Fulton.
Weavers, G. (2008) *Made You Look! Made You Talk! Made You Think!* Sandbach: Millgate House Education.

Further reading

Knight, R. (2009) Starting with what they know, *Primary Science,* 109, 22–24.
Oliver, A. (2006) *Creative Teaching – Science*. London: David Fulton.
Peacock, A. and Serret, N. (2008) When do children ask the really big questions? *Primary Science*, 105, 17–19.

Chapter 10

Promoting understanding through dialogue

Debbie Eccles and Simon Taylor

Discussion, conversation and interactions between teacher and pupils, and among pupils, can be encouraged and strengthened to improve understanding of scientific concepts. In brief, encouraging children to talk about science significantly helps their learning and understanding. Research highlights the need to shift the balance between 'teacher talk' and 'children talk' in favour of children, which may come as a surprise in some classrooms! This chapter explores a range of ideas that can quickly be incorporated into lessons to encourage productive pupil talk. The theory behind these approaches is touched upon briefly and can be explored further through the references at the end of the chapter.

Why dialogue?

It is through dialogue that teachers gain an insight into the complex webs of understanding being constructed in the minds of learners. It is also through dialogue that learners assemble their ideas to talk about and test out their grasp of a new topic. The statement by Alexander (2004) in Box 1 illustrates the huge potential for opportunities in science teaching for children to be able to talk and discuss their understanding with their teacher and their peers.

Planning and constructing opportunities for dialogue enable a teacher to become a 'fly on the wall', gaining an insight into the understanding that is being constructed in the children's brains. Listening to children explaining to each other their grasp of some event or phenomenon they have just encountered is incredibly valuable. This allows teachers to tailor their support and to become co-constructors of subsequent learning.

Teaching primary science

Box 1 Dialogic teaching

> 'Dialogic teaching is indicated by pupil talk through which children:
>
> - *narrate*
> - *explain*
> - *instruct*
> - *ask different types of questions*
> - *receive, act and build on answers*
> - *analyse and solve problems*
> - *speculate and imagine*
> - *explore and evaluate ideas*
> - *discuss*
> - *argue, reason and justify*
> - *negotiate.'*
>
> Alexander (2004, p43)

The interactions with children arising from well-constructed questioning can give learners the chance to voice their current grasp of an idea and help the teacher to identify the support children need to find their way towards a new concept. Teachers who provide opportunities in their lessons that require learners to talk about their current understanding push them into processing and re-assembling their ideas. This helps learners to make better sense of new information and ideas they have encountered.

Talking about their science activities challenges learners to think and reflect on their understanding while participating in the discussion. This simultaneously provides the teacher with really useful information about the actual learning taking place, including any developing misconceptions that can usefully inform subsequent planning. Out of this approach comes the possibility to ensure that the next learning experiences closely meet the needs of the learner or are constructed to deliberately challenge a child's misconceptions.

Effective dialogue in the classroom may help the following questions to be easily answered.

- What are the conceptions held by the children about the area of learning currently being developed?
- What are the children's stumbling blocks in understanding a specific idea or concept?
- What are the less conventional ideas held by some members of the group that they believe explain their observations?

Knowing the answers to these questions enables the teacher to plan learning experiences that can challenge preconceptions and generate some 'cognitive conflict' to encourage even deeper dialogue, lead to investigations and thus promote learner understanding. Children who are familiar with discussion and dialogue around science will learn to listen and discuss and challenge each other's ideas as they move towards a better understanding of key concepts. This is similar to the way in which peer challenge among scientists about emerging areas of research continues to push the boundaries in science.

How can dialogue be developed in science?

The answer to this question arises from the ways in which effective classroom talk is usually generated. We cannot explore all techniques and so focus on approaches that really lend themselves to science. An environment for effective classroom talk needs to be created if discussion is to become embedded and recognised by the learner as a normal part of learning.

Creating an environment for effective dialogue

There are certain conditions that support the development of effective dialogue, some of which are indicated in Box 2.

Box 2   Conditions for effective dialogue

Effective dialogue is supported by:
- mutual respect for others' opinions
- the development of effective listening skills – that is, when children are not talking they are considering and reflecting upon other children's responses
- children and teachers asking questions and offering responses
- allowing appropriate wait time in response to questions – teachers give children time to talk and produce a considered response
- teachers supporting but not intervening too early in small-group discussions
- accepted routines for response that are not competitive – for example, 'No hands up' is a technique to discourage children from competing for attention by shouting the loudest or creating most fuss, and instead involves the whole group in providing responses
- a room layout that is conducive to discussion – for example, a horseshoe or circle of chairs for the whole class
- treating mistakes as opportunities for learning, and not a matter for shame, or to be laughed at or simply dismissed.

Having established the conditions for dialogue to take place, what activities or approaches can support dialogue? Key contexts in science discussed here are the use of 'wow' events, Concept Cartoons, paired discussions, 'big fat questions' and puppets.

Using 'wow' events to encourage pupil questions

'Wow' events are examples of science that grabs children's interest and generate lots of children's questions. Sometimes this may be through teacher demonstration; at other times it may be through free exploration. For instance:

- children observe what happens when the teacher drops a mint Mentos sweet into a bottle of Coke (take care that this is done in a space where a major Coke spillage can easily be cleaned up – and stand well back!)
- children play with 'magic sand' in a tank of water
- children play with a tub of corn flour slime (made by mixing water and corn flour to a thick paste).

Teaching primary science

These activities will stimulate children to ask questions. So following the 'wow' experience, teachers may immediately want children to share with a partner the questions they want to ask about what they have just seen.

Some of the questions asked will be of the type that can be answered through further, more carefully structured enquiry. This might be where small-group discussion can continue to attempt to answer learner-generated questions, such as:

'What would happen if I put magic sand into warm or fizzy water?'
'What would happen to the corn flour slime if I left it in the classroom for a few days?'
'What would happen if more than one mint was put into the Coke, or if a fruity Mentos was used instead?'

Some of the questions that arise after carrying out an exploration might be 'why' questions (for example, *'Why does magic sand not get wet?'*). These may lead the teacher to ask for the children's ideas about what they have observed. It may also lead to the need for children to carry out research to try to arrive at an explanation of what they observed.

Using Concept Cartoons

When children are talking to each other, their guard is often down and these can be the moments when overheard conversations can provide invaluable feedback to the teacher. There are lots of opportunities to encourage this approach but a really useful, well-established resource through which pupil dialogue can be encouraged is a Concept Cartoon (Figure 1).

Figure 1   Concept Cartoons are a simple but effective resource that can be used to stimulate discussion (Naylor and Keogh, 2010, p52).

In the example in Figure 1, children discuss what will happen if the snowman wears a coat. Each of the characters in the cartoon represents ideas typically held by learners. This approach is common to all of the cartoons. Children can be asked to consider which is the character they agree with and why.

Probing children's initial responses is an effective teacher strategy that can sometimes get underneath the surface understanding of an idea into the real grasp a child holds of a particular concept.

Promoting understanding through dialogue

The simplest way to employ this is to ask *'Can you tell me a bit more about why you think this?'* The response to this may then take the teacher further into really understanding the map the children have in their mind of the concept they are constructing.

During the small-group task with the Concept Cartoon the teacher can interact with individuals, exploring why they have settled for a particular character's ideas. In small groups, this can lead to disagreements and discussion as children attempt to convince their peers as to which character has the best idea. This could then be followed by whole-class feedback where children are allowed to explain their thinking, with other class members being able to explain why they feel theirs is a better explanation. The opportunity, as in many of the Concept Cartoons, then exists for their ideas to be tested, For instance, in this example, ice cubes and different types of insulating materials can be used to find out whether or not wearing a 'coat' makes the ice cube melt more quickly. Like-minded children could work together to test their ideas. Of course, this then leads to further discussions as to which of the arguments appears to be best supported by the outcomes of their ice-cube investigation.

Paired discussions

Being able to discuss with peers allows learners the chance to start to use the new vocabulary they encounter in science. Additionally they can try out on each other their grasp of concepts without feeling too exposed. The simplest of pupil-to-pupil dialogue is with their 'talking partner' when the teacher gives the pairs 30 seconds to discuss a response to a question, thus taking out of the equation some of the stress of a question that requires an immediate answer. Teachers often wait less than a second before offering the answer themselves, but research shows that giving thinking time significantly increases the length and quality of a child's response to a question.

Big fat questions

Getting to the core of a child's understanding is a skill that can be honed and developed during a teaching career. One approach that can give a useful insight is the use of 'big fat questions' – questions that are very broad in scope. Examples include:
   'How do you know the person next to you is alive?'
   'If the Earth is spinning, why don't you get dizzy?'
   'What if all plants died?'
   'What if we had no skeleton?'

Good stem starters that encourage the asking of 'big fat questions' include:
   'What if ...'
   'How can ...'
   'Why does ...'

'What if ...' questions can be imaginative and allow for creative thinking:
   'What if there was no friction?'

Or they can require prediction related to an investigation question:
   'What if we made changes to the paper spinner?'

Teaching primary science

It is important that the learner has some evidence to draw on in relation to the question, as without this their answer is merely a guess rather than based within their experience.

Where they have experience to draw on, children can be grouped to discuss their ideas with the help of a prediction board – for example, a 'post-it' system (Goldsworthy and Feasey, 1997) to establish group or class predictions, as in Figure 2.

Figure 2 Extract of one of the planning posters from *Primarily Science* (2007), adapted from Goldsworthy and Feasey (1997).

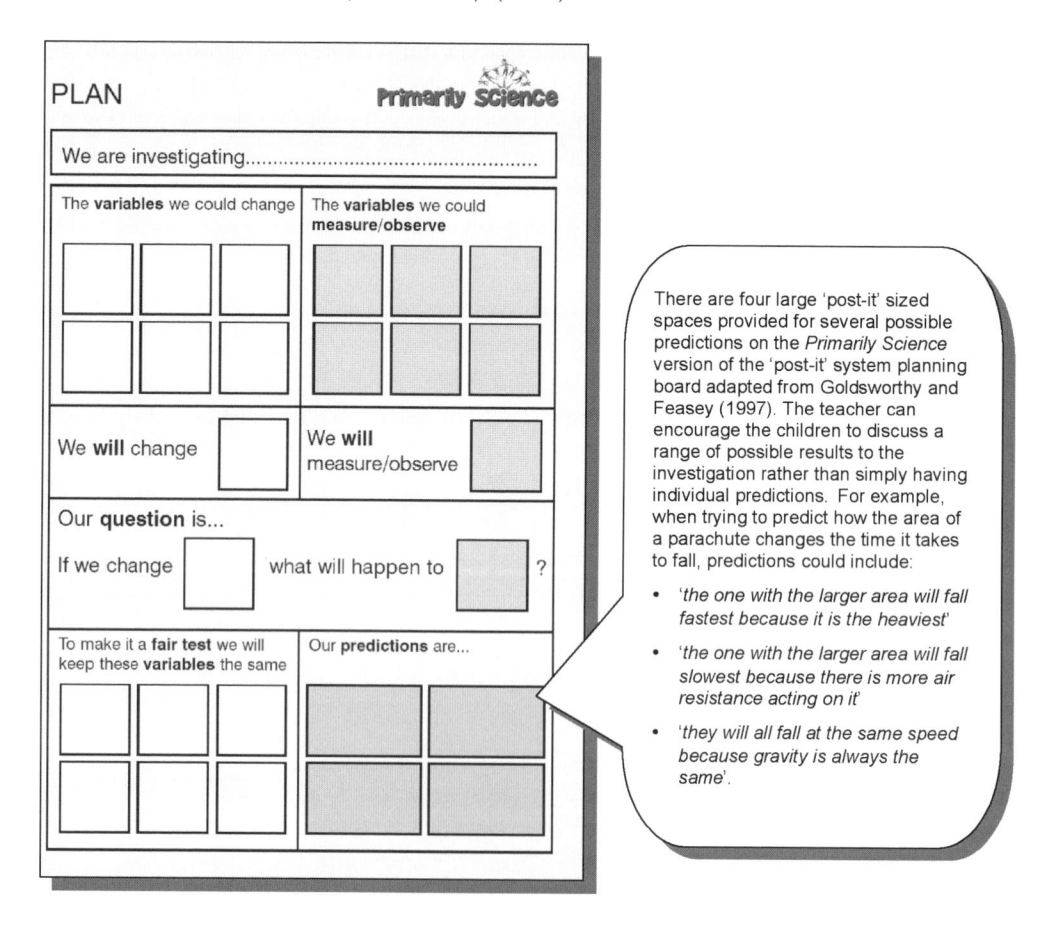

There are four large 'post-it' sized spaces provided for several possible predictions on the *Primarily Science* version of the 'post-it' system planning board adapted from Goldsworthy and Feasey (1997). The teacher can encourage the children to discuss a range of possible results to the investigation rather than simply having individual predictions. For example, when trying to predict how the area of a parachute changes the time it takes to fall, predictions could include:

- 'the one with the larger area will fall fastest because it is the heaviest'
- 'the one with the larger area will fall slowest because there is more air resistance acting on it'
- 'they will all fall at the same speed because gravity is always the same'.

In some instances children could attempt to draw graphs of what their results might look like if their prediction matches their findings from the investigation. Sketching a graph can generate a lot of discussion.

'**How can …**' questions relate to the appliance of science to real problems:
 '*How can we make the car travel faster down the ramp?*'

'**Why does …**' questions might relate to some unusual readings or unexpected outcomes from an investigation carried out by the class:
 '*Why does the paper spinner suddenly fall faster even though its wings are longer?*'

Promoting understanding through dialogue

Using puppets to stimulate talk

Another approach that can stimulate talk between teacher and children, especially where children are initially reticent to participate, is the use of puppets in the classroom.

Puppets enable discussion in a number of ways. Some teachers find it much easier to provide 'silly' answers from a puppet rather than giving these responses themselves. Children also sometimes find it easier to challenge a response offered by a puppet rather than their teacher. The puppet can provide a really effective way to challenge misconceptions. The Puppets Project (Naylor et al., 2006) has a number of characters that set problems and questions for children.

Appropriate response to pupil talk

Having encouraged pupils to engage in dialogue, it is important to consider how you respond to their questions and answers. If handled ineffectively, a teacher's response can stifle and stall discussion, whereas appropriate teacher responses can lead to an enriching and engaging learning experience for children.

Where a child offers an answer that is in line with the developing idea it is best for the teacher to acknowledge this but without the praise being too overwhelming! In some instances a teacher might want to encourage children to identify why it's a good response or what part of the answer makes it so good.

In contrast, where a response seems to be well off the mark for the idea being developed, again the answer needs to be acknowledged, but in such cases it is important to find ways to challenge *the idea*, and not the child. The reason could be a lack of specific knowledge, so one approach might be to offer some extra information and ask the child to see if he or she wants to change the response. What needs to be ensured is that children feel able to offer their ideas to the class without stress or ridicule – all ideas are up for grabs.

Sometimes a child will be hesitant and find it hard to verbalise the ideas they current hold. In these situations eliciting their understanding can be helped by offering alternatives or asking simpler questions that draw out the child's ideas little by little. Another approach may be to involve another child and ask how their ideas are the same or different.

Contentious topics as a stimulus for science talk

Some areas of science are contentious, may appear in the news and overlap into children's everyday experiences. Certain aspects of science elicit an emotional response from the learner and encourage individuals to develop and hold an opinion about them. These aspects of science can be rich seams to mine, to encourage dialogue in science (see also Chapter 12).

An approach that lends itself to explore children's opinions is to set out different views along a continuum (Ginnis, 2002). This can take the form of either a real or an imaginary line at the front of the classroom. At one end a particular view is held at the other end the opposing view is held. Children can be invited to place themselves somewhere on this line.

Some examples of some of the areas that might be explored are as follows.

- Should medicines be tested on animals?
- Should Edward Jenner have tried out the smallpox vaccine on James Phipps?
- Should we put chemical additives into foods to make them last longer?

Teaching primary science

- Are genetically modified foods a good idea?
- Should farmers use chemical sprays on crops or are organic foods better?
- Do you think parents should be able to choose the sex of their baby?

Some questions could be about the economics of science and the difficult choices science can present.

- Are the billions of pounds required to send rockets into space money well spent?
- How can doctors decide to whom they should give a kidney transplant when there is a waiting list of patients for a new one?

This approach also allows new and relevant topics to be brought to the classroom. The value of overlap between science and developing the literacy skills of speaking and listening, and also of putting talk into writing, cannot be overestimated.

In conclusion

This chapter has offered some strategies to consider when developing science talk in the primary classroom. It is recognised that effective learning more readily occurs when teachers:

- are clear in their minds about the progression in understanding that is required to access a particular scientific concept
- are able to gauge the point reached by all learners in their understanding of concepts
- plan learning experiences that move children along this progression.

Effective classroom talk provides a window into how this learning is progressing for each child. The more care we take in planning opportunities for dialogue and encouraging talk the better we are informed of the learning happening. This is the minute-by-minute assessment for learning that takes place in classrooms where children are talking about their science, and encourages them to be engaged, motivated and successful.

References

Alexander, R. (2004) *Towards Dialogic Teaching*. Cambridge: Dialogos UK Ltd.
Ginnis, P. (2002) *The Teacher's Toolkit*. Carmarthen: Crown House Publishing Limited.
Goldsworthy, A. and Feasey, R. (1997) revised Ball, S. *Making Sense of Primary Science Investigations*. Hatfield: Association for Science Education.
Naylor, S. and Keogh, B. (2010) *Concept Cartoons in Science*, Revised Edition. Sandbach: Millgate House Education.
Naylor, S., Keogh, B., Downing, B., Maloney, J. and Simon, S. (2006) Puppets bringing stories to life in science. *Primary Science Review*, **92**, 26–28.
Primarily Science (2007) *Plan Do Review Posters*.

Chapter 11

Formative feedback and self-assessment

Kathy Schofield

We assess pupils' learning for various purposes, the main ones being to help improve their learning by informing teaching, and to summarise and report on learning at various times. This chapter is concerned with the first of these, while Chapter 15 discusses the second. Here we consider two key aspects of using assessment to help learning (Assessment for Learning, or formative assessment): feedback and involvement of children in peer and self-assessment. After setting these in the context of Assessment for Learning, we discuss the rationale for, and some examples of, effective practice first for providing formative feedback and then for involving pupils in the assessment of their progress.

Assessment for Learning

Assessment for Learning, or formative assessment, is purposeful. It feeds back into the teaching and learning cycle not only in knowledge and skills but in all aspects of learning. It engages learners in their own development through a cyclical process, always guiding progress to the next steps via a positive approach using feedback and peer or self-assessment. It involves both teacher and pupils in gathering and using information about progress towards learning goals to ensure that pupils are sufficiently challenged to make progress but not expected to move on until they have a sound basis for their next steps. The definition provided by the Assessment Reform Group (ARG) captures what Assessment for Learning (AfL) involves:

Assessment for Learning is the process of seeking and interpreting evidence for use by learners and their teachers to decide where the learners are in their learning, where they need to go and how best to get there.

ARG (2002)

Teaching primary science

The ARG also identified ten research-based principles of AfL to guide classroom practice (Box 1). These principles form the basis upon which teachers build up a picture of the children's progression through collaborative learning, reviewing and reflecting upon their learning.

Box 1 Ten principles of Assessment for Learning

> 'Assessment for Learning:
> 1. is part of effective planning
> 2. focuses on how pupils learn
> 3. is central to classroom practice
> 4. is a key professional skill
> 5. is sensitive and constructive
> 6. fosters motivation
> 7. promotes understanding of goals and criteria
> 8. helps learners to know how to improve
> 9. develops the capacity for self-assessment
> 10. recognises all educational achievement.'
>
> ARG (2002)

An excellent account of implementing formative assessment as a whole pedagogic strategy in the primary school is given by Harrison and Howard (2009). Here we are focusing on two aspects, which are embodied in principles 8 and 9 in Box 1. Much of AfL takes place in day-to-day teaching where learners receive immediate feedback on their understanding of the specific aspect or topic being explored and where teachers adjust their short-term planning in line with learners' needs. AfL supports learning in the short term in the form of feedback from lessons, from lesson to lesson as the information on children's learning and understanding is evaluated and then acted upon to inform the planning and learning for the next lesson.

At other times, teachers need to stand back and reflect on the learner's overall performance across a subject or aspect of learning, drawing on a wide range of evidence. This more holistic, periodic assessment provides a clear profile of attainment against recognised criteria. It also helps identify the learner's strengths and priorities for improvement and informs the teacher's medium-term planning. Reflecting on children's learning over several lessons develops periodic assessment. This means the teacher is better able to personalise a curriculum for pupils through the constructivist approach to teaching. A constructivist view requires the understanding that learners are not passive recipients of knowledge and ideas but that these are constructed by the learners. This means providing children with the opportunities to build upon their existing ideas by constructing new ideas from experiences. These experiences need to be directed and supported yet still provide opportunity for collaboration and open exploration. It is the teachers' role to manage this effectively.

Using Assessment for Learning

To use AfL means starting from the ideas and skills that children have developed. Children need to be active in the learning process and be able to construct ideas from their experiences both in and out of school. The role of the teacher is to respond to these ideas

Formative feedback and self-assessment

and encourage children to develop their ideas. There are several points about learning to be kept in mind in responding to children's existing ideas.

First, children must be active in the process – learning has to be done *by* them, not *for* them. There are times when children need to be helped to close the gap between what they don't know and what they want to know. The skill of the teacher is to teach them the skills to enable them to 'close the gap' for themselves. So what does the teacher do/say/plan to move children's thinking forward and help them close the gap? Some strategies (Harlen and Qualter, 2009) are:

- providing new experience that may challenge existing ideas
- scaffolding new ideas
- focusing observation on aspects that may have been ignored
- linking together ideas from different experiences
- improving enquiry skills
- discussing words.

Second, in order to learn, children – as all learners – need to understand the purpose of the learning both in the short term and the long term. They also need an understanding of where they stand in relation to this ultimate goal. This requires an understanding of what constitutes 'good quality work'. Only with these two ideas in place can they work towards metacognition, which is the ability to reflect upon their own learning, thus taking it in the right direction, so they can take responsibility for it. Hence the importance of peer and self-assessment, which promote active involvement and practice in making judgements about the quality of both their own and others' work.

A third point concerns collaboration in learning. Sometimes children learn from more knowledgeable peers, while at other times they help their peers to understand. Children learn through talk, and as children talk, they also provide valuable evidence to enable the teacher to diagnose what they are learning (Chapter 10).

Feedback

Feedback should be linked to improvement; it can inform on quality of work, looking forward and therefore leading to improvement in learning. Feedback on learning can come in a variety of ways, such as written comments (marking) on written work, oral comments from the teacher to individuals or to a group or class, and discussions with other pupils. Good-quality feedback, either written or oral, avoids focusing on the child as a good or poor achiever through emphasis on an overall judgement by grading or ranking. Research has shown this not only discourages low-achievers, but also makes high-achievers avoid tasks if they cannot easily see their way to success, for failure is seen as personal rather than an opportunity to learn. The feedback advocated in formative assessment focuses on the strengths and weaknesses of the *work* and not the child, starts by recognising what is good and leads to identifying what needs to be done to improve. This allows pupils to learn from their mistakes and generates a positive effect that encourages further progression. The impact of good-quality feedback boosts self-esteem and builds resilience in learning (Naylor et al., 2004; Swaffield, 2008).

Teaching primary science

Feedback to pupils depends, of course, on teachers having evidence about the learning as a basis for taking the next steps. This evidence can be collected as part of teaching by, for example, observing children during regular work, studying their written work or other products of their activities, using concepts maps, and listening to their discussions with their peers. The essential feature that makes assessment formative is that information from evidence gathered is used to help the children take the next steps in learning. This requires information to be fed back into the teaching–learning process. Teachers and pupils can both use this information, so we have to consider feedback to the teacher and feedback to the children.

In preparation for gathering and using feedback, teachers need a clear understanding of the learning objectives and the success criteria so that these can be shared with the pupils. Box 2 gives an example of what this means for a 'sorting' activity.

Box 2   Clarifying the goals and success criteria for a sorting activity

Questions teachers ask themselves in preparing the activity:

- What do children need to know?
- What are they trying to learn (learning objectives)?
  To identify obvious differences and similarities between objects and materials.
- What will count as achievement (learning outcomes)?
  Using everyday language to describe materials during exploration. Being able to say why they have sorted in a particular way.
- What does 'good' work look like (success criteria)?
  Making use of several senses in exploring objects and materials. Giving reasons and/or choices relevant to their age and experience.
- Why are they learning this (big picture)?
  To see how this activity relates to the world around them or how this skill can be used in other contexts.

What kind of feedback to pupils?

Research by Butler has had a considerable influence on thinking about written feedback. It is summarised in Box 3, taken from Harlen and Qualter (2009).

Box 3   Research on different kinds of feedback

'In the study by Ruth Butler (1987) the effect of different types of feedback by marking were compared. In a controlled experimental study, she set up groups that were given feedback in different ways. One group of pupils were given marks, or grades only; another group were given only comments on their work and the third group received both marks and comments on the work. These conditions were studied in relation to tasks that required divergent and convergent thinking. The result was that, for divergent-thinking tasks, the pupils who received comments only made the greatest gain in their learning, significantly more than for the other two groups. The results were the same for high and low-achieving pupils. For convergent tasks, the lower-achieving pupils scored most highly after comments only, with the marks-only group next, above the marks-plus-comments group. For all tasks and pupils, comments only led to higher achievement.'

Harlen and Qualter (2009, p202)

Formative feedback and self-assessment

Experience based on these results confirms that giving marks not only produces no improvement but can wipe out the potential value of the comments (Black and Harrison, 2004).

Oral feedback can happen frequently in the primary classroom during class discussion but the teacher needs to be aware of always responding positively and ensuring all children are included. Oral feedback might highlight good practice, or it might be a question that draws out children's understanding, or might encourage children to develop their thinking skills further. For example, in whole-class discussion a strategy for including all children is to ask children not to put up their hands, but for the teacher to have all the children's names in a hat or on lollipop sticks thus making children aware that anyone can be asked a question at random. The teacher acknowledges what the children know or can do, then helps them to move forward in their learning by asking questions such as:

'Tell us more about …'
'Use one of these scientific words …'
'Explain a bit more about …'
'Describe how …'
'How else could you …'
'Think about why …'

It is important to remember the two-way process in feedback. Feedback to the teacher from a child's response may indicate a lack of understanding of a question or the need for more information. This feedback is important to the teacher and may be used to inform future planning.

Communicating the success criteria

Feedback, whether oral or written, must be in response to the task set and must clearly link to the success criteria that learners were given at the start of the session. With the focus on the task, and not the child, the teacher's comments should encourage children to think about the quality of their work, not how 'good' they are. One way to ensure the children know what the success criteria are, is to use the two characters devised by Clarke (2001): WALT (We Are Learning Today) and WILF (What I am looking for). For example:

*'**We Are Learning Today**, in science, to record our electrical circuits using circuit symbols.'* (WALT)
*'**What I am Looking For** are children who can record three different circuits.'* (WILF)

Then feedback can be directly related to the success criteria:

'Could someone else follow this circuit diagram and set up the circuit? You will need to show them clearly what to do. Think about your labels.'
'You have good clear diagrams. Could you add an explanation of why they work?'
'You have shown a labelled series circuit. Could you add a parallel circuit too?'

This approach indicates to the child the next step in their progression and, if not yet achieved, gives the child a clear learning goal. Positive feedback followed by questioning develops the child's self-esteem and creates evidence of good practice, which can then be modelled to other children.

Another method is to use KWHL (Know, Want, How, Learned) grids to highlight the learning process, like the one shown in Box 4. This type of grid can be used to scaffold learning and helps children develop their self-assessment skills.

Box 4 Class or individual KWHL grid about electricity

What do we already know about electricity?	What do we want to find out about electricity?	How will we find out?	What have we learned about electricity?

This type of grid also gives feedback to the teacher showing prior knowledge and understanding, including where the children want to take the learning forward. Feedback may be given that indicates where a child may go for help:

'Think back to your last investigation …'
'You are mixing up 'cell' and 'switch'. Check your glossary for an explanation.'
'Talk to your peers, gather their ideas, and share your own.'
'Compare your results with another child. Talk about why there are differences.'
'Ask your talk partner for help with drawing your circuit.'

Feedback that encourages children to think about how they can improve, and which is a stimulus for further thinking, is a useful tool to extend all children. This promotes children's commitment to the learning goals and assessment criteria allowing them to receive recognition for their progress, regardless how small the steps. Frequently and consistently scaffolding the language used in feedback, encouraging children's self-reflection on their learning and guiding them to identify their next steps are all essential elements for success in the development of learning how to learn.

Pupil peer assessment and self-assessment

The kind of learning with understanding that AfL promotes is enhanced when pupils are encouraged to think about what and how they are learning. As Harrison explains:

'Self-assessment is an essential component in the learning process because it helps students to gauge suitable targets for their learning. Through evaluating their own strengths and weaknesses and considering which approaches were helpful in making sense of ideas, pupils begin to build a sense … of how to help their future learning. When they can do this, they are able to steer their own learning towards the learning goal and acquire the habits of life-long learning.'

Harrison (2009, p6)

To ensure children are confident in peer and self-assessment, teachers will need to ensure they explain and share the success criteria that relate to the learning objectives and intended learning outcomes from every lesson. Many teachers introduce peer assessment before self-assessment, since it is easier to model.

Peer assessment can be developed through group work or with partners; this is a skill that will need modelling and monitoring to ensure success. Box 5 outlines some strategies that can be used to introduce the practice in the classroom.

Formative feedback and self-assessment

Box 5 Strategies for developing peer assessment

- Model the process of assessing against the criteria, using examples of work that demonstrate the intended learning outcomes, either from previous teaching or samples of other children's work.
- Critique the responses and model the approach before expecting children to work on each other's or their own work. 'Think aloud' while critiquing so that children develop the necessary language and approach.
- During investigations, 'pair and share', and give time for exchanges of ideas. This gives children opportunities to negotiate meaning for their experiences and to use the vocabulary appropriate to their level of understanding.
- Check children know the purpose of their work.
- Remind them of where this fits into the bigger picture and relates to the world around them.
- Pause at key moments during an investigation and capture their thoughts by recording. This learning journal can be shared with peers to discuss progress and identify understanding.
- Help them to assess their work and that of others using language based on the learning outcomes.
- Have regular reviews about assessment in partnership with the children.
- Give pupils examples of a variety of skills, attitudes, standards and qualities to aim for.

The success of self-assessment derives from careful coaching by the teacher using clear criteria for quality. The children begin to recognise their strengths and weaknesses by developing awareness of their own success and through the identification of problem areas in specific pieces of work. In science, this might be the understanding and articulation of key vocabulary or it might be recognising the significance of independent and controlled variables on the outcome of a fair test. To achieve success in these areas, the children will require regular effective guidance from the teacher and the opportunity to hone these skills through regular practice. Once children become secure in their own self-reflection, they might suggest their own preferred method of working – for example, creating mnemonics to embed key vocabulary or needing scaffolding in the form of given statements to sort the variables for fair testing. Children should be encouraged to talk through the success criteria with their peers; working collaboratively encourages change and builds confidence.

Asking the children to comment on their own and each other's work in a positive way develops self-esteem for all children as they begin to recognise each other's strengths. This is essential to developing the self-assessment ethos, so highlighting good recording or demonstrating correct techniques are fundamental to the children's understanding of what is required of them as learners. They need inspirational targets set by other children, not just by the teacher.

Reviewing progress in AfL

While pupils' involvement in their own formative assessment has an important role in learning, it is not to be achieved overnight. It may require quite fundamental changes in the conditions and habits of the classroom. So a review of progress will help in its gradual introduction. This should be a review of what had gone well, what needs to be changed, what the children thought and liked about the assessments and most importantly incorporate a celebration of achievements. The celebration of achievements should include all elements of the assessment, not just knowledge gained but new skills learned, and examples of good practice where children have carried out peer and self-assessments. This may include work, displays, photographs or interviews with the children to build up the overview of Assessment for Learning.

This review helps children know how to improve, and reinforces the self-assessment practice – for this to be successful, children need to take an active part in the learning process. Self-assessment is a skill necessary for continued learning throughout life. It is a means of children acquiring a set of effective learning practices taught by their teachers. This requires teachers to understand learning, and help children to reflect upon their learning and improve on their own learning journey. This can only be developed through continuous interaction and discussion both with their peer group and their teacher.

The teacher's approach to peer assessment clearly requires a class atmosphere where cooperation and collaboration, rather than competition, are encouraged. When they have confidence in gaining help from a structured exchange with a peer, children begin spontaneously to ask each other for their opinions. The recognition of being able to help themselves and each other enables learning to continue when the teacher is occupied with those who need extra help (based on Harlen *et al.*, 2003, pp132–133).

In conclusion

Our knowledge of how children learn lends support to the use of formative assessment so that children can learn through constructing their understanding. Key aspects of this are two kinds of feedback. The first is feedback to the teacher from observing and interacting with children, enabling the teacher to use this information to inform decisions about activities that are matched to the needs of the children. The second is feedback from the teacher to the children to help them in improving their work and moving forward. We have considered some ways of doing this and the nature of the information that is most helpful. However, pupils are less dependent on feedback from the teacher when they themselves assess their own work. The ability to do this requires a good grasp to the goals of their work and the criteria for judging good quality. Helping children to develop these practices serves to help them reflect on their learning and to begin to take responsibility for it.

References

ARG (Assessment Reform Group) (2002) *Assessment for Learning: 10 Principles.* Available online at: www.assessment-reform-group.org/CIE3.PDF

Black, P. and Harrison, C. (2004) *Science Inside the Primary Black Box.* London: nferNelson.

Clarke, S. (2001) *Unlocking Formative Assessment.* London: Hodder and Stoughton

Harlen, W. and Qualter, A. (2009) *The Teaching of Science in Primary Schools* (fifth edition). London: David Fulton.

Harlen, W., Macro, C., Reed, K. and Schilling, M. (2003) *Making Progress in Primary Science. Study Book.* London: Routledge Falmer.

Harrison, C. (2009) Assessing the impact of assessment for learning 10 years on. *Curriculum Management Update*, November 2009.

Harrison, C. and Howard, S. (2009) *Inside the Primary Black Box.* London: GL Assessment.

Naylor, S., Keogh, B. and Goldsworthy, A. (2004) *Active Assessment: Thinking, Learning and Assessment in Science.* Sandbach: Millgate House Publishers.

Swaffield, S. (2008) Feedback: the central process in assessment for learning, in Swaffield, S. (ed) *Unlocking Assessment.* London: David Fulton

Chapter 12

Developing interest in science through emotional engagement

Paul McCrory

It seems as if teachers are constantly being exhorted to 'make science fun' nowadays. Where is the evidence that this approach can really help to improve the pupils' understanding and knowledge? How can hard-pressed teachers, working to deliver a given curriculum, find the time to do this in practice? Is it even possible to make all topics in the science curriculum fun? In fact, isn't there a danger that this approach will suggest to pupils that science itself cannot ever be fun unless we artificially make it so? This chapter discusses these important questions and offers a practical toolkit of some techniques that teachers can use to increase interest in their science lessons through fostering positive emotional reactions.

The neglect of the affective domain

Across the Western world there is widespread concern about the decline in interest in science, and in its uptake both as a subject to study and as a career to pursue. Research evidence suggests that, in the UK at least, many pupils start to turn away from science as young as the end of their primary school years, and that this disaffection escalates during early secondary school (Osborne and Dillon, 2008). Crudely speaking, two of the most often-considered learning outcomes are centred on the cognitive domain (understanding, knowledge and skills) and the affective domain (feelings and attitudes). Most teachers instinctively seem to recognise the need to interest their pupils in the classroom, yet they often complain that the short-term cognitive imperative of today's assessment-driven classrooms will always take precedence over the need for any longer-term affective outcomes.

The 'education versus entertainment' debate

There is a long and controversial history to teaching approaches that exploit entertainment techniques to 'make science fun' for pupils. Critics of such methods have branded them unrealistic, dishonest and ultimately unsustainable. They argue that many of the concepts and skills that children are required to master in science are in fact abstract and intellectually demanding.

In Western society, and in our classrooms, there is often a deep-seated distinction drawn between education and entertainment. Education is traditionally seen as 'work' (and typically characterised as important, serious, difficult and unpleasant), and entertainment is perceived as 'play' (associated generally with being vacuous, frivolous, easy and pleasurable). The different baggage of associations that we each hold around the terms 'education' and 'entertainment' perhaps lie at the root of many of the fierce debates in this area. The uneasy tension between education and entertainment essentially derives from a 'trade-off' model of placing these experiences at opposite ends of a continuum – the more you have of one, the less you can have of the other. The implicit – and dangerous – assumption behind this perspective, however, is that education cannot ever be enjoyable in and of itself, and that teachers continually have to 'sweeten the pill' of learning by adding entertaining distractions. This model is typified by one of 'Mickey's Ten Commandments' that Disney's Imagineers reportedly use to guide how they integrate education into an entertainment-based medium: 'For every ounce of treatment, provide a ton of fun.'

We live in a culture increasingly dominated by diverse forms of entertainment, but every variety of entertainment shares one common characteristic – at their core they are simply about creating an emotional response from humans. It is, of course, possible to design experiences for pupils that are both educational (in the sense of increasing understanding and skills) *and* entertaining (in the sense of being emotionally engaging). This is not to pretend that all scientific concepts and learning experiences are immediately appealing to pupils. There is an important 'delayed gratification' aspect of science education, which was well-captured by Claude Bernard, the nineteenth century scientist, when he observed that learning science was like '*entering a kitchen full of awe and wonder*', but cautioned that the problem was '*the long dark hall you had to go through to get there.*' Sadly many pupils never get to emerge from the gloom of the hall to experience the delights of the kitchen in their science classes. They never sustain their engagement long enough to be able to stand on their achievements and survey the breath-taking way that science can unify seemingly diverse phenomena, or appreciate the awesome power of science to help explain and predict the everyday world around them.

Some forms of entertainment can be frivolous and easy, but this is certainly not true of all entertainment. Millions of young computer gamers are willing to spend months learning the most fiendishly difficult games because they enjoy being tested by and eventually overcoming the intellectual and physical challenges that are thrown at them. The computer gaming industry has an intriguing term to describe this vital element of game play – 'hard fun' arises from activities that are enjoyable largely because they are difficult. Perhaps one of the biggest misconceptions about education is that pupils want the teacher to make the subject easy for them. The art of teaching is, like a good computer game, to pitch the challenge at a level that is tantalisingly above the competence of the learner so that it appears achievable and they are motivated to master it. As their skill increases, so does the difficulty of the tasks. By reading pupils closely and structuring activities carefully, teachers can use this concept of 'hard fun' to embrace the many challenging aspects of science education, and actually turn them to their advantage.

The importance of emotional engagement in science education

There is a very wide range of positive emotions that teachers can foster through the way they teach science – for example, curiosity, anticipation, uncertainty, surprise, intellectual joy of understanding, wonder, sense of imagination, amusement, sense of beauty, and amazement. The principal justification given for the importance of these affective qualities to science education is simply that if the emotional reward gained from learning science is increased, pupils will be more motivated to study science in school and also more likely to engage with science in their everyday lives. Developing positive emotional responses in the classroom also helps to cultivate effective relationships between the teacher and the pupils. There are, however, several other reasons why affect is increasingly being considered a powerful ingredient in modern theories of learning – for example, the value of emotional responses in their own right, and the role emotions play in attention, interest and cognition.

The clear utilitarian benefits of science education for society and the national economy have been used to justify the privileged position of science in many curricula alongside the core skills of literacy, numeracy and information technology. The dominance of this practical justification, however, has had an unfortunate consequence; compared with the more personal arguments often made for education in the arts and humanities, science education appears to have lost its soul. The emotional responses a child can have to a beautiful work of art or a moving poem rarely have to be defended or measured in terms of how useful they are to the child's future career, society's ability to make democratic decisions, or the economic well-being of the nation. Curiosity and a sense of wonderment at the way the world around us works are precious parts of being human. These powerful feelings are just as valuable outcomes of engagement with science as they are of the arts. The positive emotional reactions that children can experience from science are surely an essential part of their cultural entitlement and are important in their own right.

Attention is a necessary, but not sufficient, condition for *any* learning outcome. This statement seems so obvious that it is easy to take it for granted when teaching. In fact, many psychologists argue that the most important role of attention, and perhaps one of the most significant functions of our brains, is the ability to filter out the deluge of competing sensory stimuli and memories to focus our scarce attention on the information that is really important to us at any one time. Without this one skill it would be impossible for our brains to make any sense of our conscious experiences. Neuroscience (Chapter 5) indicates that one of the main criteria that the brain uses to sift information is the emotional value it holds. So embedding emotional stimuli throughout a lesson will immediately capture and help to maintain the attention of pupils.

The fundamental question of what pupils actually find interesting about science is, surprisingly, an under-studied area. Psychologists recognise two different types of interest:

- **individual interests** – the narrow enduring interests that each pupil has already developed, often from their previous experiences (for example, insects, cancer treatments)

- **situational interests** – stimuli from the content or the way in which it is presented that spontaneously create short-term interest for almost all pupils (for example, forensic science contexts, explosive demonstrations).

Situational interests are generally more effective in the classroom because they are more likely to engage the largest number of students at once and are more under the control of the teacher than individual interests. One of the most effective sources of situational interest is any sort of emotional response.

We have already discussed how emotions influence the cognitive processes involved in securing attention, but affect also plays a vital role in one of the most important cognitive elements of learning – memory. For reasons of survival, our brains appear to be designed to privilege information associated with emotional arousal. Furthermore, one of the strongest messages beginning to emerge from the relatively recent application of neuroscience to educational research is that it is no longer possible to separate cognition and affect (Chapter 5). Even though in the past we may have tried to neatly divide these brain functions, they are, in fact, inextricably linked with one another (Damasio, 2006). So, even if a teacher is solely concerned with improving understanding or skills, rather than any motivational or attitudinal changes, it turns out that they cannot ignore the role of positive emotions in their pupils' learning. The approach of emotional engagement, far from simply being a concession to motivation, is actually at the centre of how children attend, remember and think.

Hunting for hooks – increasing interest in science

A study of the rather limited educational research into situational interest reveals that there is a wide range of types of stimuli or 'hooks' that are universally interesting to pupils – including novelty, incongruity, uncertainty, curiosity, humour, imagination, choice, control, empowerment, involvement, challenge, complexity, comprehension, social interaction and relevance. Most of these types of hook contain both affective and cognitive components. For example, the comprehension hook clearly involves understanding the material as well as experiencing an intellectual joy at this realisation.

The fundamental principle for emotional engagement is that throughout the lesson teachers should either find or insert emotional hooks to grab and hold the attention of their pupils. As Figure 1 shows, when teaching any topic, the content and the situational interests of the pupils will obviously overlap to a greater or lesser extent depending on the topic in question.

Figure 1   Internal and external emotional hooks.

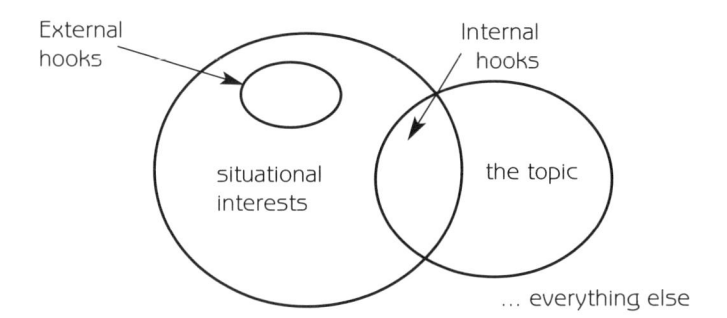

Teaching primary science

Many concepts and activities in science have a high intrinsic interest for most children – they already possess numerous strong internal emotional hooks. The process of scientific thinking and investigation, for example, is full of curiosity, wonder, surprise and joy of understanding. Research suggests, however, that when teachers think about increasing student interest in a topic, they automatically tend to consider how to 'make' the content more interesting by adding external hooks, rather than consider ways of finding and bringing out the inherent interest that is already within the content. To illustrate this distinction, consider the popular demonstration where vinegar is added to a zip-lock bag containing baking soda and the bag is sealed. If the teacher deliberately chooses to place the primed bag nearer the pupils than strictly necessary, in order to provoke a greater sense of group involvement and jeopardy, then this would be an example of an external hook; whereas the unavoidable and suspenseful delay before the inflating bag eventually bursts is an internal hook that the teacher simply exploits.

External hooks should, where possible, be related to the content or process in some meaningful way, and they need to be used with great deliberation so that they enhance rather than harm cognitive learning outcomes. If they are used strategically throughout the delivery of a less immediately appealing topic, these devices may increase the vigilance of pupils so that they remain attentive to capture the next rewarding emotional hook. In this way it is possible that their attention may be held long enough for them to discover some of the deeper satisfaction possible from understanding such topics.

Table 1 presents a sample of emotional engagement techniques, involving both internal and external hooks, which teachers can use in the classroom to increase situational interest in science. Some of these techniques can be used more frequently than others depending on the topic being taught and how well they suit the existing classroom persona of the teacher.

Table 1 Examples of emotional engagement techniques.

Technique	Emotional engagement technique
self-disclosure of the character of the teacher	Pupils are endlessly fascinated by their teachers and by finding out more about them as human beings. For example: • teachers revealing aspects of their personality through the persona they present in the classroom • sharing appropriate and relevant personal stories with pupils.
modelling emotions	The positive or negative emotions of a teacher are extremely contagious to pupils. Teachers should exaggerate and vary their verbal and non-verbal expressiveness to clearly demonstrate to pupils how they feel about the topics they teach. Enthusiasm has been shown by research to be a particularly important emotion to model when teaching (Patrick et al., 2000).

Developing interest in science through emotional engagement

Technique	Emotional engagement technique
empowerment	Give pupils a real, or apparent, sense of control of the direction of the lesson and regular opportunities to feel involved and empowered. For example: • appearing to be 'one step behind' pupils • following-up their questions and investigation ideas as much as possible • giving pupils choice about the themes to use to cover particular topics.
first form of suspense – provoking curiosity	Curiosity is perhaps the most powerful emotional engagement device available to teachers – an emotional itch that we feel compelled to scratch. It involves making pupils aware of the small, tantalising information gaps in their knowledge so that they will do almost anything to close these gaps. For example: • posing intriguing questions • teasing pupils with 'a menu' of what is to follow later in the lesson • creating 'cliff-hanger' endings to a lesson.
second form of suspense – creating uncertainty	This is when pupils think they know what might happen next, but complications keep them hooked until the final resolution. To most people, some degree of conflict and uncertainty is appealing. For example: • deliberately making mistakes and allowing things to 'go wrong' in the lesson • facilitating group discussions and debates about controversial ethical issues and process issues in science.
third form of suspense – building anticipation	In this form of suspense, pupils know exactly what will happen, but this event is delayed as much as possible. The greater the delay, the more unbearable the anticipation. For example: • inserting a stall deliberately before completing a demonstration or revealing an answer • covering a piece of equipment with a cloth until you are ready to dramatically unveil it at the end of the lesson.

Teaching primary science

Technique	Emotional engagement technique
generating surprise	Novelty or surprise is a very powerful way of grabbing the involuntary attention of pupils. The human brain is essentially a pattern-sensing machine, and we seem to enjoy detecting patterns and then, occasionally, having our expectations confounded. For example: • exploiting counter-intuitive demonstrations • using variety in the range of teaching methods employed.
telling stories about scientific discoveries or applications	Stories are perhaps one of the oldest and most powerful ways of learning or passing on information through the ages. Good stories have the power to captivate even the most reluctant pupils. They are like 'emotion simulators' for our minds – they allow pupils to visualise the situation they hear described and to feel emotions as if they were the characters in the story.
humour	There are many ways to use moderate humour effectively in the classroom. The type of humour that a teacher uses will obviously depend on their personality, but most teachers will find it easier to exploit the situational humour that arises naturally through events and interactions in the classroom, rather than telling jokes as such.
fostering wonder and imagination	These profound emotions can be quite dependent on the topic being taught, but are more likely to be induced by expressions of the teacher's appreciation for the visual and intellectual beauty to be found in science. For example: • openly admitting that there are questions that science cannot currently answer • posing 'what if' questions to provoke pupils' imaginations • linking science with other creative subjects like art, music, creative writing and drama.
provoking short-term negative emotions	It is possible to grab the attention of pupils through the careful use of short-term, moderate negative reactions. For example: • using the 'gross factor' to provoke a disgust reaction • encouraging a slight fear about the outcome of an apparently dangerous demonstration.

In conclusion

For strong evolutionary imperatives, the human brain appears to be programmed to find learning, at the appropriate level of challenge, emotionally rewarding. This chapter has attempted to explore some of the subtleties and dangers that lie behind teaching approaches that claim to 'make science fun'. It suggests that the strategic use of emotional engagement hooks throughout a lesson can help to retain the attention of pupils, improve their recall, engage them cognitively and increase their interest in science. It is perhaps reassuring to realise that psychological and neuroscience evidence is increasingly demonstrating that it is not a question of whether teachers should focus on short-term cognitive outcomes *or* on the generally longer-term affective impact of their teaching. Effective teaching appears to depend on simultaneously engaging both cognitive and affective processes in the brains of pupils.

References

Damasio, A. (2006) *Descartes' Error.* London: Vintage Books.

Osborne, J. and Dillon, J. (2008) *Science Education in Europe: Critical Reflections.* London: Nuffield Foundation.

Patrick, B.C. et al. (2000) 'What's everybody so excited about?' The effects of teacher enthusiasm on student intrinsic motivation and vitality. *The Journal of Experimental Education,* **68**(3), 217–236.

Chapter 13

Creativity in teaching science

Brenda Keogh and Stuart Naylor

What is creativity in teaching science? Why is it important? How can we enhance it? These are the questions raised in this chapter. The starting point for tackling these questions is to look at some of the issues through the eyes of a novice teacher and those of more experienced teachers observing her lesson.

Scene 1
A discussion between a school mentor (Jasmin) and a university tutor (Joe), after a lesson observation.

Jasmin: I liked the way that she began the lesson with a story about her sister in New Zealand.

Joe: Yes, it helped to contextualise her teaching so that the children could see the point of the lesson. The way that she led into the problem about day and night was lovely.

Jasmin: You could see how puzzling about why her sister is usually in bed when she phones really generated cognitive conflict and got the whole class engaged and thinking.

Joe: I liked the way she let them talk about and explore lots of possible ideas. They were far more engaged than in my last visit, when she talked at them far too much. They were thinking more creatively too.

Jasmin: I was concerned about her getting the children to choose how to solve the problem. I thought it would take too long, but it didn't, and they seemed to learn a lot. Sending emails to her sister in New Zealand was a brilliant way of recording their ideas. They can't wait for the replies to come.

Joe: It's tempting just to teach right answers, but that's much less engaging, and it doesn't guarantee that the children will have learned anything.

Creativity in teaching science

Scene 2
A discussion between two trainee teachers, later that evening.

Roger: So how was your tutor visit?

Rena: Better than I expected. The lesson went really well, and I got some great feedback – from the children too.

Roger: You must be relieved.

Rena: Yes, especially after my last disaster. I've learned from my mistakes though, which is funny really – one of the things they said last time is that I ought to help children learn from things that go wrong.

Roger: It's weird that, isn't it? My mentor was telling me about using misconceptions in my teaching! I've always done my best to avoid them, but she explained how they are great for getting children arguing about science.

Rena: Yes, arguing . . . Who would have thought we would want to get children arguing? But they get so involved! Now I can make sense of what tutors in college were saying when they talked about dialogic teaching.

Roger: I don't know about you, but I find it hard to suspend judgement about their ideas when they are discussing. It's easy when they get the wrong answer, but much harder when they come up with the right answer.

Scene 3
And what about the children? Here's what one child said when she got home.

I love science! Today our new teacher said that every time she phones her sister in New Zealand she is in bed and she can't work out why. I thought that's easy, it's because the Sun goes down there when we're in bed, and comes up here when they're in bed. But Billy said that wasn't right, it's because the Sun doesn't shine down there in our summer. Everyone had different ideas. It was fun finding out. We used the computer, but other groups used books, models and stuff. And her sister's going to send us an email about our questions! Shall I tell you about how we get night and day?

What can we learn from Rena and Roger reflecting on their teaching? What insights are they developing into why and how they might make their teaching more creative?

What is creativity in teaching?

Creative teaching in science is about providing the stimulus and the space for pupils to explore their own ideas. It's about being inventive and imaginative:

> *'Creativity involves breaking out of established patterns in order to look at things in a different way.'*
>
> Edward de Bono (1971)

It can involve taking some risks, since the outcome may not be known in advance. Mary Lou Cook is reputed to have said that *'creativity is inventing, experimenting, taking risks, breaking rules, making mistakes, and having fun'*. Creativity seems to fit with that lovely description of research, of making the strange familiar, and the familiar strange.

Some definitions of creative teaching seem to assume too much of teachers. It isn't helpful to suggest that only creative individuals can teach creatively. Even if some teachers are more naturally creative than others, creativity in teaching can be developed and enhanced, like other skills. Our research into using puppets to teach science (Simon et al., 2008) indicated that teachers who claimed not to be very creative recognised that using puppets for a short time helped them to be more creative and led to creative responses from the children.

We shouldn't assume that being creative in teaching science always involves teaching cross-curricular topics, or that linking science with art and drama is necessary to encourage creativity. A wide range of strategies can promote creativity. Working towards a creative learning environment will help children to be creative in their learning, and creative children will help teachers to be more creative in their teaching.

Why is creativity important?

Why is creativity important? Because it works. Creative teaching fits naturally with science education, for doing science inevitably involves creativity. Creativity begins the scientific process. It's there when pupils wonder whether and why things happen, when they build on what they know in an attempt to make sense of what they don't yet know, and when they invent creative hypotheses that help them to reason about the world. During the process it helps them devise suitable investigations and identify some of the hidden variables that might be misleading or confusing. At a later stage creativity helps them to look for different interpretations of the evidence, not simply for what they expected, and to think of alternative possible explanations for what they observe.

But perhaps that misses the point. The main reason why it's good to be creative in teaching science is because it makes our teaching better. Learning isn't a purely cognitive, academic process; feelings matter too (Hodson, 1998). Creative teaching helps us to take pupils' feelings into account. When we teach science creatively our lessons are more interesting and pupils are more engaged. Creative teaching is more likely to get pupils to think, to reason, to argue, and to be creative in their own thinking.

The value of creative teaching is recognised in various official documents, in statements such as:

'The most important goal for science education is to stimulate, nurture and sustain the curiosity, wonder and questioning of children and young people.'

Learning and Teaching Scotland (2009)

'Opportunities to develop critical and creative thinking should be planned ...'

QCA (2009)

Creative teaching runs as a subtext throughout the Scottish Curriculum for Excellence; it is evident in the most recent national curricula for England, Wales and Northern Ireland, which strive to nurture:

Creativity in teaching science

- successful learners who can think creatively and independently
- confident individuals who relate to others and manage themselves
- responsible citizens who evaluate issues and make informed choices and decisions.

Working towards these aims requires teaching that is engaging, interactive, thought-provoking and creative. How can young people develop into critical and creative thinkers if teachers don't model the process of thinking critically and creatively for them?

How to be creative in teaching science

There are several sources of generic strategies that support creative teaching and learning. For example, Best and Thomas (2007) offer a wide range of strategies such as analogies and metaphors. Ryan's (1990) *Thinker's Keys* and Futurelab's (2009) *Thinking Guides* include approaches such as listing the disadvantages of an item and using this to find ways to overcome them. These kinds of strategies can be valuable for engaging pupils and promoting dialogue, especially when applied to worthwhile scientific ideas. Creative strategies that are illustrated in scientific contexts can be found in White and Gunstone (1992), Naylor, et al (2004) and Adey (2006).

Let's go back to the scenarios at the start of this chapter, where Rena and Roger are beginning to understand how to work towards a more creative classroom culture. Here's what Rena wrote in her professional development portfolio.

> I think the penny has dropped about making my science lessons more creative. Today's lesson was really enjoyable for me and for the pupils. It's still a challenge to hold back and let their ideas flow, but here's what I want to do in my lessons from now on.
>
> My ten top tips!
>
> - Use questions and problems, not just information and instructions.
> - Use misconceptions. Share them with pupils.
> - Create cognitive conflict. This leads to engagement, challenge and thinking.
> - Provide plausible alternatives with no obvious right answer.
> - Suspend judgement about pupils' ideas - otherwise they stop thinking.
> - Use dialogic teaching to promote discussion.
> - Expect mistakes and uncertainty. View mistakes as an essential part of learning, not as a problem, and learn from them.
> - Contextualise my teaching wherever possible.
> - Be creative at the middle and end of lessons, not just the beginning.
> - Be fascinated with the way the world works. Share a sense of wonder with the pupils.

What do you think about Rena's list? Which of these do you do already? Do they influence how children respond? What else can you do?

Teaching primary science

Illustrating creativity in teaching

So how can we put creative teaching into action? Let's take another look at Rena's professional development portfolio.

> *Wednesday 5th March – Making science problematic*
>
> Presenting children with problems instead of instructions is working well. I just have to remember not to jump in too soon. I've begun to ask interesting questions to get children thinking about things they haven't thought about before. I like these two:
>
> - Will a black card make a darker shadow than a white card?
> - What would it be like if we had eyes in our feet?
>
> I'm trying to get them thinking of creative questions too. Jasmin suggested a 'What if … ?' display, with children invited to collect interesting scientific questions under that heading. They love it. One of them has written 'What if we go up in a space rocket? Will we still get day and night, or will it be night all the time?'
>
> *Friday 7th March – Cognitive conflict; suspending judgement*
>
> We took the last 15 minutes to talk about some of the 'What if … ?' questions. Kevin reckoned that he knew whether you get day and night if you go up in a space rocket, so I got him to tell the class. Then instead of saying 'Well done', I asked if anybody had a different idea. Nikki came up with a completely different way to look at it. I could instantly see how suspending judgement worked. If the answer was obvious, nobody would have thought any more about the question. As it was, several of them tried to find out more over the weekend, and I hadn't even asked them to do this for homework!
>
> *Wednesday 12th March – Using misconceptions; plausible alternatives with no obvious right answer*
>
> I used a Concept Cartoon for the first time. I was worried that it might reinforce some misconceptions, but it didn't. It was about why the Moon changes shape, which I thought was quite challenging. I asked them to choose which person they agreed with and why. I was surprised that they had so many ideas between them. Because they couldn't agree, they were really keen to find out more. Letting them choose their own way of finding

out worked really well. Between them they had so much evidence. The teacher's feedback noted how engaged the children were, even the less confident ones. Next time I'll try to capture some of their ideas in the Concept Cartoon by adding some blank bubbles.

The science coordinator has been on a PUPPETS course (www.puppetsproject.com). I watched her use the puppet today. It presented alternative ideas in a way that she couldn't. The children treated the puppet's problem as an authentic problem, instead of the teacher pretending. The children weren't intimidated and shared all sorts of ideas with the puppet. It looks like puppets can be as creative as you want them to be. I think it will be liberating to talk through a puppet and say anything I want! I'll try it on my next placement.

Friday 14th March – Problems, or information and instructions

I've gone backwards! My teacher suggested using the Jack and the Beanstalk story. But I was so anxious that the children learned about the conditions for growth that I had already decided what they should do with the seeds. It was only when Ali asked what would happen if they planted the seeds upside down that I realised, but it was too late. The beans were all neatly planted.

Wednesday 19th March – Mistakes and uncertainty; creative middles and ends

My last science lesson! Today we checked our plant investigations. We were all surprised by the plant in the cupboard. I hadn't expected it to grow, but it had – long, thin and pale! Previously I would have closed the door quickly so the children wouldn't see it, just in case it wasn't meant to be like that. But I am glad I didn't. We all learned so much about plants by trying to work out why it happened. Their group video diaries and individually designed seed packets were really effective at showing how much they had learned. And we finished with another story. I remembered about how George de Mestral invented velcro after looking at burrs, so we used this to talk about how plants might get their seeds to new places.

Teaching primary science

More illustrations

We hope that Rena's portfolio illustrates how principles can translate into action in the classroom. Here's a small selection of other ways to build creativity into lessons.

Urban myths as starting points for enquiry

These include the well-known 'facts' that water always swirls anti-clockwise in a basin in the Northern Hemisphere, and placing a spoon in the neck of a bottle of fizzy drink will stop it going flat. The best has to be Murphy's Law of Toast, which states that toast always lands butter-side down on the floor. A fascinating account of the physics involved in this is given in Matthews (2001).

Real-world problems

The British Science Association CREST Award activities are a goldmine of ideas for real-world science problems (see *Websites*). Although they are designed for out-of-school settings, there are many creative ideas that fit into the science curriculum. For example, under the theme of waste disposal and recycling, possible investigation questions might include the following.

- What is the perfect thickness for tomato sauce, and what tests would you do to find which sauce is best?
- Does the nature of a teapot affect the quality of a cup of tea?
- How does wearing a hood affect our hearing, and what are the implications for road safety?

The ASE website includes sections such as *Hot Issues*, which lists recent news stories that help to bring a global dimension to science and provide creative ideas for teaching. The *Science Across the World* section acts as a brokering service between schools that wish to make international links, to collaborate on topics such as drinking water supply or waste disposal. Links to *Primary Upd8* give access to a vast range of news items that have been developed into creative classroom activities.

There are many other organisations and websites that provide ideas and resources, such as the Primary Science Enhancement Programme, where a typical activity might be exploring the problems faced by a glue manufacturer who makes a glue that is too thick, so it won't flow through the factory pipes properly.

Cross-curricular links

Jarvis (2009) provides numerous interesting examples of activities that link science with other subjects. For example, an oral history account from an air raid warden during the Second World War connects to an investigation of the best material to use for blackout curtains. The Virtual Colour Museum (see *Websites*) has a range of creative links between science and art, with interactive demonstrations and animations that can be used in the classroom. These examples don't require teaching a whole topic through a cross-curricular approach, but they do challenge the view that subject boundaries are fixed and impenetrable (see also Chapter 7).

Creative ways of communicating

Drama can be engaging, powerful and memorable; that's why people go to the theatre. We can use its power to communicate scientific ideas. Examples of science drama could include representing what happens to particles of solid as they dissolve in a liquid, or using movement to illustrate pushes, pulls and balanced forces. Nickerson (2009) provides further background.

It isn't necessary to be a drama teacher or use scripted role plays. Small-scale examples of children taking on a role, such as by using Concept Cartoons (Naylor and Keogh, 2010), can be very effective. Children are simply asked to take one character and think about why that character is making that comment, and then to present what they think to the rest of the class.

Lesson endings

Ideas can be captured from children in creative ways by getting them to generate a set of instructions, write a letter, produce a cartoon strip, create an advertisement, generate a news report, create questions for an interview, produce a photo montage, develop a PowerPoint presentation and so on.

In conclusion

Let's keep in mind the purpose of being creative in teaching. It isn't another requirement to meet, or target to aim for. When teachers are more creative in teaching they enjoy their job more, children are more engaged, and learning is more effective. Isn't that what we all want?

One last thought. We can kill creativity as well as help it to grow. Creativity dies where teachers:

- always tell pupils what to do
- stifle pupils' ideas with their own
- only value products, not processes
- don't allow time for pupils to struggle
- praise everything
- see creativity as bad behaviour.

References

Adey, P. (2006) Scientific thinking: how can we accelerate and generalise it? In Wood-Robinson, V. (ed) *ASE Guide to Secondary Science Education*, pp205–212. Hatfield: Association for Science Education.

Best, B. and Thomas, W. (2007) *Creative Teaching and Learning Toolkit*. London: Continuum.

De Bono, E. (1971) *Lateral Thinking for Management: A Handbook of Creativity*. New York: American Management Association.

Futurelab (2009) *Thinking Guides*. Available online at: www.exploratree.org.uk

Hodson, D. (1998) *Teaching and Learning Science*. London: Open University Press.

Jarvis, T. (2009) Promoting creative science cross-curricular work through an in-service programme. *School Science Review*, **90**(332), 39–46.

Learning and Teaching Scotland (2009). Available online at: www.ltscotland.org.uk/curriculumforexcellence/buildingthecurriculum/guidance/btc1/scn/intro.asp

Matthews, R. (2001) Testing Murphy's Law: urban myths as a source of school science projects. *School Science Review*, **83**(302), 23–28.

Naylor, S. and Keogh, B. (2010) *Concept Cartoons in Science Education* (second edition). Sandbach: Millgate House Education.

Naylor, S., Keogh, B. and Goldsworthy, A. (2004) *Active Assessment: Thinking, Learning and Assessment in Science*. Sandbach: Millgate House Education.

Nickerson, L. (2009) Science drama. *School Science Review*, **90**(332), 83–89.

QCA (2009) Programmes of Study. Available online at: http://nationalstrategies.standards.dcsf.gov.uk/node/16065

Ryan, T. (1990) *Thinker's Keys for Kids*. Australia: South Coast Education Region, and available online at: www.thinkerskeys.com

Simon, S., Naylor, S., Keogh, B., Maloney, J. and Downing, B. (2008) Puppets promoting engagement and talk in science. *International Journal of Science Education*, **30**, 9, 1229–1248.

White, R. and Gunstone, R. (1992) *Probing Understanding*. London: Falmer.

Websites

Association for Science Education: www.ase.org.uk

British Science Association: www.britishscienceassociation.org

Primary Science Enhancement Programme: www.psep.org

Virtual Colour Museum: www.colour-experience.org

Primary upd8: www.primaryupd8.org.uk

Chapter 14

Using and serving the environment

Carolyn Yates

All environments present opportunities for learning science. Natural landscapes provide rich, diverse, multi-sensory experiences; interactions with the human-made environment instil respect for human endeavour and an awareness of the impact of humankind on the natural world. The first part of this chapter considers children's ideas about the living and other things they see in their daily lives and how these ideas can be developed into scientific understanding through the use of process skills. The second part is concerned with helping children to understand how human activity is affecting the natural environment and what can be done to minimize the negative impact.

Why use the environment?

Children, like scientists, learn about the world by using all their senses – by looking, listening, touching, smelling and tasting it. From these interactions ideas are tested, links made between cause and effect, similarities and differences compared and mental models about how the world works created. As children grow and move around more independently, so the boundaries of their environment expand.

While it is always fun to explore any aspect of science outside, it is useful to keep in mind which aspects of science knowledge and skills are particularly enhanced by the opportunities offered through the environment. Biology, ecology and earth sciences require active engagement with the environment, but learning in other sciences, too, can draw on objects and events outside the classroom. Skills developed through interactions with the environment include:

- measuring
- observing
- recording in lists, tables, spreadsheets and graphs

Teaching primary science

- drawing and photographing
- keeping a nature diary or log book
- data collecting
- processing and data logging.

Helping children develop ideas about the environment

Having a broad understanding of how children's concepts about the world around them develop over time and through experience helps the teacher plan suitable learning pathways (Allen, 2010). Environmental education for the Early Years should focus on encouraging young children to explore and enjoy the world of nature. The teacher's role is to help them by asking questions that focus their attention, and to encourage them to use their full range of senses – what they see, smell, touch and hear – to ask themselves questions.

Young children learn best through daily, direct and concrete experiences that relate to what is already familiar and comfortable (Moore and Wong, 1997). School playgrounds and gardens provide natural habitats that nourish children's awareness and support their learning (Louv, 2005). Children can be asked both 'big' questions (for example, *'What is a garden?'*, *'Does everyone have a garden?'*, *'What are gardens for?'*, *'How is gardening different from farming?'*) and 'small' questions (for example, *'How many legs does this insect have?'*, *'What do we need to grow our sunflower seeds?'*) By helping children find out the answers to their questions through investigations and research in books and on the internet, teachers model scientific habits. *'I don't know the answer to that but let's try and find out'* is a motivating response.

A playground can be enriched as an environment by adding bird feeders, windsocks, flower and vegetable pots, rock piles, and logs. Children can have daily access to this outdoor laboratory, with plenty of opportunity to develop skills of manipulation, sensory engagement, and self-initiated explorations. Children need to be shown how to handle plants and animals safely and respectfully (ASE, 2001). Involving a class in creating and protecting an outdoor habitat for wildlife will develop scientific knowledge, skills and an attitude of curiosity to the natural world. Monitoring and recording the changes that occur daily and through the seasons builds understanding of the cyclical nature of the world around us.

Investigating life and living things

Most young children have difficulty with grouping living things into plants and animals, let alone using scientific classification systems. Scientists group living things into Bacteria and viruses, Protista (simple one-celled and few-celled organisms), Fungi, Plants (flowering and non-flowering), Vertebrates (animals with backbones) and Invertebrates (animals without backbones). Children tend to use 'animal' or 'plant' inconsistently – for example, they may suggest that flowers are plants but grass is not; a cat is an animal but a person is not. Young children often do not recognise trees as living although they understand that seedlings are alive. They may not recognise that trees, vegetables and grass are all plants, with shared characteristics. Children and biologists do not have the same ideas about the meaning of main biological and ecological concepts, such as 'animal'. Most children think only large land

Using and serving the environment

mammals are animals. They may think whales, jellyfish and starfish are all fish. Many children up to the ages of about 11 and 12 think that plants, fungi, eggs and seeds are not living.

Classifying organisms and objects, such as rocks and stones, using characteristics in a consistent way is an important reasoning skill that first starts to develop when children naturally group things by their similarities and differences. Primary and lower secondary pupils will use criteria like number of legs, body covering and habitat to decide whether things are animals. Older pupils frequently use characteristics that are common to both plants and animals (for example, reproduction and respiration) as criteria.

Children have difficulty understanding that an organism can be classified as both a bird and an animal. Children need to practise sorting and grouping living things in many different ways – for example, according to:

- whether they live on land, in the air or in the sea
- size – for instance, is a plant taller than humans or smaller than humans?
- skin covering – for instance, does an animal have bare skin, feathers, fur or scales?
- number of legs.

Finding and examining invertebrates or plants in their immediate environment provides children with opportunities for this. Children need to wear gloves before they collect materials for closer study back in the classroom. Other equipment needed is suggested in Box 1.

Box 1   Essential equipment for exploring different habitats

- hand lenses and magnifying glasses
- collecting trays
- pooters
- clean jam jars with lids with holes
- tweezers (forceps)
- small-headed paintbrushes
- paper and plastic specimen bags

There are plenty of colourful, well-illustrated books, keys and picture cards to help children name their specimens. It is a good idea to build up a resource bank of identification materials, appropriate to the school's immediate environment. Library services can lend collections of identification books related to other habitats like waterways, the seashore, woodland or heathland.

As well as creating their own sorting sets based on easily observable criteria from real animals and plants, it helps if teachers develop children's reasoning by using collections of pictures of living and non-living things. The pictures could include the Sun, seaweed, a baby, a jellyfish, a jumper, a feather, a box of cereal, a train and some shells. About 20 cards provide the right level of challenge for children from six years old. Asking children, working together, to put the cards in groups and explain their reasoning gives the teacher instant access to their ways of reasoning and plenty of opportunity to develop an emerging logic to define 'living' and 'non-living'.

Some children may believe fire, clouds and the Sun are alive, but others think plants and certain animals are non-living. Children typically use criteria such as 'movement', 'breathing', 'reproduction' and 'death' to decide whether things are alive. Getting the 'right' answer is not as important as providing the children with opportunities for high-quality decisions. Some children will begin to differentiate between 'non-living' and 'never lived'. They might say things like *'The bird's feather isn't alive but it's been on a living thing, but this stone is not dead – it's not ever, ever lived.'* This sort of talk indicates that they may be ready to look at the processes of life more scientifically. Life processes for all animals include nutrition, movement, growth and reproduction; growth, nutrition and reproduction are common to plants.

Exploring habitats

Children between the ages of five and seven, particularly those living in urban areas, may believe that nothing happens without a human cause – they may think that people made hills, for example. Children are aware that animals and plants live in different places. They may say *'A sheep grows a warm coat so it can live in cold places. A polar bear grows a white coat so it can hide in the snow and stay warm'*. They assume the animal can choose this attribute. The idea that animals adapt to their environment is challenging. Putting a bird table at ground level, another at a higher level and also hanging bird feeders in trees, all containing different types of bird food, can help to demonstrate the idea of adaptation. Children will observe that different varieties of birds feed at the different food sources.

Visiting different habitats, such as a field, a pond or a hedgerow, to observe and identify what lives there, describing the place, recording the physical conditions of light, water and temperature can help to make the link between the types of animals and plants that live there and the conditions. Observing the same places over the changing seasons helps to strengthen the idea of relationships between the physical conditions of the habitat and the features of the organisms living there. Encouraging the children to draw, photograph and discuss their observations gradually builds an understanding of the ways living things interact with their environment (De Boo, 2004). Studying a habitat leads to thinking about food chains. Children tend to think of food chains in relation to the food they eat, such as:

hen eats seeds ➤ hen lays eggs ➤ I eat eggs for my breakfast

Encouraging children to grow their own food plants and to observe and record the plants' development, then harvest and eat the plants, is a lively and engaging way to explore the relationships between germinating and growing factors (sunlight, warmth and water) and their own need for food to grow and be healthy.

The Earth in space

Common misconceptions that young children hold include that the Earth is sitting on something, that it is larger than the Sun, that it is flat and round like a pancake and that it is the centre of the solar system. While it is hard to challenge these ideas through interaction with the environment, direct observation can challenge other misconceptions: that stars and constellations appear in the same place in the sky every night and that the Sun rises in the east and sets in the west every day. Parents and carers can be asked to help their children keep observation logs of both weather conditions and, where there is the opportunity, the sky at night. Keeping records of the school's environment visible over time builds knowledge about seasonal changes.

Asking children what they think causes different weather conditions is revealing. Russell et al. (1993) reported from their research:

> 'While many children were able to explain that rain comes from clouds, their explanations of the relationship between clouds and rain vary. Both infants and juniors tend to report that rain occurs as clouds become heavy ... Infants tended to suggest that rain comes from particular clouds which hold the rain until they 'burst'.'
>
> Russell et al. (1993, p67)

Serving the environment

As children become older, their cognition and moral development shift from egocentric concerns to engaging with wider relationships and issues. They develop an understanding of cause and effect: when they do not water the plant pots on the windowsill, the plants will wilt and die; if they do not feed the pet rabbit daily and with the right food it will not be healthy; the vegetable garden needs regular weeding or the crop will not grow. This lays a foundation for realising that the care they take of the environment is linked to the care everyone needs to take for all ecosystems and all animal and plant species.

Big ideas such as recycling, protecting endangered species and energy conservation become a focus of interest and offer opportunities for scientific research and investigations. Children shift from externally set rules – such as '*We pick up our litter because we are told to do this*' – to autonomy through belief and conviction: '*We need to make the world a better place for all living things so we need to be careful of how much litter we create and what we do with it*'. By upper primary age, children may be ready to make the links from local to national (government policy) to international – the big questions about global warming, climate change, extinction of animals and plants, energy conservation and renewable and non-renewable energy sources.

In 2006, The Department for Children, Schools and Families (DCSF) launched the Sustainable Schools Framework (see *Websites*). Its aim is for every school to be a sustainable school by 2020. The key idea is 'education for sustainable development', indicating that schools are to take an integrated approach through the teaching provision, learning opportunities and the curriculum, as well as the school's values and in its engagement with local people and partners in the community. Guidance on creating a policy about using the school environment for learning, teaching and becoming a sustainable school is available through the website. Box 2 gives an example of a school policy.

Box 2 Extract from a school policy on environmental awareness

> It is important for our school community to have an awareness and understanding of the effects of our actions upon the environment in which we live, work and relax. We need to take responsibility for our own actions and we need to have a sense of duty and care for the world in which we live.
>
> The ways in which we will strive towards this goal are to reduce the amounts of materials we use and waste we produce, re-use materials wherever possible, restore what is deemed to have been destroyed and respect our neighbours and our environment.

Climate change

All kinds of factors influence our climate, from massive events on the Sun to the growth of microscopic creatures in the oceans, with subtle interactions between many of these factors. There is a growing body of evidence that points to the conclusion that the world is warming, and that it is highly likely this warming is due to human activity increasing levels of greenhouse gases in the atmosphere. It is assumed that, if emissions of greenhouse gases (particularly carbon dioxide and methane) continue to rise, the warming will too, with increasingly serious consequences. Damage would come indirectly from rising seas, land ice melting, lack of rain in some areas, heavier rains in others and climate disruptions. The scientific debates and disagreements focus on how fast and how high temperatures will rise. Newspaper articles and children's news programmes stimulate debate and teachers have access to many excellent resources (to be found, for example, on the Curriculum for Excellence for Outdoor Learning and the Primary Upd8 websites) to help children make decisions about how best to serve their school and home environment in the light of these big issues – that is, to become 'responsible citizens'.

Waste and decay

In the UK we generate enough waste every hour to fill the Albert Hall. Everyday waste changes over time. Young children often think that waste matter will stay the same or that the wind, animals or people will move it away. Some will mention that things left outside change colour or go rusty. This could be explored further with upper primary pupils, by setting up a 'controlled experiment' (Box 3).

Box 3 Investigating decay

> This investigation helps children see that rotting and decay are caused by chemical, biological and physical processes. Two net bags are each filled with a piece of paper, some orange peel, a pebble and an iron nail. One bag is buried and then regularly dug up to be examined, while the other is left outside exposed to the weather. Observing the changes in each shows children that decay is a gradual, inevitable consequence. They may begin to grasp the need for decomposing agents by comparing the amount and speed of decay of the objects in the two bags. They will appreciate that different waste materials decay at different rates, and thereby come to understand that recycling and re-using helps to reduce the amounts of slow-decaying substances filling landfills or being deposited out at sea.
>
> (**Note:** Don't let children handle waste material unless fully equipped with litter grabbers and gloves.)

Through visits, discussion and research on the internet and in libraries, children can increase their awareness of what happens to household waste. Plastic bags present a huge problem. Children in the upper primary school realise the problem when they consider the facts. Each year about thirteen billion bags are used and thrown away in the UK. Each bag will be used for an average of 20 minutes, and takes up to a thousand years to decompose. Most will litter the countryside. Others find their way into the seas, where they are mistaken for food and kill up to a hundred thousand marine mammals each year, as well as countless birds. Many countries have taken the initiative to ban or phase out plastic bags, including

China, South Africa, India and Kenya. Many schools are spearheading local campaigns to stop plastic bags being used in local shops.

Energy saving

Through implementing energy reduction measures, most schools can save as much as 10% on utility bills (water and heating), which, even for a small primary school, can be large amount of money. UK schools spend approximately £450m on energy each year, three times as much as they do on books, about 3.5% of their budgets. In many schools, children are already taught about the smaller measures, such as turning off the lights at the end of lessons. Beyond that, children can help calculate the school's energy usage, and identify ways to cut it. They can use a school neutral carbon calculator (see *Websites*) to help calculate their 'carbon footprint' and understand how their school can reduce its emissions.

In conclusion

There are several reasons for including studies of the environment in children's science education. It makes science relevant to daily life, encourages a sense of respect and caring for the natural environment, provides satisfaction in being able to find out about the world around us and may lead to life-long interest in living things. In order to benefit in these ways, children need to be able to explore, observe and test out their ideas about causes and explanations. Thus teachers need to be aware of the ideas that pupils are likely to have so that they can ensure opportunities, through enriching the school environment if necessary, to develop more scientific ideas and skills.

References

Allen, M. (2010) *Misconceptions in Primary Science*. Maidenhead: Open University Press.

ASE (2001) *Be Safe!* (third edition). Hatfield: Association for Science Education.

De Boo, M. (2004) *Nature Detectives: Environmental Science for Primary Children*. ASE and Woodland Trust.

Louv, R. (2005) *Last Child in the Woods: Saving our Children from Nature Deficit Disorder*. Chapel Hill, NC: Algonquin Books.

Moore, R.C. and Wong, H. (1997) *Natural Learning: Creating Environments for Rediscovering Nature's Way of Teaching*. Berkeley, CA: MIG Communications.

Russell, T., Bell, D., Longden, K. and Mcguigan, L. (1993) *SPACE Research Report Rocks, Soil and Weather*. Liverpool: Liverpool University Press.

Websites

Foundation for Environmental Education: www.fee-international.org

BTCV: www2.btcv.org.uk

Commission for Architecture and the Built Environment (CABE): www.cabe.org.uk/education/green-day

The Carbon Trust: www.carbontrust.co.uk/energy/assessyourorganisation/surveys-for-schools

Teaching primary science

Curriculum for Excellence through Outdoor Learning:
   www.ltscotland.org.uk/outdoorlearning/index.asp

Project Genie: www.projectgenie.org.uk/Teachers.aspx

Primary Upd8: www.primaryupd8.org.uk

Sustainable Schools Framework: www.teachernet.gov.uk/sustainableschools

LTScotland website has a variety of tools to measure energy footprints etc.:
   www.ltscotland.org.uk/sustainabledevelopment/findresources/globalfootprint/learners/footprintcalculator/index.asp

Chapter 15

Assessing pupils' learning

David Brodie

It is only human to make casual observations and judgements of everything around us, including each other. Formal assessment may not be quite so much built into us, but it has still been around for a very long time. This chapter considers the assessment of pupils' learning in science and how it can be carried out to serve the two purposes of helping progression and of reporting on what has been attained at various times. Northern Ireland, Scotland, Wales and England each have their own approaches to assessment, and in all of these home nations change is ongoing. The main section of this chapter gives an account of the Assessing Pupils' Progress (APP) project in England, but it begins with a brief summary of practice in the other three countries of the UK.

Assessment practice in the UK

In Northern Ireland, reporting to parents is a statutory requirement of every school, on an annual basis and not only at the end of a Key Stage. Across the whole of the Province, the option of centrally set and marked formal tests has been kept open, in that pupils '*may be assessed using such computer-based assessment method as the Department may specify*'. It is not, however, proposed that 'computer-based' methods provide the only format, but it is recognised that assessment '... *is most effective when it is used not only to chart progress but also to move pupil learning forward by providing timely and constructive feedback*'. School principals have considerable freedom about how they assess and report, and the non-statutory guidance for science provides a summary of the principles of Assessment for Learning.

In Scotland, the curriculum is non-statutory, and only national 'guidelines' are provided by Government. The new national guidance, 'Curriculum for Excellence', states that '*Assessment practices will follow and support the new curriculum. This will promote higher quality learning and teaching and give more autonomy and professional responsibility to teachers.*' It goes further to say '*Teachers can gather evidence of progress as part of day-to-*

day learning, and specific assessment tasks will also be important in assessing progress at key points of learning.' Teachers' assessment of levels attained is supported by a National Assessment Resource (under development 2009/10), explicitly for purposes of quality assurance and also to support teachers in achieving consistency and confidence in their professional judgements. The new National Assessment Resource is to be more than a bank of assessment items for tests. It will allow teachers to collaborate and develop a shared understanding of standards. In addition, it will provide guidance on a wider range of assessment approaches using media such as graphics, video, audio and interactive resources as well as the more familiar text. It will also include illustrations of learners' work to support teachers in developing a shared understanding of standards that they can apply consistently. The new assessment system is designed to provide ongoing feedback to teachers, parents and children and young people about steps that need to be taken to maximise individual progress.

The situation in Wales was, several years ago, the same as that as in England, but with devolution of powers to the Welsh Assembly Government it moved quickly apart, and Wales abandoned national tests at Key Stage 3 much sooner than was the case in England. The Welsh system replaced them with school-based assessment using 'levels' that have origins in the previous 'England and Wales' system. This makes a commitment to formative assessment in its introduction, stating that *'Ongoing formative assessment – assessment for learning – lies at the heart of good teaching'*, and claiming that it helps teachers to *'... build up an extensive knowledge of your learners' strengths, as well as the areas that need further development, and you will use this knowledge to help you plan for the next steps in their learning.'* There is an emphasis on 'next steps', which outline the actions that result from the diagnostic benefit of a particular classroom observation or set of observations. It also recognises both the need to work with inevitable complexity and the need for workability based on criteria, or 'level descriptions', that make due demands on teacher professionalism: *'It may be that ... no one level description provides an exact fit'* with a learner's work, so that the teacher must decide which description provides a 'best fit' to a learner's performance. Teachers need a sound working familiarity with the descriptions, and the confidence to make judgements.

There are recognisable themes in the above – a movement away from externally set and marked paper tests and towards teacher assessment, and very significant influence of the 'Assessment for Learning' movement. The Assessing Pupils' Progress (APP) project that operates in England follows the same pattern, and the rest of this chapter is based on the writer's experience of developments in England, in supporting pilot and later work on the APP project. It uses APP as an example by which to explore some key principles and practicalities of assessment.

The APP project

On one hand, for all funded activity, including learning and teaching, quality assurance matters. On the other hand, the concept of assessment in order to enhance progression in a semi-continuous interaction of assessment, planning and activity has emerged more strongly into consciousness relatively recently, most particularly under the banner of 'Assessment for Learning' (Chapter 11). Both quality assurance and progression are required, so those who aspire to design a curriculum and its assessment must deal with challenges that include the strong desirability of fitting assessment for both of these purposes into a single package. APP is an attempt to meet such a challenge.

Assessing pupils' learning

An overview of APP might be helpful before addressing the question of whether it succeeds in filling dual QA and progression roles. A first point is that APP is not statutory. It provides guidance, not rules. The guidance is for good practice based on ideas of assessment for progression.

Every teacher already makes assessments, formally at intervals and informally on a daily basis. APP makes use of progressive levels, from 1 to 8 (and 'Exceptional Performance' so that there is no ceiling) as defined by the National Curriculum for England and its associated Level Descriptions. It thereby provides a structure that allows teachers' existing expertise and knowledge of individual pupils to be recognised. Indeed, failure to take advantage of these very human resources would be wasteful.

The teacher uses APP to assess in order to provide due direction and support for learners through an upwards progression. As the guide on this ascent, the teacher needs a map – provided in the form of a grid of Assessment Guidelines. All learners must make the journey, whether or not they reach the highest ground, and can do so best if they, too, know where they are going. A map, like any other model of a greater reality, has predictive power. It allows planning of a route, even before the journey begins, and then a means to check progress on a very regular basis and thereby to make adjustments to details of the pathway to the highest practicable point. Playing with the analogy a little more, it is interesting to consider what provides the landscape that is being mapped. Arguably it is the curriculum itself, as specified in England by the National Curriculum and its Level Descriptions.

The APP map

The APP 'map' for science is presented as a grid, or Assessment Guidelines, with five columns addressing different aspects of science and eight rows for the levels of progression, 1 to 8. The five columns provide five Assessment Focuses or AFs:

AF1:   **Thinking Scientifically**, dealing with abilities in describing and explaining processes and phenomena, including through critical use of models and evidence

AF2:   **Understanding the Applications and Implications of Science**, requiring learners to develop and show awareness of the significance of scientific and technological developments to themselves and to wider society

AF3:   **Communicating and Collaborating in Science**, involving use of scientific vocabulary and conventions, creation of data presentations in various formats, use of secondary sources, and working with others

AF4:   **Using Investigative Approaches**, for which the learner plans and carries out investigations, with due attention to safety

AF5:   **Working Critically with Evidence**, requiring assessment and interpretation of gathered data.

For each Assessment Focus, and for each of the eight levels of achievement, there are between three and five Assessment Criteria, presented as bullet points. Each cell in the five-by-eight grid therefore has a small set of these bullet points (Figure 1).

Figure 1 The structure of the APP Assessment Guidelines, showing just three of the eight levels. The AFs are the five Assessment Focuses, and the panels within each cell are the bullet-pointed Assessment Criteria.

	AF1	AF2	AF3	AF4	AF5
6					
5					
4					

The Assessment Guidelines make little mention of specific content. But scientific information, principles and concepts, as well as applications of these by the pupil, are necessary for achieving the competencies. The criteria do not provide crude tick boxes but demand some intelligent interpretation. They are *indicative* of a level; they represent that level but they do not provide a full description. At Level 5, for example, for Assessment Focus 3, Communicating and Collaborating in Science, a criterion requires that pupils might '*Use appropriate scientific and mathematical conventions to communicate abstract ideas.*' That can take very many forms, such as use of arrows to show size and direction of forces, and it can be done with different levels of competence. Thus to provide support to teachers in making judgements of a pupil's level of progression, APP does not consist of the Assessment Guidelines alone. There is a considerable library of Standards Files, where collections of pupils' work at the full range of levels illustrate good practice in the 'levelling' decision-making progress. The files illustrate that evidence of a pupil's level can take many forms – which could be written reports on investigations or on some specific scientific model, or could be a physical model, a presentation, or even merely the pupil's spoken word. The system values teachers' judgements, as it must since it provides assessment for progression and it is the teacher who will be guiding the progression of the assessed child.

Can APP support both formative and summative assessment?

A key question is whether such a system can fill a dual role, providing quality assurance at the same time as supporting progression. To begin to answer this question it is useful to compare APP to the system that existed before, with formal national tests taken at the end of Key Stages – the SATs.

SATs provided some assurance of 'quality'. They came into being because elected politicians felt that it was their role to see to it that such assurance was provided – a very reasonable perception. The tests did offer good reliability, or replicability of outcome, as is likely to be the case for sets of formal questions requiring short and highly focused answers. That is, they produced numerical results that could be produced again, with a modest margin of error, for a child for whom a new test of the same kind is given. Since they took place at the end of Key Stages, however, they provided no information for teachers or learners for guided progress within a Key Stage; they did not offer assessment for progression. Also, by dominating what happened in classrooms, the SATs assured quality of a limited kind. They made only modest assessment, and encouraged likewise modest teaching, of understanding

Assessing pupils' learning

that the learner could apply to new situations, and less again of competencies of working, often collaboratively, in order to carry out tasks such as sourcing and selecting information or making meaningful observations and investigations. They paid no heed to the motivational benefits of task-based goals or contextual and active approaches to concepts. They did not ensure such quality at all.

SATs had good reliability, but their weakness was validity. That is, it has to be questioned whether what they were assessing were attributes that have much value in the world. Validity is intended to be a strength of the APP approach, bringing in 'thinking' (AF1), 'understanding' (AF2), 'communicating and collaborating' (AF3), 'investigating' (AF4) and 'working critically' (AF5). APP supports and promotes direct teacher assessment, in keeping with its designed role as assessment for progression. But universal confidence in teacher assessment does not exist, and for assurance the world requires confidence. There would be a strong argument for operating the two styles of assessment in parallel, unless APP can be seen to approach the same levels of reliability as SATs and thereby be seen to be superior overall. The possible threats to reliability of teacher assessment come in three forms:

- the fundamental uncertainty of single observations of any phenomenon
- the danger of lack of commonality of standards between teachers, schools and regions
- the concern that some teachers are not up to the job, either because they are incapable of making judgements or because they allow crude self-interest to dominate their decisions.

APP makes an attempt to address these threats.

Strengthening the reliability of APP

While a single observation may have considerable uncertainty, multiple measurements, as proposed by APP, provide better precision of overall judgement.

The APP Assessment Guidelines on their own, since they are not rigid statements but require thoughtful input from the assessing teacher, leave open the possibility that teachers, however professional they try to be, will not always make the same judgement. The project begins to address the danger of divergence of judgement by providing Standards Files, made up of collections of evidence of pupil achievement (in many formats since APP itself presents no restrictions on these) with commentary on level decisions. Study of these files is a prerequisite of proficiency in making confident judgements and thereby inspiring confidence amongst those outside the classroom.

The Standards Files might not be quite enough to achieve full commonality of level of judgement as is required for assessment for quality assurance, and the possibility of poor standards of professionalism, in some place and at some time, must be dealt with. During the pilot projects for both Primary Science and Key Stage 3 Science, APP was seen to work best with a system of 'moderation' that took the form of 'peer review', with an emphasis on 'peer' so that discussions were not 'top-down' from a supposed authority figure but were discussions amongst professionals. During the pilot projects these meetings, when chaired by a professional with the confidence to avoid dominating proceedings, were also seen to have professionalising and motivating benefits for participants.

That leads to the matter of necessity of workability in many thousands of classrooms. Initial familiarisation is a barrier to ease of use of the APP Assessment Guidelines. Their basic tabular structure is quite simple but it carries a lot of information, and at first sight it is only a little more meaningful than a map would be to one who had never seen one before. The ability to use a map through quick glances surely comes later, once a familiarity has been established, and the same is true of the Assessment Guidelines.

APP makes no demands for storage of vast quantities of paper material. Indeed, it encourages use of some assessment evidence that need not be paper-based at all, including direct teacher observation in the classroom. 'Peer review' – backed up by some real evidence (paper or otherwise) and by spoken argument to colleagues who are not from the same school, or from any school, and who are neither hostile nor necessarily sympathetic – provides accreditation of a teacher's professionalism, grants trust to a teacher, so that in general their judgement regarding what they have seen in the classroom becomes accepted. Those classroom observations, after all, have huge validity and it would be wasteful not to exploit them. An essential role of anyone who claims a position of leadership then becomes one of supporting peer review.

In case the point has been missed, APP does not require that entire cabinets should be filled with catalogued work from pupils. What is necessary is that a teacher making judgements about pupils can show – to peers in the first instance but thereafter to anyone else who makes legitimate enquiry, such as parents, headteachers and local authority or government appointees – that their judgements of pupils' levels of progression are soundly based on the Assessment Guidelines and on national standards as illustrated by the Standards Files and confirmed through peer moderation processes.

In conclusion

Teachers need information on a continuous basis about all pupils in order to move them forward in learning. They also need to be able to summarise learning and to be able to demonstrate, with some confidence, how far their pupils have progressed. Both these purposes are integral to the teacher's role and are supported in different ways in the countries of the UK. We have described the APP project in England, which is a well developed way of serving these purposes.

Websites

Northern Ireland:
www.opsi.gov.uk/sr/sr2007/nisr_20070045_en_1
www.nicurriculum.org.uk/key_stage_3/assessment
Scotland:
www.scotland.gov.uk/Topics/Education/Schools/curriculum/assessment
www.ltscotland.org.uk/curriculumforexcellence/sciences/principlesandpractice/assessment.asp
www.ltscotland.org.uk/learningteachingandassessment/assessment/index.asp
Wales:
http://wales.gov.uk/docs/dcells/publications/090806ScienceGuidance.pdf
England:
www.nationalstrategies.standards.dcsf.gov.uk/node/157236

Section 3

Provision for science at the school level

Chapter 16

School-level planning

David Simon

Teachers need to plan the opportunities they provide for children's learning within a context of shared values and overall planning at school level, so that children experience a coherent programme as they pass through the school. As noted in Chapter 6, we can think of planning as being needed at three main levels: long-term planning across the whole school for a whole year cycle; medium-term planning of sequences of lessons; and short-term planning at the class level. This chapter deals with the first two levels of planning, which operate across the whole school. It begins by considering planning of the curriculum content. In a later section it deals with other decisions at the school level that constitute a school policy for science and ensure consistency and continuity in the opportunities for teaching and learning science.

Planning the science curriculum

Long term

Two contrasting approaches to curriculum planning have been used at various times in the primary school. One is aptly described as 'subject-based', in which science is likely to be taught in discrete science lessons, perhaps two 45-minute lessons per week. In the other 'topic-based' approach science is taught in topics that also develop learning in other areas. Each approach has advantages and disadvantages.

A benefit of a subject-based approach is that content can be clearly planned, giving confidence that the children will have covered all that they should have over a term, year or Key Stage. But this approach can lead to curriculum overload – by dealing separately with the demands of every subject a time pressure is created, causing difficulty in covering the requirements of the curriculum or guidelines. This approach can also have a limiting impact on practical work in science, much of which cannot fit into discrete, relatively short, periods of time.

Topic-based approaches are more consistent with the ethos of primary schools, particularly as the more integrated approach is seen to be a better reflection of how learning takes place in everyday life. Science will be taught with other subjects, making it easier to create links between the learning in the different subjects: design and technology

School-level planning

projects often involve electrical circuits; geographical work on rivers, or settlements near water, is supported by learning about the water cycle; making and playing musical instruments can link science, design and technology and music. When these links are effective, the learning is enhanced in all the subjects. A disadvantage of this approach is that, although curriculum coverage is planned, teachers can over or underplay different subjects in the topic. So it is possible for the less confident science teacher merely to pay lip service to the science within a topic. At its worst, topic-based learning can be very weak, with obvious and inconsequential links made between subjects, almost by word association. In this situation, the learning in all of the subjects may suffer.

In practice most schools sit somewhere between these two extremes. Most schools take a topic-based approach, in the knowledge that some topics are more heavily weighted towards particular subjects. This balance ensures that the curricular links remain sensible, coherent and effective for learning.

The size of a school has a bearing on the organisation of the curriculum. A one-form entry primary school would seem to be an easy model. For example, in an English school, with six years of primary education, the whole curriculum may be divided into six parts and assigned to Years 1 to 6. However, it is accepted that there are benefits in teachers working together, so perhaps planning three two-year cycles is better, allowing the teachers in Years 1 and 2, 3 and 4, and 5 and 6 to plan together and ensuring full coverage over a child's journey through the school. In larger schools the teachers are likely to be working in teams, facing different problems, particularly the management of resources. In schools of less than one-form entry it may be worth considering a three-year cycle across Reception and Years 1 and 2, and a four-year cycle across the junior years. In Scotland, the natural planning periods are the stages identified in Curriculum for Excellence: Early (pre-school and primary 1), First (to the end of the fourth year of primary) and Second (up to the end of primary). In Northern Ireland, the Foundation (Years 1 and 2), Key Stage 1 (Years 3 and 4) and Key Stage 2 (Years 5, 6, and 7) form the obvious planning phases, while in Wales the planning periods are Foundation Stage (pre-school and Years 1 and 2) and Key Stage 2 years, either in a four-year cycle or in two two-year periods (Chapter 21).

A school's long-term curriculum plan for science should fit on to one side of A4 paper. Its aim is to show that the school has coverage of all that is expected within the required curriculum, generally organised as blocks, or units of work, assigned to year groups or within a cycle. This may be annotated with curriculum reference numbers or these may be left to medium-term plans. The more cross-curricular the approach, the more important it may be to specify what is to be taught, whereas a unit called 'electricity' is fairly self-explanatory. A topic-based plan would list the agreed topics for each year, briefly noting under each the part of the Programme of Study (or 'experiences and outcomes' in the case of the Scottish Curriculum for Excellence), as illustrated in Table 1.

Table 1 Example of a long-term whole-school plan.

Reception Curriculum reference	Me and my family ( )	Our garden ( )	My house ( )	Toys ( )	Stop, look and listen ( )	Changing times ( )
Year 1 Curriculum reference	Living things ( )	Seeds and flowers ( )	Ourselves ( )	Pushes and pulls ( )	Bits and pieces ( )	Sounds ( )

and so on

Provision for science at the school level

When planning the long-term curriculum it is essential to refer to the appropriate national curriculum or guidelines (see Chapter 21 for the different ways in which these are set out in the countries of the UK). Although this sounds very obvious, in recent years there have been other documents that teachers have used for planning, such as QCA Scheme of Work (QCA, 1998), neglecting the original curriculum document. The result is that teachers may continue to teach content that is no longer required, unnecessarily adding to the perception of pressure and of excessive content to be covered.

A useful approach to planning is to consider the knowledge content of the curriculum. This is in Attainment Targets 2, 3 and 4 in the English National Curriculum, in 'The World Around Us' in the Northern Ireland curriculum, the three areas of the Welsh curriculum and the five science organisers of the Scottish Curriculum for Excellence. Planning involves perusing each of the relevant areas to decide whether there are any 'chunks' that make effective units of work. An example of how to select appropriate chunks is given in Box 1.

Box 1 Identifying 'chunks' for planning work on electricity

> In the National Curriculum for England, all the electricity work in Key Stage 1 appears to go together well. Consider whether that chunk is an appropriate amount of learning for one unit of work, or whether there is too much. Does it need splitting into two units, allowing return a year later for some progress? In this case, since electricity features in the Key Stage 2 curriculum, one unit would seem to be fine. Should it be allocated to Year 1 or 2? This will need to be considered later, after looking at Key Stage 2.
>
> At Key Stage 2, the electricity content would seem to make a sensible unit of work. If it is split up, the content in each part would be rather too small. However, learning about electricity once over four years does not seem enough, especially if it were in Year 3 or 4, for this would miss the opportunity for some children to further their understanding when older. This would seem to be a good opportunity for a cross-curricular link where the children return to electricity in the upper junior classes in a problem-solving situation – through a design and technology project, for example. This will allow some children to develop their knowledge and understanding of electricity, others to add to their understanding of any areas that they previously found difficult, and all the children to further develop their learning through problem solving.

The example in Box 1 suggests that electricity appears three times across Key Stages 1 and 2. Sensibly, these could be in Years 1, 3 and 5, or 2, 4 and 6. Returning to areas that are consistent across Key Stages 1 and 2 every other year is generally good practice in science. It allows for prior learning to be built upon, providing good continuity, yet also providing enough new learning for progression.

Returning to areas more than every other year can be confusing for children, and teachers. In the electricity example, sharing the learning over the four year groups of Key Stage 2 would mean spreading it very thinly. Teachers, by the time they have differentiated their lessons, could end up delivering very similar lessons in preceding or succeeding years.

Many of the statements in the National Curriculum or equivalent can easily be formed into chunks for upper and lower junior classes. Some areas form easy chunks, but may be better taught together in topics with other learning. Consider the required learning about

School-level planning

microorganisms in the National Curriculum. On the one hand this could form a relatively small unit of work, but on the other it could be developed within other units of work, such as food chains, food and health. Children may then pull together the threads that run through different areas of science and make their own links.

Once all the chunks have been worked out, they need to be shared out across the long-term plan, ensuring that there is a balance of biological and physical science in each year. There are also some practical considerations to be taken into account in this planning, such as the demand on resources and the seasons of the year.

Medium term

For classroom teachers, the school's medium-term plans are the most useful for planning sequences of lessons. They flesh out the bare bones of the curriculum references in the long-term plan, although leaving scope for teachers to plan their delivery and short-term plans. As suggested in Box 2, teachers in England, Wales and Northern Ireland may also go beyond the bounds of the statutory curriculum (in Scotland the curriculum guidelines are non-statutory).

Box 2   Beyond the statutory curriculum in England

> The National Curriculum is the minimum entitlement that children should experience. There are many other elements of science that could be taught in primary schools. In some cases this will be happening, as it were, out of habit. So, for example, in recent years many children have been taught about the digestive system, despite it not having been included in the National Curriculum for many years. On the other hand, it might not be a matter of habit but a conscious decision that a rudimentary knowledge of the digestive system is valuable. Equally, in the various revisions of the curriculum, content relating to forces has been reduced each time, but some science coordinators believe that there is still a need, and the time, to teach some of the excised content.
>
> Beyond content that was at one time in the National Curriculum, there are elements that could be called science, or perhaps general knowledge, that a school may teach. Examples are a 'Space' topic in Key Stage 2 or 'Dinosaurs' in Key Stage 1. While knowledge and understanding of The Earth and Beyond is within the National Curriculum, children often learn about far more, including planets and constellations. Both of these examples provide contexts that children find particularly stimulating, interesting and enjoyable in which enquiry skills can be developed using information from secondary sources including books and the internet.

Medium-term plans must specify the learning intentions that need to be taught within the unit of work. The statements in the National Curriculum are not learning intentions, and need to be more specific. For example:

> *'Pupils should be taught how to represent series circuits by drawings and conventional symbols, and how to construct series circuits on the basis of drawings and diagrams using conventional symbols.'*

Provision for science at the school level

This could be broken down into the following learning intentions:

- there are standard symbols to represent electrical devices in circuit diagrams
- straight lines are used to show connections between devices
- series circuits show devices connected one after another
- the shapes of wires in an actual circuit do not matter.

If teachers then effectively plan their lessons or activities from the learning intentions on the medium-term plans, there is an element of quality control within the system. As in any subject, it is important that teachers focus on the intended learning.

Beyond the learning intentions, there is much to be included in the medium-term plans, such as specific science vocabulary, links to other areas, use of ICT, resources, health and safety advice, and particular assessment opportunities and expectations. Where relevant they may include arrangements for visits or visitors and ways in which parents can help. Medium-term plans could also provide activities, but it is important that class teachers retain ownership of their teaching; if activities are dictated then this is diminished.

The medium-term planning must also specify which elements of enquiry skills ought to be included. The National Curriculum states that:

> *Teaching should ensure that 'scientific enquiry' is taught through contexts taken from the sections on 'life processes and living things', 'materials and their properties' and 'physical processes'.*

Similar statements can be found in other curriculum documents (for example, Scottish Government. 2009). It is vital that the investigative skills are explicitly taught. While many children will pick up some aspects of scientific thinking and processes by doing investigations, it is important that they become aware, through discussion and reflection, of how they are working. As these aspects occur to some extent in all activities it is useful to provide more guidance and suggested activities for the teachers – for example, by reference to *Making Sense of Primary Science Investigations* (Goldsworthy and Feasey, 1997).

The school policy for science

The school policy for science:

> '... should be a clear expression of values and aims and should inform teachers, governors, parents, children and the wider community about what the school sees as important in science.'
>
> Harlen and Qualter (2009, p305)

The science policy may be a separate document or a section of a more comprehensive Teaching and Learning Policy. In either case, it should cover a number of areas, such as in Table 2. It should be developed with staff, particularly the science coordinator, and should reflect the practice that is occurring in the school. There is an expectation that teachers will follow the policy and any changes made after development, trialling and reflection. Helpful advice on policy construction is also given by the ASE, and by CLEAPSS (2006) in its publication for science coordinators.

Table 2 Outline of a school policy document.

Section headings	Outline of content
Aims and objectives of science	What makes science special? Why is it important for primary-aged children to learn science? How does it fit into the bigger picture of learning (Chapter 1)?
Organisation of the curriculum	This will not require a lengthy narrative and may just be the one page long-term plan described above.
Medium-term planning	A statement to make explicit expectations for the planning of the teaching of investigative skills and the development of positive attitudes towards science (Chapter 12).
Assessment, recording and reporting	Explaining: • the use of assessment to help development within a unit of work • the system for providing summative assessment (Chapter 15) • the policy on marking in science (Chapter 11).
Role of the coordinator	Setting out some aspects of the coordinator's role that are specific to science – e.g. is the coordinator responsible for the tidiness of the resources (Chapter 17)?
Resources	Setting out the procedures for obtaining consumable resources and for keeping others in good order. An appendix may be the best place to record a list of resources and where they are kept (Chapters 8 and 17).
Health and safety	There are specific health and safety issues in science. These may be collated here or perhaps just include a reference to *Be Safe!* (ASE, 2011).
Involving parents; homework policy	Explaining: • how parents are kept informed about what their children are learning • how they are encouraged to visit the school • any particular resources or programmes used with parents • how parents may support learning through helping children conduct an investigation at home, visiting science centres or buying their child a book (Chapter 20).
Transfer	Describing what happens at transfer from pre-school to primary and primary to secondary school, what special preparations are made, what records are passed on, whether there is a transition unit of work started at one school and finished at the other (Chapter 19).

Section headings	Outline of content
Visits, visitors and outdoor education	Stating the importance of learning outside the classroom. Setting out the expectations for making use of visits or visitors – teachers may, for example, expect to have a visit for a history topic, but not think the same for science. Depending on the locality, there may be a need to set a minimum guarantee to ensure local resources are used – i.e. 'while at our primary school children will visit the Science Museum' and so on (Chapter 20).
Equal opportunities	Stating how differing interests, experience, ability and motivation are taken into account in maximising learning opportunities for all children (Chapter 6).
Appended forms, lists, letter templates, documents	A collection of lists and forms that teachers may need at various times, such as when planning a visit out of school, or needing to communicate with parents.

In conclusion

Teachers' lesson planning needs to take place within the frame of decisions made at school level, which ensure consistency in certain procedures while providing freedom to adapt content to suit individual pupils. Whole-school curriculum planning is necessary so that pupils' encounters with content support progressive understanding of scientific ideas as they move through the school. A school policy provides a framework that should be supportive, and not restrictive, of the decisions of individual teachers. Teachers should have ownership of the policy through participation at key points in its development.

References

ASE (2011) *Be Safe!* (fourth edition). Hatfield: Association for Science Education.

CLEAPSS (2006) *A Guide for Primary Science Coordinators* (L255) Uxbridge: Brunel University.

Goldsworthy, A. and Feasey, R. (1997) *Making Sense of Primary Science Investigations*. Hatfield: Association for Science Education.

Harlen, W. and Qualter, A. (2009) *The Teaching of Science in Primary Schools* (fifth edition). London: David Fulton.

QCA (1998) *A Scheme of Work for Key Stages 1 and 2*. London: Qualifications and Curriculum Authority.

Scottish Government, Learning and Teaching Scotland, HMIe and SQA (2009) *Curriculum for Excellence: Sciences. Principles and Practice*. Edinburgh: Scottish Government. Available online at: www.ltscotland.org.uk/curriculumforexcellence/sciences/principlesandpractice/index.asp

Chapter 17

The science subject leader

Liz Lawrence

Effective subject leadership is central to developing and sustaining high-quality science provision. This has traditionally been the role of a named science leader or coordinator, preferably with some interest or expertise in the subject, and in many schools this style of subject leadership continues. However, curriculum change and evolving ideas about school leadership have led to an increase in alternative structures. This chapter illustrates some of these different models and describes the core functions of subject leadership and management that must be carried out in order to ensure effective teaching and learning of science.

The importance of subject leadership

Inspections of primary schools suggest a correlation between good teaching and provision, leading to high standards, and effective subject leadership. The report *Success in Science* (Ofsted, 2008) states that:

> 'In the schools where science was thriving, the coordinator had good support from senior management, was well organised and had a very clear understanding of the strengths of provision and the areas for development.'
>
> Ofsted (2008)

An effective subject leader will set high expectations and ensure that colleagues have the subject knowledge and support to plan and teach good lessons with progression and challenge. They will put in place procedures for assessment and monitoring and act on information that these provide. But whether this happens is dependent on the value the school places on professional development of subject leaders and the opportunities they are given to genuinely lead their subject within the school (Box 1).

Provision for science at the school level

Box 1 The established and supported subject leader

> Emma is the science coordinator at a junior school in Surrey. The school is successful in science and Emma attributes her positive impact to the value the headteacher places on subject leadership and the systems in place to support her. Central to this is the investment of time needed for her to access CPD, be active within ASE and carry out her role in school. Dedicated leadership time is provided, to be spent only on high-impact activities such as monitoring and support. In recognition of the expertise Emma has developed, the headteacher also operates a clear distinction between his responsibility for seeing science within the whole-school overview and her relatively autonomous role as leader of the subject. This has given her the freedom to develop new approaches, such as piloting national assessment materials by trialling them in her classroom, with phased dissemination to colleagues supported by coaching.

The responsibilities of the subject leader

The current professional standards for teachers in England (see Training and Development Agency website) do not address the role of the subject leader directly. However, the standards for 'excellent teacher' describe attributes, knowledge and understanding and skills that are required for effective leadership. These include contributing to the professional development of colleagues, knowing how to improve the effectiveness of assessment practice and taking a leading role in developing, implementing and evaluating policies and practice that contribute to school improvement.

However, for a concise definition of the responsibilities of a subject leader it is useful to revisit the *National Standards for Subject Leaders* (TTA, 1998), which identifies the core purpose of subject leadership as being to:

> '... *provide professional leadership and management for a subject to secure high-quality teaching, effective use of resources and improved standards of learning and achievement for all pupils.*'
>
> TTA (1998, p4)

This short definition contains the primary purpose of subject leadership: the direct and positive impact on standards that the effective subject leader, in the dual roles of leader and manager, is working for. Characteristics of a school where science subject leadership is highly effective would include:

- a shared vision for what high-quality science education in the school will look like, based on knowledge of best practice in curriculum planning, teaching and assessment and nationally benchmarked expected standards

- good pupil progress and attainment in knowledge, understanding and skills, demonstrated and facilitated by robust assessment processes and a focus on Assessment for Learning

- a curriculum that meets the needs of all pupils, includes appropriate and purposeful links to other subjects and fulfils statutory requirements

The science subject leader

- a high standard of teaching, informed by strong subject and pedagogical knowledge and teacher confidence
- pupils who enjoy and are stimulated by science and show positive attitudes and behaviours in response to the high expectations of teachers
- effective communication and celebration of science throughout the school community
- systems in place to review and support continuing development.

All teachers will be clear about expectations with regard to what is taught, how it is taught, what the standards are and how they will be assessed. The subject leader will model, support, monitor and review (Box 2) to ensure that the whole school is able to move forward together.

Box 2 Effective use of self-review

> Sean is the science coordinator in a large London primary school. Last year, as part of a rolling programme across all subject areas, he led a detailed audit of science. This involved initial identification of key issues followed by gathering evidence through lesson observation, work scrutiny and interviews with pupils and parents. All teachers were observed and also carried out paired observations of colleagues; this degree of involvement ensured that teachers saw the process as developmental rather than judgemental. There was also active involvement of a teacher from the local secondary school. A full report, informing the subject development plan, was written and presented to staff and governors. As a result the detailed scheme of work has been rewritten with older pupils focusing less on separate units and formal revision and more on practically revisiting concepts through studies themed around forensic science, healthy living and sustainability. There are also plans for improved communication with parents via the school website and pupil blogs.

Carrying out the role

One of the most important skills the subject leader requires is the ability to prioritise. The competing demands of their own classroom, routine management tasks and leading teaching and learning in science can seem overwhelming and too much time can be spent on activities that have little real impact on standards and quality. In addition to fulfilling the role within the school, it is also important not to neglect personal professional development. Reading, engaging with professional networks, including the ASE, and attending CPD activities enable the subject leader to respond effectively to the developing needs of the school and to external changes.

The easiest functions to fulfil are the management roles, sometimes categorised as those of provider and administrator. Most of these can be carried out without being released from teaching. Although necessary, they are reactive in nature and may not have lasting impact. They include:

- auditing, budgeting for, selecting and deploying resources, including people, accommodation and expertise

Provision for science at the school level

- acting as an informal source of subject-specific advice and signposting additional resources and external sources of information and CPD
- providing documentation, such as relating to policy and scheme of work, and advice and guidance on assessment activities and on health and safety.

Even with resource management and ordering delegated to support staff, this is an area that can be very time-consuming. Lack of resources or inability to find them when needed is cited as a reason why some teachers avoid practical science activities. Removing simple barriers is important but once systems are in place minimal time should be spent on lower-level tasks. (See Chapter 16 for discussion of planning and schemes of work.)

One management area that cannot be neglected is responsibility for health and safety. Primary science is statistically very safe but subject leaders still need to take responsibility for keeping their knowledge and reference sources – such as *Be Safe!* (ASE 2001, 2011) – up to date. They also need to ensure that health and safety procedures feature in policy documents, that risk assessments are known about and adhered to and that colleagues are aware of sources of advice from, for example, the ASE, CLEAPSS, SSERC and Local Authority advisors, and situations in which that advice should be sought. As with other aspects of the role, this requires systems and monitoring.

The aspects of the role that should be of greatest concern are those having higher impact. These are usually more proactive in nature and can often be linked to whole-school priorities to provide additional leverage for changes to be made. Their performance relies on the ability to engage with colleagues and implement a rigorous cyclical process of information gathering and analysis, focused planning and intervention, and systematic evaluation. They also require whole-school commitment, as some aspects of the process need to be carried out during lesson time. Core activities are:

- **monitoring** of planning, teaching and learning, including lesson observations, book scrutiny, learning walks and pupil interviews – outcomes of this must be acted on, remembering that it is a supportive and developmental process where it is as important to nurture and publicly share good practice as to identify and challenge weaknesses or non-compliance
- **tracking pupil progress** and attainment – this also includes ensuring that assessment practices provide meaningful and accurate data to inform day-to-day and strategic planning and meet any statutory reporting requirements
- **analysing information and making judgements** to inform next steps in improving practice
- **setting priorities** – embedding a few key changes rather than making many superficial ones
- **modelling good practice and trialling new ideas** – balancing the role of expert with that of lead learner for the subject
- **establishing the school as a learning community** that supports and develops colleagues and shares good practice through school-based CPD, including mentoring and coaching – this could be expert coaching by the subject leader and/or external specialists or peer coaching within the school

- **motivating colleagues** by effective communication that emphasises their contributions to the common goals, celebrates achievements and builds on existing good practice – this may also include organising special events such as science weeks and focus days, which bring everyone together with a common purpose.
- **engaging with the wider school community** and other communities and networks beyond the school including other subject leaders, primary school cluster groups and local secondary schools.

It is not necessary for one individual to carry out all these functions but, if they are distributed, a coherent development plan and good communication are crucial.

For each individual subject leader, the balance between these different activities will vary according to their own experience of subject leadership and seniority within the school, the school context and needs, the management structure and leadership style favoured by the head and how much release time can be provided. In contrast to the experienced subject leader of Box 1, the case study in Box 3 demonstrates how a new subject leader is prioritising the demands of the role.

Box 3   Using a whole-school priority as a lever for change

> Gurjeet is a recently qualified teacher working in an infant school. She has recently become the science coordinator. Although keen to overhaul the scheme of work, run a science week and develop an environmental area, she has recognised that what she has inherited is functioning, if slightly outdated. Science is not a priority area for the school and extensive changes will need to be postponed until she has more experience. The school is currently focused on achieving Healthy Schools status and this provides an opportunity for her to work with other subject leaders to develop those health-related aspects of science, design and technology and PE, which support the Healthy Schools priorities. She will gain supported experience of implementing change in a small, defined area, including planning a special event, involvement of parents and writing a whole-school policy. Gurjeet hopes that successful developments in this aspect of science will support her case for addressing many of the wider changes she has identified.

Changing models of subject leadership

In recent years, an increased focus on middle leaders in school and a consequent re-evaluation of how they work has led to shifts in emphasis within the subject leader role. In addition, changes to pay structures, curriculum and assessment have prompted some schools to re-assess the whole structure for undertaking the functions of subject leadership. Schools that previously had many subject leaders have consolidated responsibilities among a smaller number of middle leaders whose roles may not include the traditional subject focus. In some areas, high staff mobility has necessitated the development of models, which address concerns that one person, who may leave the school and be difficult to replace, is the repository of all the subject expertise (Box 4).

Provision for science at the school level

Box 4 Distributing subject expertise between several individuals

> The headteacher of a large London primary school is developing a model of subject leadership that is less dependent on the expertise of one individual – one which addresses issues of succession planning and leadership development. The headteacher has appointed four phase leaders, each with responsibility for two year groups, to lead English, mathematics and science within their phase. There is also a coordinator for ICT across the school. Phase leaders undertake leadership and core subject CPD and are responsible for disseminating to senior leaders and their phase group, organising whole-staff training and monitoring impact. This system is in its early stages. In order to develop a whole-school view, opportunities will also be provided for leaders to teach classes outside their phase. They will thus be able to work together as a team and subject leadership will be less vulnerable to changes in personnel.

With many schools moving towards curricula that organise subject content into areas of learning or creative themes, and subject hierarchies being redefined by assessment and curriculum changes, structures based on individuals or teams taking responsibility for several linked subjects are evolving. For example, in one school in England, the headteacher anticipated changes in the primary curriculum by restructuring responsibilities around the six proposed 'areas of learning' (Chapter 21). Each area is the responsibility of a team led by a senior or middle leader and includes representatives from all phases, chosen for their particular interests and expertise. Most teachers belong to more than one team. The teams are responsible for drawing up overviews of the whole curriculum, individual subjects and themes, looking at skills progressions and writing action plans. They will also have a development and quality assurance role through monitoring planning and a programme of peer observation. Currently in its early stages, this model intends to build capacity within the school and develop a more relevant and connected curriculum.

A further change is the increased emphasis on schools working together. This may involve a leading school sharing good practice with a less successful school or several schools working together for mutual support.

Box 5 describes changes in some Northern Ireland schools following the implementation of the revised Northern Ireland Curriculum (Chapter 21).

Box 5 Implementing the revised Northern Ireland Curriculum

> The revised curriculum includes science and technology, history and geography as contributory subjects of 'The World Around Us' (TWAU). This has resulted in schools reviewing both their curriculum plans and management structures. In some rural small schools, Development Action Teams are assigned to review provision for the learning area if it is a priority on the School Development Plan. They build on existing practice and make appropriate links among the three TWAU elements. This does not preclude the discrete teaching of any of the subjects as long as a balance is achieved in their exploration. Other small schools absorb the changes, with the existing science coordinator assuming the responsibility. In a large Belfast primary school the principal and the three individual subject organisers agreed to work as a team with the science coordinator leading staff in the restructuring of plans and topics, again starting with existing themes and resources. This model worked very successfully, causing minimum disruption and maximum cooperation along the lines premised in the curriculum document.

Strengthening subject leadership

Although there are many successful schools with effective subject leaders, there are concerns that clear routes to science subject leadership do not exist. Many new subject leaders have limited scientific knowledge and have had few opportunities during initial training or their early career to observe and learn from good practice in primary science teaching and leadership.

In *Success in Science* (2008), Ofsted comments on issues relating to both the trainee and the subject leader:

> *'Overall, primary trainees spend too little time on relating the teaching of science to what is known about the way that pupils learn at various stages of their development ... their understanding of how to plan and sequence activities in a way that will help pupils progress is limited ... During their blocks of school experience, they also spend too little time working with science coordinators.'*

> *'... in schools where management and leadership were weaker, too few coordinators had received sufficient training to prepare them for the role.'*
>
> Ofsted (2008)

There are many generic middle leadership courses for more experienced teachers but anecdotal evidence suggests that, in an increasing number of schools, teachers are taking on science subject leadership at an earlier stage in their career. Generic courses do not address the subject and pedagogical knowledge needed to support colleagues and make subject-focused judgements and decisions. CPD targeted at the specific needs of the science subject leader is an important part of raising standards.

A positive development in this respect is the Primary Science Quality Mark (Chapter 18), through which the coordinator, supported by external training and mentoring, leads a development process to celebrate and enhance the school's science provision. Pilot schools have noted how the process of self-evaluation and action planning created *'a culture of positive attitudes to science with science enthusiastically discussed and celebrated.'*

Continued improvement in science provision and standards is dependent on the schools having the capacity, individual or distributed, in subject knowledge and leadership skills, to drive the improvement cycle and ensure that the activities outlined above have real impact on the experiences and attainment of pupils.

In conclusion

Science subject leadership combines generic middle leadership skills with the particular management, subject knowledge and pedagogical demands of a practical, resource-heavy subject, which may have high-stakes targets associated with it. Although schools are using a wider variety of structures to provide subject leadership, successful models all demonstrate the features described in this chapter. Good schools with effective science provision and high standards value the subject and have clear systems in place that empower subject leaders to make and evaluate evidence-based changes.

References

ASE (2001) *Be Safe! Health and Safety in Primary School Science and Technology*. Hatfield: Association for Science Education.

ASE (2011) *Be Safe! Health and Safety in Primary School Science and Technology* (fourth edition). Hatfield: Association for Science Education.

Ofsted (2008) *Success in Science*. Jun 2008, ref: 070195. London: Ofsted. Available online at: www.ofsted.gov.uk

TTA (1998) *National Standards for Subject Leaders*. London: Teacher Training Agency. Available online at: www.all-london.org.uk/Resources/subject_leader_standards.pdf

Websites

Association for Science Education: www.ase.org.uk

CLEAPSS: www.cleapss.org.uk

Scottish Schools Equipment Research Centre (SSERC): www.sserc.org.uk

Training and Development Agency for Schools (TDA): Professional Standards for Teachers in England: www.tda.gov.uk/teachers/professionalstandards/using.aspx

Chapter 18

Continuing professional development and the role of Science Learning Centres

Jane Turner

'Given the nature of teaching, professional development and learning should never stop.'

Pollard (2005)

Whatever the stage of their career, all primary teachers need to engage with continuing professional development (CPD), either personally as participants, as colleagues responsible for assessing and meeting the CPD needs of others, or as organisers or presenters of CPD both in and out of school. This chapter is designed to help primary teachers, science subject leaders, senior management team members, consultants and CPD providers make informed decisions about professional development in science for primary teachers. Why is CPD necessary, what types are available and where, and how can its impact be evaluated, maximised and accredited?

Why is science CPD for primary teachers necessary and worthwhile?

Being a primary teacher is a challenging job. The long list of TDA standards for Qualified Teacher Status (TDA, 2007; see also *Websites*) is evidence of the complexity of skills, knowledge, understanding and expertise that a newly qualified primary teacher requires; and that is just the beginning. A newly qualified primary teacher embarks on a career where the pace of change is fast and constant. CPD can help teachers to respond to change imposed either from within school or externally from the local authority or national government. CPD can mediate new initiatives and strategies and offer teachers a context in which to exercise and refine their own professional judgements. CPD is a crucial element in career progression, enabling teachers to fulfil performance management objectives, build on Masters credits gained on PGCE training, and to meet professional targets such as threshold criteria or leadership role requirements.

Provision for science at the school level

Teaching science is just one part of a primary teacher's complex and challenging role, yet a high proportion of primary teachers feel they particularly lack the confidence, expertise and training to teach current science curricula effectively. This is not surprising. Primary teachers are required to be experts in many subjects and the list keeps growing. Many teachers do not have an academic background in science and therefore lack personal confidence in the subject. It is difficult for teachers to keep up to date with the fast-changing nature of developments in the subject itself and also the pedagogy that supports it. The need for and value of professional development that raises primary teachers' capacity and enthusiasm for teaching science is very clear.

> 'Good-quality continuing professional development is considered key to improving primary teacher confidence; teachers who have carried out any professional development in science appear more confident in nearly all aspects of science teaching.'
>
> Murphy et al. (2005)

What forms can CPD take?

The TDA defines continuing professional development (CPD) as:

> 'Reflective activity designed to improve an individual's attributes, knowledge, understanding and skills. It supports individual needs and improves professional practice.'
>
> TDA (2007)

This definition encompasses a lot more than 'courses', the traditional 'one day away from the classroom' experience, designed to give a group of teachers insight into new knowledge or skills and an opportunity to share professional expertise with other colleagues. CPD in science for primary teachers can and does include accredited or non-accredited courses of different lengths. However, primary teachers also develop their professional capabilities through subject association membership and attendance at events, in-school coaching and mentoring, working with colleagues from cluster schools, working with external consultants, action research projects, independent reading, watching Teachers TV and web-based research. The format by which CPD occurs may vary but the aim of supporting teachers' needs and improving professional practice is consistent.

What impact can good CPD have?

Having recognised the need for professional development in science and the varied forms it takes, how can primary teachers judge its effectiveness? Guskey (2000) proposes five levels for measuring the impact of CPD, outlined in Box 1. This model works very well when considering the possible impact of any type of primary science CPD and is, therefore, a useful tool for primary teachers and their senior management colleagues, as well as CPD providers, to use when planning for professional development.

Continuing professional development and the role of Science Learning Centres

Box 1 Guskey's five levels of impact of CPD

1. Participant reaction. How satisfying and enjoyable did the teacher find the CPD event or experience? Was it worthwhile? Was the content useful and manageable, did the activities facilitate learning and development and was the context relevant?

2. Participant learning. In addition to enjoying the experience, what knowledge, skills and attitudes does the primary teacher perceive he or she has learned? Has he or she gained a clearer understanding of previously confusing scientific concepts, learned the theory and rationale behind new ideas or innovations, or become more knowledgeable about how young children learn and acquire scientific ideas? What pedagogical skills have been acquired? Is he or she more able to use questions more effectively or develop children's enquiry skills? How have the primary teacher's attitudes or beliefs changed? Does he or she feel more enthusiasm for teaching science, and recognise its value in the primary curriculum?

3. Support and change in the organisation. Has the primary teacher been able to translate the learning achieved through the CPD experience into his or her professional practice? Have the appropriate resources and time been made available? Has the timetable, class structure or assessment regime in his or her setting been flexible enough to allow for change? Has senior management supported the implementation of new skills and knowledge?

4. Participant use of new knowledge and skills. Is what the primary teacher learned being used, and being used well? This can only be judged after sufficient time has passed to allow a teacher to adapt new ideas and practices to his or her own setting.

5. Student learning outcomes. What is the impact on the children? This may be measured simply by comparing levels of attainment, but measures of attitudinal and behavioural change may be equally valid if the aim of the professional development was to change, for example, children's motivation for science or capacity to work independently.

By considering these five levels, primary teachers, subject leaders, school senior management and CPD providers can make considered decisions about the impact that they intend the professional development to have. The next question to consider is where that CPD can be accessed.

What opportunities exist for science-specific CPD for primary teachers?

There are many opportunities for science-specific CPD run by local authorities (though provision is patchy), science subject associations including the Association for Science Education, independent consultants and universities. These may be face to face or online, in school or at an outside venue.

Provision for science at the school level

Science Learning Centres

The National Network of ten Science Learning Centres (SLCs) – nine regional centres in England and the residential National Centre based in York, which covers the whole of the UK – opened its doors in 2004, following the recommendations of the Roberts Report into science education (Roberts, 2002). Jointly funded by the Department for Children, Schools and Families(and now by DfE) and the Wellcome Trust, the network provides high-quality, short-term and longer-term professional development for teachers of science, including technicians and teaching assistants, in all phases of education. The main aims of the network are to improve science education and to bring contemporary science into the classroom.

The network works closely with a wide number of stakeholders across the science education and STEM communities, plus local authorities to coordinate, develop and deliver CPD. Over 19 600 SLC training days were delivered in 2008–9 with both primary and secondary teachers reporting very positively about the impact of the CPD on their practice. However, as a result of the additional funding for secondary teachers and the relatively higher profile of science in the secondary education agenda, take up for CPD from secondary teachers has been considerably higher than that of primary teachers and it is of concern to the network that large numbers of primary teachers still have not heard of the Science Learning Centres (Sharp and Hopkin, 2007). The network is working with stakeholders at all levels to raise awareness of the significant value of, and increasing need for, high-quality science CPD for primary teachers, children and schools, and thereby increase demand and potential impact.

The issue therefore for the SLCs, as for other providers of primary science CPD, is to ensure that the CPD they offer meets teachers' needs and is effective.

How can CPD have maximum impact?

There is certainly no 'one-size-fits-all' model for science CPD for primary teachers, but the elements that make professional development effective, whatever the format, are widely acknowledged (Adey et al., 2004). These elements have profoundly shaped the structure and implementation of the Science Learning Centre CPD programme and courses.

CPD that supports individual primary teachers' needs and improves professional practice in science teaching in primary schools should be:

- highly relevant to a teacher's need
- sustained
- collaborative
- embedded in the culture of the school
- continuing throughout the primary teacher's career.

Relevant

Professional development needs can be identified in a variety of ways. It may be simply that a teacher recognises that he or she is shaky on a particular area of science subject knowledge, isn't confident using a particular piece of equipment or is unsure about planning and assessing practical science activities. These types of personal capability needs may also become evident through lesson observation. Sometimes a teacher is feeling jaded and needs an input of new ideas. The need for CPD is often raised when a teacher moves into a new role, perhaps becoming the science subject leader. However, CPD needs are not always linked to deficit. Often individual teachers have a personal wish or ambition to develop a particular new skill or embark on a piece of research.

Sometimes a need is externally imposed – for example, the Government may be introducing a new curriculum, pedagogical approach or assessment regime and the teacher needs to understand the implications and implementation requirements. It may be imposed by a decision made by the school senior management – for example, to implement a new teaching and learning strategy in science, develop an outdoor environmental area, or participate in an award scheme such as Eco Schools or the Primary Science Quality Mark (see *Websites*).

Often, and most productively, personal and school needs overlap. Teachers who reluctantly have CPD imposed on them do not make the most willing learners and it is unlikely that significant personal professional development will occur in this situation. Ideally, performance management should be the system by which school and teacher professional needs are identified and combined and it is important that a teacher spends time with a senior colleague to identify the right type and content of CPD to meet his or her and the school's needs. In common with other good CPD providers, the Science Learning Centres always advertise the methodology and intended outcomes of their courses. Reviewing this information against the identified needs in consultation with a senior colleague is a prerequisite of attending an SLC course, enabling a teacher to make a sensible decision about whether it will be the right professional solution for him or her.

Sustained

A quick fix is rarely an effective one. It takes time to embed a new skill or piece of scientific understanding into pedagogical practice. For CPD to be effective, it needs to offer teachers a framework for embedding freshly gained enthusiasm, confidence, new ideas, skills and understanding into their own long-term classroom practice. It is a truism amongst CPD providers, but a useful one, that simply passing on a trick to do in class tomorrow is not the mark of good CPD. What a good CPD provider should be aiming for is a change in professional skills and behaviour that continues to develop and becomes part of the teacher's own professional repertoire, perhaps even being extended to colleagues, and is evident many months after the CPD event. The Science Learning Centres, like other high-quality CPD providers, have action planning built into all their programmes, be they one-day or extended external courses, or whole-school in-service training, ensuring that primary teachers distil the key learning points from the course into a few achievable actions to follow up in school. These may include implementing new teaching and learning strategies, acquiring and using resources, reading deeper into the subject, or instituting organisational change. This action plan has several functions.

- It reminds the busy primary teacher, who deals with many subjects, exactly what it is they had planned to do in science as a result of the course.
- It is a valuable reflective tool for analysing the impact of the CPD.
- It provides evidence of professional development for performance management or career progression or accreditation.
- It also enables the Science Learning Centre or other CPD provider to evaluate the impact of the CPD it has provided.

Provision for science at the school level

Collaborative

Primary teachers, like children, are very good at, and enjoy, learning from and with each other. CPD therefore should offer opportunities for teachers to work with colleagues from their own school and outside to share and try out ideas and skills. This can be facilitated by a variety of teaching and learning approaches on courses, in school or via network groups. These may include practical and problem-solving group activities, field work, workshops with scientists, mentoring and coaching, planning and teaching with a colleague, or a primary teacher watching someone else – for example, a museum or field study centre educator – teach his or her class. These activities can all be sustained though follow-up online or face-to-face collaboration.

All SLC courses are supported by a dedicated web portal, which – as well as providing an extensive resource bank and acting as an electronic CPD portfolio for individuals – enables course participants to continue the collaboration begun at the face-to-face event.

Embedded

It is very difficult for a primary teacher to initiate change in his or her professional practice if it is not supported by the school. Stenhouse (1975) defined three critical characteristics of what he called the 'extended professionalism' that is essential for curriculum research and teacher development:

> '[1] the commitment to systematic questioning of one's own teaching as a basis for development
>
> [2] the commitment and skills to study one's own teaching
>
> [3] the concern to question and to test theory in practice.'
>
> Quoted in Pollard (2002)

These may be interpreted as personal teacher characteristics, but they are characteristics that require CPD in order to be realised. However, without a primary school ethos that recognises the value of professional development, viewing its teachers as learners and supporting experimentation and change, it is unlikely that a teacher will be able to achieve this 'extended professionalism'. Testing theory in practice – whether learned from individual reading, at a course or conference, or by working with colleagues – needs the permission of peers and senior management. This may be perceived as risk taking unless colleagues are aware of the intended aims and outcomes of the changes to practice.

Continuing

As primary teachers proceed from being newly qualified – to climb up the pay, expertise and maybe management ladders – they may undertake a wide range of roles, such as subject leader, phase leader, assessment leader, mentor and member of the senior management team. All of these roles will require a revised acknowledgment of professional needs and careful decisions about the type of professional development that will meet them.

How is CPD structured, valued and accredited?

There are many frameworks that can support and accredit primary teachers' professional development, offering CPD that is relevant to their needs at the time, but also builds into a portfolio that will support their career progression – for example, the Masters Qualification in Teaching and Learning, the GTC Teacher Learning Academy and programmes offered by the National College (see *Websites*). These frameworks are not subject specific, but nevertheless provide valuable ways of developing and accrediting primary teachers' professional knowledge, skills and understanding, of which the teaching and learning of science is an important part.

However, there is now also a science-specific way in which primary teachers' professional development, expertise and commitment can be accredited, in the form of Chartered Science Teacher status.

Chartered Science Teacher (CSciTeach) is a chartered designation that has been developed through a close partnership between the Association for Science Education (ASE) and the Science Council. As a specialist section of the Science Council's Chartered Scientist (CSci) register, CSciTeach provides science teachers, including primary teachers, with a professional status that recognises and rewards their demanding combination of skills, knowledge, understanding and expertise. The award allows for a range of different routes to be taken by individual teachers as they build a portfolio of evidence of achievement under headings that include professional qualifications, experience, a commitment to working with colleagues to develop science education beyond the classroom and to continually updating their professional expertise and competence.

Since September 2006, 18 primary ASE members have been awarded CSciTeach, a significant achievement for non-specialist primary teachers. However, it is not surprising that the majority of primary educators who have attained CSciTeach status in the first few years of the award work in the higher education or advisory sectors. As accreditation for professional development and achievement gains currency, particularly in light of the Masters Qualification in Teaching and Learning (see *Websites*), it is to be hoped that more primary teachers will be able to demonstrate their suitability for CSciTeach status and will participate in the professionally satisfying application and awarding process.

Funding for CPD in primary science

This chapter has discussed the purpose, value, impact and supporting structures for professional development in primary science but has not considered the thorny question of cost. At the moment funding arrangements vary within the UK but allocation in most primary school budgets for science has been meagre in comparison to literacy and numeracy, and is likely to be further reduced. The number of Local Authority Primary Science advisors has fallen significantly. Secondary Science has taken up the lion's share of national and regional government and industry financial support for science education.

In conclusion

However, the outlook is not all gloomy. The Wellcome Trust has awarded the ASE and the Science Learning Centres funding to roll out the training-led Primary Science Quality Mark Award across the UK (see *Websites*). The TDA is championing the role of CPD in terms of school improvement, and teacher retention, and is leading the process to make teaching a Masters Level profession. Many NQTs begin their careers with Masters credits accrued from their PGCE courses on which to build. Much more is now understood about the impact and value to individuals and schools of high-quality, professional development. Primary teachers and their senior colleagues need to assert their entitlement to good quality, effective CPD in primary science.

References

Adey, P. with Hewitt, G., Hewitt, J. and Landau, N. (2004) *The Professional Development of Teachers: Practice and Theory*. Dordrecht: Kluwer.

Guskey, T.R. (2000) *Evaluating Professional Development*. Thousand Oaks, CA: Corwen Press.

Murphy, C., Beggs, J., Russell, H. and Melton L. (2005) *Primary Horizons: Starting Out in Science*. London: Wellcome Trust.

Pollard, A. (ed) (2002) *Readings for Reflective Teaching*. London: Continuum.

Pollard, A. (2005) *Reflective Teaching*. London: Continuum.

Roberts, G. (2002) *SET for Success: The Supply of People with Science, Technology, Engineering and Mathematics Skills*. London: HM Treasury.

Sharp, J.G. and Hopkin, R.C. (2007) *National Primary Science Survey (England)*. Lincoln: Bishop Grosseteste University College Lincoln.

Stenhouse, L. (1975) *An Introduction to Curriculum Research and Development*. London: Heinemann Educational Books.

TDA (2007) *Professional Standards for Teachers*. London: Training and Development Agency for Schools.

Websites

General Teaching Council for England: www.gtce.org.uk/tla

Master in Teaching and Learning (MTL): www.tda.gov.uk/teachers/mtl.aspx

National College: www.nationalcollege.org.uk/schools

Primary Science Quality Mark: www.psqm.org.uk

Training and Development Agency for Schools (TDA): Professional Standards for Teachers in England: www.tda.gov.uk/teachers/professionalstandards/using.aspx

Chapter 19

Points of transfer

Martin Braund and Kathy Schofield

Points in our lives where we move from one phase to another have significant impact. From childhood to adolescence, from being single to having a partner, changing jobs, retirement – these are often stressful times. We have probably forgotten what it was like for us on that first morning in a new school, nervous in the new environment but expectant and excited too. Going to school is a 'rite of passage' in our early lives and later, at transfer to secondary school, an entry into adulthood. The curriculum attempts to portray science learning as a continuous and progressive experience, but for many children that journey is anything but smooth or exciting. This chapter sets out the key points to bear in mind to make children's learning journeys in science as productive as possible.

Transitions and transfers in science

Key moments of educational *transition* are listed below. Where these transitions coincide with changes of school, they are called *transfers*. The following are common in England, Wales and Northern Ireland:

- from pre-schooling (for example, Kindergarten or nursery, now called Early Years Foundation Stage) to formal schooling, Key Stage 1 (may involve transfer)
- from Key Stage 1 to Key Stage 2 (may involve transfer)
- from Key Stage 2 to Key Stage 3 (nearly always involves transfer)
- from Key Stage 3 to Key Stage 4 (involves transfer in some middle school systems)
- from Key Stage 4 (GCSE) to sixth form or to work-based training (can involve transfer – for example, from school to a college)
- from sixth form to university or college, or to work (always involves transfer).

There are also more minor points of transition: from one school year to another within the same school, from one topic to the next and, at the smallest scale, from one activity to another within lessons. All can impact on children's learning, sometimes in negative ways.

Provision for science at the school level

For example, a change of teacher from one year to another might mean children having to adjust to new behavioural codes and ways of working.

The role of the science subject leader or coordinator, using school policies and structures, is to recognise these transitions and try to minimise, by careful monitoring and evaluating, the disruption they might cause. For example, schools might adopt common policies on behaviour management and codes of conduct that must be applied equally and consistently throughout the school. Equally, for science there should be an agreed policy on progression identifying when and how key skills, concepts and vocabulary are introduced throughout the course of the children's education. This could also mean supporting staff when they move between classes or stages by providing in-house training, especially if the school has a parallel intake and/or mixed year groups. All aspects of teaching and learning within science need careful consideration if they involve significant changes for the children and teachers. Good assessment evidence should be passed on to support future planning following transfer as this helps to smooth change. This should include information on topics covered, types of enquiry used and the levels of skills, knowledge and understanding achieved.

What are problems of transfers for children's learning in science?

Research exploring transfers from one stage or one school to another suggests there are *social* and *pedagogical* factors that impact children's learning in science. The social factors are well known: different friends, learning in a new and bigger place, feeling of isolation and nervousness, many teachers instead of one, and new work regimes such as homework that affect home life. Apparently these effects of social change are short-lived and so it is the pedagogical issues that we will concentrate on. These are that:

1 children might repeat work, often without sufficient increase in challenge, sometimes in the same context and using identical procedures or equipment

2 teaching environments, teaching styles and teachers' language might be very different, particularly after transfer to secondary school – the different learning cultures of a new school can take time for young children to adjust to

3 teachers in new schools (particularly secondary schools) might not make use of, or refer to, children's previous science learning experiences – information supplied by one school or stage might not be used effectively to plan work for the next steps in learning

4 teachers in new schools may distrust the assessments made by the previous school – this is sometimes why secondary schools justify 'starting from scratch' when planning new learning as they think children do not really know or understand work previously covered

5 many secondary schools receive children from several primary schools, and find the consequent variety of children's prior knowledge and understanding to be a major concern.

Smoothing transfer from early learning to infant class

One of the main factors affecting the transfer from Foundation/Reception class to infant classes is the style of teaching. These early years are all about exploration and enquiry through collaborative and experiential learning where children are given a range of opportunities to investigate their surroundings. This approach is designed to develop their knowledge and understanding of the world around them. Children are actively encouraged and supported to show curiosity through exploration in a variety of settings created and supported by their teachers. These often involve objects children are familiar with and, similarly, places where they feel secure. It is within this secure setting that young children experiencing science-based activities can begin to develop generic life-long skills. The acquisition of these skills is the first step towards independent life-long learning. Therefore the challenge for infant school teachers is to build on these skills and develop the children's knowledge and understanding further while maintaining an ability to inspire curiosity.

Communication plays a key role in the smoothing of the transition from a play-based, child-led approach to science common in many Early Years settings. Science in the first two years of school has a more structured approach leading to most children developing some science enquiry skills by the end of their infant school years. It involves the children in communicating their ideas to their peer group and their teacher and using knowledge and understanding they have acquired throughout this phase. Therefore, the role of the teacher is to provide a means of enhancing these communication skills alongside the acquisition of knowledge and understanding in a way that mirrors the children's development stages.

Early schooling should continue to be about everyday experiences and exploration, while incorporating good-quality questioning techniques. There should be lots of time provided for speaking and listening to build towards group activities. Group activities help create independence and ownership of investigations. A good method of introducing structure to investigations is to use resources such as 'Puppets' or 'Discovery Dog' (see *Websites*), which consist of simple stories and are accompanied by a CD. These types of resources allow children to develop empathy with characters and to create familiar starting points for generating investigations. Puppets build confidence as children can use them to express ideas or questions through the character of the puppet in a non-threatening manner.

Children should be at the heart of the learning environment and so displays or arrangements should always involve decisions made by the children. Creating interactive displays that enable children to handle objects or answer questions can be very rewarding. This collaboration between teacher and children is very much part of the early transition process, initially learning together with a long-term view towards children taking responsibility for their own learning.

Towards the end of the first two years of school most children will have acquired the ability to read, opening up another dimension to be nurtured by the teacher, namely opportunity to pursue a particular interest in a science topic through accessing non-fiction books. Science books should be part of all classrooms, including pre-school, so that those children who are curious can be provided with the means to develop their interests at an early stage.

Provision for science at the school level

Smoothing transfer from infant to junior classes

By the end of their first two years in school most children will have become familiar with the way science is taught, they will understand that they can investigate through the use of different types of enquiry and that science has a unique vocabulary to be understood if they are to develop their knowledge of the subject further. The next phase in their progression (from infant to junior classes) largely builds on these skills and greatly increases their knowledge and understanding, including introduction of new vocabulary. The key to successful transition at this phase is to get to know the children through careful assessment of their scientific abilities – both their knowledge and understanding of the key concepts, and their investigative skills. Later work revisits key concepts so recognising and acknowledging children's prior knowledge and understanding becomes crucial. Revisiting topics and building on previously learned concepts helps provide progression within a 'spiral' curriculum that enables more complex skills and ideas to be used as topics are explored in more depth. Table 1 highlights the challenge for junior teachers.

Table 1   Aspects of progression from infant to junior years.

Development from …	To …
using everyday language	increasingly precise use of technical and scientific vocabulary, notation and symbols
personal scientific knowledge in a few areas	understanding in a wider range of areas and of links between these areas
describing events and phenomena	explaining events and phenomena
explaining phenomena in terms of their own ideas	explaining phenomena in terms of accepted ideas or models
participating in practical scientific activities	building increasingly abstract models of real situations
unstructured exploration	more systematic investigation of a question
using simple drawings, diagrams and charts	representing and communicating scientific information using more conventional diagrams and graphs

Progression involves children on a journey through science, building on ideas and concepts they already have and changing their understanding by greater depth of study. It is important to know what children understand in order for them to make progress. It is also important to know where they are going in order to help them on the next steps of their journey. Therefore teachers are responsible for building children's independence while maintaining their enthusiasm for the subject by sharing the roles and responsibilities for planning and investigating. The role of the junior teacher is to ensure all children in their care receive opportunities to achieve their full potential in science. As a result, consideration must be given to those children struggling with literacy even though their knowledge and understanding of science concepts is strong. An environment where children feel emotionally secure is guaranteed to raise their self-esteem (Chapter 12).

The emotional environment, especially in junior science classrooms, should be one where every child is valued no matter how small, or how strange their ideas might seem. Science should be an interactive subject where the teacher challenges children to put forward their ideas, make and test their predictions and generally voice their thinking in science. The value of talk and discussion is essential in science and the classroom environment should be one of encouragement and celebration. Good planning by junior teachers incorporates talking and thinking time so children can explore scientific concepts fully. If children are allowed to discuss their ideas they become more engaged with their learning and have opportunities to construct their own knowledge and understanding. These strategies will help towards a smooth transition from primary to secondary school.

Smoothing transfer from primary to secondary school

Children arriving at secondary school with enthusiasm for science may soon find their positive attitudes to science eroded if all they meet is a diet of repetition of work and fewer chances to be independent and to investigate science through practical work. Four conditions in secondary schools have been recognised that allow children a better chance of progression and continuity in their science learning after transfer:

1. **Learning environment.** The learning environment reflects best practice of primary schools, including provision of colourful displays relevant to children, celebration of work carried out in the first few weeks in the new school, encouragement of paired and group discussions and use of older children to act as working partners or mentors.

2. **Assessment.** As well as the summative assessment records passed on with pupils, assessment at both sides of transfer should be focused on and involve individuals, pairs or groups of children, drawing on the best practices of formative and diagnostic assessment. Children should have oral feedback from science teachers as regularly as they did from their primary class teacher (Chapter 11).

3. **Progression in learning.** The science learning journey began before the age of four and it is natural to revisit areas of knowledge to make our thinking better and to develop a more complete understanding of the world. The skills and procedures of science are a common toolkit that is expanded as children learn and can do more. Teachers should talk to children about what they have done before, value their efforts and help them look forward to next steps in their learning.

4. **Liaison and collaboration.** There should be regular high-quality sharing of practice each side of transfer, using co-planned bridging projects or work of the schools' own devising, and two-way teacher exchanges.

Provision for science at the school level

Strategies that schools use to provide these conditions include:

- meetings and open days
- jointly planned teaching projects
- sharing practice.

Meetings and open days

These often involve children working in teams, solving problems using a variety of basic laboratory skills – to solve a 'murder' mystery, for example, or build and test water-cooling systems. Such activities help children from different primary schools to get to know one another and their teachers to learn something about the practical capabilities and ideas of the new intake. Open days where science demonstrations based on advanced abstract concepts, such as static and current electricity or with plenty of explosions might be theatrical and exciting but promote a false sense of what science is really like and the collaborative skills children will draw on in practical lessons.

Jointly planned teaching projects

A popular way of addressing discontinuities between primary and secondary science is through jointly planned teaching. One approach is to plan some activity that children start towards the end of primary school and continue when they arrive in secondary school. Schemes in this area are variously described as transition units, link projects and bridging units and have been developed by a number of groups of schools, local authorities and universities. Some points to bear in mind when planning these projects are shown in Box 1.

Box 1   Points to consider when planning bridging work or transition units

- Use contexts for lessons that are about science in the real world (for example, investigating bungees, making drinks, designing a school garden).
- Make sure that children experience a similar lesson structure either side of transfer, which they are familiar with and understand.
- Make sure that there are at least some familiar teaching approaches used either side of transfer, such as Concept Cartoons or planning posters.
- Make the best of equipment available in secondary school that children will not have used before.
- Value the work that children did at primary school. Refer to the results of investigations that children have done or ask them to tell other children in the class what they found out.

Evaluation of projects shows that they have to be carefully planned, or children might think they are doing the same old primary work again, when what they really want to do is get their hands on the Bunsen burners! For example, one project involved children proving dough and making bread. In the primary school the work started with observations of yeast activity in a plastic dish followed by research on how bread is made in a bakery. The children were provided with a letter inviting them to find out whether a proving oven is needed to help bread dough to rise better, setting the context for the children's investigations. When they arrived in their secondary schools, children reported their findings and received a further letter inviting them to discover at what temperatures dough might best be proved and for how long. Their investigations at secondary school involved modelling yeast activity using test tubes, delivery tubes and ICT tools to measure, record and graph carbon dioxide production, thereby ensuring that sufficient progression in the investigations and use of equipment took place. Advice on how to get the best from these jointly planned projects can be found in Braund (2008).

The ASE has produced a pupil 'passport' that supports bridging through a choice of investigations and structured follow-up (see *Websites*). The intention is that teachers issue children with colour or black-and-white copies of the passports and children collect 'visas' (icons) awarded by the teacher to mark achievement in scientific skills. Achievement 'visas' can be awarded by the teacher using their own criteria or can be tied to suggested investigations that can be started in the primary school and continued after transfer. The passport acts as a stand-alone transfer record or can be part of more structured bridging.

Sharing practice

This involves teachers watching teaching in the alternate setting to the one in which they teach, or going into another school to do some of the teaching. If they can be arranged, two-way exchanges work best and provide the Y6 teacher with a chance to follow up her or his children in their new setting. The secondary teacher should visit the primary school as the 'learner' rather than 'the expert'. Remember that few primary teachers have the level of subject knowledge that the secondary science teacher must have, but they are experts in effective ways to teach science to children of this age. Whatever the liaison, it must be one of mutual respect and professionalism. Co-observations of teaching should be planned well ahead and roles agreed. It is important to always have a professional discussion together following the observation to share teaching ideas and insights (for a framework to guide this, see Braund, 2008, pp128–134).

Co-teaching, where teachers go into each other's schools to do some teaching, can be most rewarding. This is often a good way to teach shared projects like bridging units. In the York transition projects primary school teachers and first year secondary school teachers planned and co-taught at least one lesson in each other's schools. Even for the most experienced teachers, the insights gained from sharing practice with primary colleagues can open eyes.

> *'I would have thought they (primary teachers) would have given more instructions. They let the kids do more than we do. We like to think we are doing all this (independent work) but you know … my goodness … they are doing it more than we do.'*

Given the right use of protocols to establish purposeful sharing of each other's practice, these methods are effective no matter what stage of transfer is considered.

In conclusion

There are many points of transition and transfer in children's school experience and, although most attention is given to the primary-to-secondary transfer, there may be problems of repetition or lack of continuity for various reasons when children move into infant classes and from infant to junior classes. Transfer at all points is eased by liaison and collaboration of staff on each side of the move, good assessment and records that can be

Provision for science at the school level

trusted by the receiving teachers, and knowledge of how pupils have been taught as well as what they have learned. Visits of pupils to their new class or school, co-teaching by staff and the development and study of bridging units before and after the move reduce the anxiety that many pupils feel about leaving familiar territory and prepare them for the next stage of their progress.

References

Braund, M. (2008) *Starting Science ... Again?* London: Sage.

Websites

Discovery Dog Investigations Packs from Millgate House Education Ltd:
   www.millgatehouse.co.uk

Puppets Project resources from Millgate House Education Ltd: www.millgatehouse.co.uk

Magazines containing articles relating to transfers and transition: www.ase.org.uk

Current information on EYFS and transition from KS1 to KS2:
   www.nationalstrategies.standards.dcsf.gov.uk

A number of primary–secondary transfer projects are described and some professional development materials are available at: www.azteachscience.co.uk

The children's' passport is available as part of a set of resources produced by the ASE for science year (2002): www.sycd.co.uk/who_am_i/passport/activity.htm

Chapter 20

Human resources to support primary science

Joy Parvin

Primary teachers have to be skilled in teaching a broad range of subjects and as the world becomes increasingly technological, new areas of learning are added. Information and communication technologies are ever changing, and science and its technological applications continue to advance. Teachers need support of different kinds – some in relation to the subject matter and some in helping with practical subjects – in meeting the demands of teaching science, design and technology. This chapter explores the different sources of support that are available for primary schools in the UK: teaching assistants, scientists and technicians who may visit the school or be visited by children, other adults with relevant expertise and experience, and older students from secondary schools or higher education.

Teaching assistants

Many schools have teaching assistants, who support the teacher on a regular basis each week directly in the classroom. Some may be present to support pupils in the classroom with specific learning, behavioural or physical difficulties, while others have a broader remit to support the teacher in a variety of ways across a range of subjects. Whatever the remit, there are many ways in which teaching assistants can support science in the classroom, from developing exciting and interactive displays to supporting assessment of practical enquiry skills. Teaching assistants may need some support to develop their confidence in these areas, and can obtain this continuing professional development (CPD) through courses currently provided by the ASE and, in England, by the Science Learning Centre (SLC) network.

The role of teaching assistant has changed dramatically in the last ten years in England and Wales. Teaching assistants have been given greater responsibilities, and can now progress to the position of Higher Level Teaching Assistant, or HLTA, if they wish (TDA, 2006). Teaching assistants are now expected to support the curriculum and HLTAs expected to teach the curriculum,

Provision for science at the school level

with inspection bodies across the UK recognising this important role. However, in many primary schools, teaching assistants are rarely asked to support the science curriculum, with their focus often being on literacy and numeracy, and on supporting less able pupils.

Yet the practical and enquiry-based nature of science begs for the input of more than one adult with a class of 30 children. Teachers can find practical work with a large class daunting, but with the presence of another adult who is able to help children to handle and use equipment, measure appropriately and solve problems the challenge can become not only surmountable but enjoyable. Teaching assistants can also play a vital role in developing and reinforcing children's use of scientific vocabulary, thus supporting children's literacy during science lessons. There are many resources available to support this role. For example, Feasey (2009) offers suggestions for games that teaching assistants can support, as does the CPD unit *Discussions in Primary Science*, available from AstraZeneca (see *Websites*).

There is also a strong argument for teaching assistants to support formative assessment in the classroom, particularly of enquiry skills, involving collaborative teamworking, discussion and decision making. It is difficult for a teacher to assess children individually, or even in groups, in relation to these transient skills that are not necessarily captured on paper or other recorded format.

All this means that it is vital that teaching assistants have the skills and knowledge to support science in the primary classroom in a variety of ways, and that they are offered professional development opportunities in order to do so. The network of SLCs in England offers courses for this purpose, varying in length from twilight sessions to four-day courses provided by the National Science Learning Centre at York. The model used at the National Centre splits the course in two parts, providing assistants with a period of time on returning to school to try out some of the strategies covered during part one, followed by the important sharing of experiences with other assistants on returning to part two of the course. These courses develop teaching assistants' abilities and confidence, to support the teaching, monitoring and assessment of science. In the words of one course participant:

> 'The course has given me much more confidence in science and [shown me] how to support not only less able but also gifted and talented children.'

Figure 1 Teaching assistants carrying out scientific enquiry during a Science Learning Centre course.

Human resources to support primary science

Scientists, technicians and engineers

Many more primary schools are taking advantage of options available to engage with scientists, technicians and engineers from local companies to enable children to visit the workplace, or to bring the workplace into the classroom. These experts in their field, with a little encouragement and time spent planning with the teacher, can demonstrate the relevance of science to their work as well as offering inspirational role models to our young scientists and engineers of the future (Parvin, 1999; Evans et al. 2004).

At first glance, the idea of contacting people in industry can appear to be very daunting. Teachers can be put off by the time it might take to set up such links, yet teachers who engage in such activities will testify as to how rewarding this kind of engagement can be. There are organisations that can help teachers to establish links with local companies, so that the teacher is not wholly responsible for recruiting the 'right people' to work in the classroom, or to visit in their workplace. A teacher involved in one such programme, Children Challenging Industry, commented:

> 'Our aim was to enhance the investigative science in school, and to provide the teaching staff with training which would give them a range of industry links. Our pupils have thoroughly enjoyed solving real-life scientific problems through class-based investigations. Following our industry visit to Grosvenor Chemicals, many children expressed the wish to be a scientist when they grew up. Their follow-up work and comments demonstrated how their perception of the chemical industry had changed from a negative to a positive one.'

This programme is available to schools in the north of England via a team of advisory teachers, and is available via distance learning through the Primary Science Enhancement Programme (PSEP; see *Websites*) to all other teachers and schools. The programme encourages the use of industry as contexts in which to teach scientific skills and concepts. These industrial contexts, or stories, often start with a letter from industry to the children, asking for their help to solve some scientific problems and challenges that the company faces. These letters, though fictitious, are based on issues that real companies have faced, and may continue to face. They require the children to carry out scientific enquiry in small groups, to develop good discussion and teamworking skills, and to report their findings back to the company.

An example of such a letter is shown in Figure 2, which is based on the processes of a real company that makes the products described (Jackson and Parvin, 2003). This kind of starting point can be used by anyone making links with a local business, with the consent of the company concerned.

The children are then asked to carry out various investigations, in this case regarding the 'runniness' or viscosity of liquids and how this property can be changed. The children work in company teams, all working as scientists, but all with an additional role and responsibility – modelling teams in industry. One such role is the Communications Manager, and this child reports back the team's plans, data, challenges and conclusions or recommendations to the rest of the class. Another child in the team is the Resources Manager, who has the job of collecting and returning equipment and resources required for their practical investigations. This is a great classroom management strategy to prevent everyone moving around the classroom at once, while giving the groups independence over the choice of equipment for their tests.

Provision for science at the school level

Figure 2 Fictitious letter requesting help.

Industrial Polymer Resins Ltd

Consett
County Durham

Dear Research Group

We produce special inks for chocolate-makers, who use them to print the names of sweets on the wrappers. We also make the main ingredient in the glue for sticking the wrappers together. We have found that the best starting ingredient for the ink and glue is a liquid from trees. Unfortunately, our new recipe is causing us problems. It makes a very thick liquid that does not flow easily through our pipes. It is also very hard to stir, and we need a lot of electricity to run our stirring machines. This is very expensive!

We understand that your research group is investigating liquids, and would be pleased if you could suggest ways we can solve this problem.

We need as much data as you can provide, including any measurements you make of runniness of different sorts of liquid. Any suggestions you can give us, which will make our liquid flow more easily, would help us very much.

We look forward to hearing from you in the near future.

Kind regards

J. Wellington
Managing Director

Following their classroom investigations, the class visit a relevant company (in this case, one that transports liquids other than water around the site), to see the processes and meet the scientists, engineers, technicians and many other people involved in the workplace. The company personnel have been trained by the advisory teachers and have spent a great deal of time planning the visit, prior to the children arriving on site. During this training, the personnel have the chance to try out the classroom practical investigations, to find out what primary children are likely to know when they arrive on the site, and to support them in planning a relevant site tour and any laboratory-based activities for the children.

It is not always possible to arrange visits of this nature, and so another option is to invite an 'ambassador' from industry in to school. There are Children Challenging Industry (CCI) ambassadors across the north of England, and there are STEM ambassadors available across the country. These are coordinated by STEMNET, and can be contacted via their website (see *Websites*). Both CCI and STEM ambassadors undergo training to support these classroom visits. Also, as for all adults working with children across the UK, even if they will not be left alone with the class, they provide CRB (Criminal Records Bureau) checks during these training sessions. These ambassadors are encouraged to be as interactive as possible with the children, and to bring large photographs (often in PowerPoint presentations) showing the production areas, laboratories, and colleagues engaged in science and technology. They are also encouraged to bring pieces of equipment to show simple demonstrations to the children. These demonstrations are best linked to (1) the science the children have been carrying out in the classroom and (2) the work of their company, to demonstrate the applications of the children's work or the research carried out by industry.

If neither the site visit nor the industry ambassador is an option, teachers can look for websites that offer short video clips showing people working in industry that are tailored to meet the needs of primary children (for example, PSEP; see *Websites*). Alternatively, persuade a governor or parent that works in industry to visit the children.

School governors, parents and other adults linked to the school

Close to home, school governors and parents can have a valuable role in exciting primary children about science and its applications in the real world. Among the parent and governor population can be found a hidden wealth of scientists working in the medical professions, industry, academia and elsewhere. It is worth taking the time to 'find' them and invite them in to the classroom to share expertise with the pupils. The school could send a 'volunteers wanted' letter to governors and parents, asking them if they work in a scientific or technical job, and would be willing to share their expertise with children in school. Sometimes, relatives of teachers or other school staff can also provide a pool of potential helpers.

As with the student volunteers discussed in the next section, the key to success is in planning exactly what the adult will do in the classroom. This should avoid the problem encountered in one school when, during a science week, an enthusiastic parent brought a prototype racing car from the engineering department in which he lectured, only to discover that he could not get the car through the school hall doors. He then proceeded to talk to classes of children outside in a very windy playground, which resulted in a great deal of distraction as the leaves whipped up around them!

As well as planning the resources that will be used, the content of any talk or presentation should be discussed at reasonable length. The adult should be encouraged to be as interactive as possible, asking questions of the children rather than delivering facts, engaging children in short demonstrations, and bringing in equipment, materials, objects and photographs for the children to handle.

Teachers may find that some of these adults are already registered as ambassadors, and have therefore received training on working with young people. This does not remove the necessity to plan, but the time spent planning can be reduced. For example, one CCI ambassador, trained to work with 7–11-year-olds, was begged by her 5-year-old son to visit his class. Due to confidence she had gained from the training, she felt able to plan a session that excited the children greatly, and certainly made the little boy very proud of his mum!

In addition to describing their own science-based work, informed adults can help teachers with the difficult questions children raise. Every week there are science stories in the newspapers or on the television. What do children make of these stories, and how do teachers support children in their engagement with them, and formulation of opinions about them? These can be challenging areas for primary teachers to deal with, and the support of others with greater expertise can help the classroom teacher in their endeavours. These 'expert' adults with their additional knowledge and skills can inform and enliven day-to-day classroom activities and discussions. There are many willing volunteers out there, who are

Provision for science at the school level

keen to impart their love of science, and only need a little encouragement and an idea of what children already know to engage in a meaningful way with our young people.

Figure 3 A Children Challenging Industry Ambassador excites some five-year-olds.

Older students studying science and engineering

Another group of potential role models lies in the student population of our secondary schools, colleges and universities. Many of these pupils have gone on to choose to study science beyond the compulsory age and often have a passion for their subject. In England, this would include those only just over the age of 16, who are still relatively close to primary children in age and therefore seen to be 'cool'.

All primary schools have a secondary school in their locality, and if this school is a specialist school for science, technology, engineering or even entrepreneurship, even better. There is probably some kind of transition activity in place, but it may not involve the secondary pupils as role models. Ideally, these pupils will be post-16 students, as they have then made the choice to study science, and should therefore be able to convey their enthusiasm for the subject, and be able to discuss with primary children the reasons for their choices. One such model, SPLATS, which is offered by an organisation called Sphere Science (see *Websites*), helps sixth form students to develop their communication skills before working with primary-aged children. In the words of one Head of Science of a secondary school involved, SPLATS is:

> '... *an excellent project that both sets of students gained a lot from. The greatest improvement was in the students' confidence in their own presentation and communication skills. It achieved all that I had hoped, and in a number of areas exceeded my expectations.*'

Human resources to support primary science

If there is a university nearby, it may run schemes for student volunteers to spend placements in primary schools. The scheme may be run by individual departments, or centrally by the university. Either way, a school could place a specific request for a science student, and thus engage a positive and young role model, choosing to go on to study science. It is important to spend time planning with the student, to maximise the impact of the time the student spends in the classroom. During this planning, the teacher reminds the student about the level at which the children are working; otherwise, students tend to want to explain everything at a molecular level, forgetting that they would not have understood this at the age of nine or ten! In addition to the planning, the student is invited in to a lesson where the children, in small groups, talk about their science. The language the children use to explain their work helps the student to grasp the level of the children's knowledge.

It is important that the student has time to talk to the children, again in small groups, about the choices he or she has made, and about what life is like as a science or engineering student in a university. This can have quite an impact on children who have never thought about going to university before, and can raise their aspirations to do so. Further, research shows that children's interest in and attitudes towards science tend to be formed in the primary school and are already declining by the age of 11 (Murphy and Beggs, 2003). This is part of a general pattern for pupils' attitudes towards most school subjects to become less positive with age (Tymms et al., 2008) but unless children are enabled to make better-informed judgements, these attitudes are inevitably influenced by myths and hearsay about science.

It may also be possible to arrange a visit to a university science department, as many departments carry out outreach work, though this is often aimed at secondary rather than primary-aged pupils. There have been schemes in recent years to encourage visits of this kind, but there are challenges for the universities to face, such as timing of visits and safety precautions. For the schools, as for all visits, parental permission is required.

Figure 4 Primary school pupils visit Manchester University's chemistry department to practise separation and filtering techniques.

In conclusion

There is a range of ways in which teachers can have help in the classroom and can extend their pupils' engagement with science within and beyond the classroom. The key to success is planning the input that other people can have to children's work, both in the classroom and during visits. Wherever possible, the other adults should have received training and support from one of the many schemes and organisations mentioned here. For more information on schemes and organisations that offer support, advice and training, visit the STEM Directories website (see *Websites*) where a comprehensive list of what is available nationally and regionally can be found. Involving adults in the classroom not only motivates pupils, but it can give teachers new inspiration as well.

References

Evans, C., Hogarth, S. and Parvin, J. (2004) *Children Challenging Industry: Analysis of CCI Project Data 5 years On*. Available online at: www.cciproject.org/reports/documents/5yearOn.pdf

Feasey, R. (2009) *Jumpstart! Science Games and Activities for Ages 5–11*. London: Routledge.

Jackson, B. and Parvin, J. (ed) (2003) *Runny Liquids*. Chemical Industry Education Centre, York: University of York.

Murphy, C. and Beggs, J. (2003) Children's attitudes towards school science. *School Science Review*, **84**(308), 109–116.

Parvin, J. (1999) *Children Challenging Industry: The Research Report*. York: Chemical Industry Education Centre, University of York.

TDA (2006) *Guidance to the Standards for the Award of HLTA Status*. London: Training and Development Agency for Schools.

Tymms, P., Bolden, D. and Merrell, C. (2008) Science in English Primary Schools: Trends in attainment, attitudes and approaches. *Perspectives on Education*, 1, 19–42. London: The Wellcome Trust.

Websites

AstraZeneca: www.azteachscience.co.uk

Children Challenging Industry: www.cciproject.org

National Centre for Learning Science : www.sciencelearningcentres.org.uk

Primary Science Enhancement Programme: www.psep.org

Sphere Science: www.spherescience.co.uk

STEM Directories: www.stemdirectories.org.uk

STEMNET: www.stemnet.org.uk

Section 4

The national and international context

Chapter 21

What are we teaching? Science curricula across the UK

Wynne Harlen, Peter McAlister, Barbara Harrison, Philippa Minto and Nancy Bilderbeck

National curricula were introduced in England, Wales and Northern Ireland, and national guidelines in Scotland, for the first time around 1989/90. Several revisions during the 1990s alleviated some of teachers' problems in implementation, but in the early 2000s it became clear that more radical revisions were needed to ensure that primary school education took its part in preparing children for their future in an increasingly scientific and technological world and for life-long learning.

The separate reviews in the four countries resulted in new curricula, which diverge to a greater extent than previously and are at various stages of being implemented. This chapter very briefly maps the changes in each country, identifying some common trends and some differences in how children are introduced to science in the primary years. The ASE website is a good source of information about any further changes within the UK.

England

The curriculum in place for the primary school in England is the 1999 revision of the National Curriculum. Initially introduced in 1989, the National Curriculum was revised on several occasions in response to recurring complaints about being crowded and over-prescribed. In 2002, it was extended to include the Foundation Stage.

The ages 5–16 are divided into four Key Stages, the first two being in the primary school (KS1 Years 1 and 2, ages 5–7; KS2 Years 3–6, ages 8–11). In its initial form, the National Curriculum comprised ten foundation subjects: English, mathematics, science, design and technology, history, geography, art, music, physical education and (for secondary schools) a modern foreign language. English, mathematics and science were designated as 'core' subjects and as such were the first to be specified and in far greater detail than other foundation subjects. Religious education, although required, was not part of the National Curriculum.

What are we teaching? Science curricula across the UK

In the revision in 1999, information and communications technology was added, as were non-statutory programmes of study for citizenship and for personal, social and health education. In 2007, a revised National Curriculum for KS3 and 4 was published by the QCA and implemented in 2008.

The Programme of Study for each subject indicates the knowledge, skills and understanding to be taught and the 'breadth of study' or range of experiences and contexts to be included at each Key Stage. Some of these experiences or contexts are given as examples; others are required by law to be taught. For science at KS1 and KS2, knowledge, skills and understanding to be taught are set out in four sections:

1 **Scientific enquiry** – ideas and evidence in science; investigative skills

2 **Life processes and living things** – life processes; humans and other animals; green plants; variation and classification; living things in their environment

3 **Materials and their properties** – grouping materials; changing materials; separating mixtures of materials (KS2 only)

4 **Physical processes** – electricity; forces and motion; light and sound; the Earth and beyond (KS2 only).

Under each sub-heading are bullet points listing what 'pupils should be taught' (DfEE and QCA, 1999).

What children are expected to learn is set out in terms of Attainment Targets specified initially at ten progressive levels to cover the age range 5–16, subsequently reduced to 8 levels and 'exceptional performance' beyond level 8. At the same time, detailed level specifications of the Attainment Targets were changed to broader and simpler Level Descriptions for each of the four sections of the Programmes of Study. Box 1 gives some examples of Level Descriptions for 'scientific enquiry' and 'physical processes'.

Box 1 Examples of Level Descriptions in the National Curriculum for England

> *'Science enquiry: Level 2 (target level for the end of KS1)*
> *Pupils respond to suggestions about how to find things out and, with help, make their own suggestions about how to collect data to answer questions. They use simple texts, with help, for finding information. They use simple equipment provided and make observations related to their task. They observe and compare objects, living things and events. They describe their observations using scientific vocabulary and record them, using simple tables when appropriate. They say whether what happened was what they expected.*
>
> *Physical processes: Level 4 (target level for the end of KS2)*
> *Pupils demonstrate knowledge and understanding of physical processes drawn from the Key Stage 2 or Key Stage 3 Programme of Study. They describe and explain physical phenomena (e.g. how a particular device may be connected to work in an electrical circuit, how the apparent position of the Sun changes over a day). They make generalisations about physical phenomena (e.g. motion is affected by forces, including gravitational attraction, magnetic attractions and friction). They use physical ideas to explain simple phenomena (e.g. the formation of shadows, sound being heard through a variety of materials). (The examples in brackets are non-statutory).'*
>
> DfEE and QCA (1999)

The national and international context

Reviews of the primary curriculum

Dissatisfaction with the National Curriculum continued to mount from 2005 onwards, fuelled partly by the lack of improvement in national test results from 2001 onwards but also by the contrast between the Government's urge for education to be 'personalised' and the requirements to follow what was still seen as a closely prescribed curriculum. While a revised Key Stage 3 curriculum was implemented in 2008, it was not until 2008 that Sir Jim Rose began a review of the primary curriculum.

In fact, there were two reviews of the whole primary school curriculum in England, both reporting in 2009. One was a fundamental review of primary education, funded by a private foundation and therefore independent of the Government. It was based in the Faculty of Education of the University of Cambridge and led by Professor Robin Alexander. As well as the curriculum and assessment and testing, it considered matters as diverse as children's development and learning, the relationship between schools and other agencies, teachers and their training, the structure of primary education as a whole and its relationship to pre-school and secondary provision. Work began in 2006 and interim reports were available on the internet (Cambridge Primary Review, see *Websites*) from 2007 and the final report was published in 2010 (Alexander, 2010).

Then, in January 2008, the Government launched a separate review, confined to the primary curriculum in England, conducted by an ex-chief inspector for primary education, Sir Jim Rose. This review recommended a new primary curriculum for England organised around six broad areas of learning:

- understanding English, communication and languages
- mathematical understanding
- scientific and technological understanding
- human, geographical and social understanding
- understanding the arts
- understanding physical development.

It also set out 'Essentials for learning and life' (literacy, numeracy, ICT capability, learning and thinking skills, personal and emotional skills, and social skills).

The proposals set out what children should be taught in each of these areas at 'early', 'middle' and 'later' stages across the primary years. This contrasts with the divisions for Key Stages in the 1999 National Curriculum.

The content for the early stage was intended to dovetail with the curriculum for the Early Years Foundation Stage, and in *Scientific and technological understanding*, economically described in 11 statements, many begin with 'to explore ...'

For the middle stage the statements of what children should be taught were set out separately in relation to skills 'across the area of learning', 'design and technology' and 'science'.

In the later stage the science was broken down into 'energy, movement and forces', 'material behaviour', 'life and living things' and 'the environment, Earth and solar system'. Although the number of statements under each heading was small, there were many notes indicating the detail of what should be included.

Implementation of the new curriculum was planned for 2011, but the required legislation was not passed through Parliament before the general election of May 2010 and it was not supported by the new coalition government. Thus England is the only one of the four home countries not to have a new primary curriculum in the first decade of the twenty-first century.

Northern Ireland

Throughout the 1990s and until 2007 the primary curriculum in Northern Ireland was similar in structure to the National Curriculum in England. Introduced in 1990, the Northern Ireland Curriculum included 'science and technology' as a compulsory subject throughout primary and secondary education. As in England, complaints about overcrowding and the burden of testing and reporting led to several revisions and in 1999 a major review of the whole curriculum was announced by the Department of Education. The resulting New Northern Ireland Curriculum was phased in from 2007.

Primary education in Northern Ireland has three phases:

- Foundation (Years 1 and 2, ages 5 and 6)
- Key Stage 1 (Years 3 and 4, ages 7 and 8)
- Key Stage 2 (Years 5, 6, and 7, ages 9–12)

The new Northern Ireland Curriculum for the primary school is set out in the same way for each of these three phases; statements describe a progression through the seven primary years. In each phase there are six areas of learning (plus religious education):

- language and literacy
- mathematics and numeracy
- the arts
- the world around us
- personal development and mutual understanding
- physical development and movement.

The world around us

In Key Stages 1 and 2, primary science and technology has been downgraded from 'core' status to that of a contributory element of *The world around us* learning area, along with geography and history. At Foundation Stage there are no contributory elements.

The world around us learning area is defined differently from the other six learning areas in that it is set out in four interrelated strands that apply to the primary Key Stages. These are:

- interdependence
- place
- movement and energy
- change over time.

The national and international context

Each strand contains 3–8 broad statements that vary according to Key Stage and are open to interpretation from the perspectives of geography, history and science and technology. The strands are prefaced by the following statutory requirements, which recognise the importance of developing subject-based and generic knowledge, skills and conceptual understanding.

Foundation:

> *'Teachers should enable children to develop knowledge, understanding and skills in relation to …'*
>
> CCEA (2007, p38)

Key Stages 1 and 2:

> *'Through the contributory elements of History, Geography and Science and Technology teachers should enable pupils to develop knowledge, understanding and skills in …'*
>
> CCEA (2007, p86, p88)

Some examples of statements are given in Table 1.

Table 1 Examples of statements in the Northern Ireland Curriculum for the *Movement and energy* strand of *The world around us* learning area.

Foundation Stage: strand of Movement and energy	
Pupils should be enabled to explore:	**Children are learning:**
How and why do things move, now and in the past?	• to recognise things around us that move
How do things work?	• some of the ways in which things are made to move • an awareness that they move things by pushing or pulling them • an awareness of what makes everyday things work
Where do living things move?	• that living things move on the ground, underground, in the air and in water
Why do people and animals move?	• some of the reasons why people and animals move from place to place
Where do people and animals move to?	• that some people and animals move to other places at different times of the year
What sources of energy are in my world?	• that light comes from a variety of sources • that sound comes from a variety of sources • an awareness of sound and light in their immediate environment • that electricity can be dangerous
How and why are they used?	• that we use light and sound to keep us safe

What are we teaching? Science curricula across the UK

Key Stage 1: strand of Movement and energy (H = history; G = geography; SandT = science and technology)	
Pupils should be enabled to explore:	Children are learning:
Sources of energy in the world	• some of the ways in which light and sound are used to keep us safe in road safety and our everyday lives (SandT) • that the strength of a push or pull can make things speed up or move more slowly (SandT) • some of the ways people lived in the past before electricity (H)
How and why people and animals move	• that animals move in a variety of ways (SandT) • how seasonal change causes animals to move (SandT) • that changes to the environment can cause people and animals to move (SandT) • how people in the past travelled from place to place (H) • how people travel and products are transported from place to place in the locality (G) • that weather affects the movement of people, goods and animals (G)
Changes in movement and energy over time	• to recognise how models and machines allow movement and how this has changed over time (SandT) • how transport has changed over time (H)

Across the whole curriculum there is emphasis on:

- **cross-curricular skills** – communication; using mathematics; using information and communications technology
- **thinking skills and personal capabilities** – managing information; thinking; problem solving and decision making; being creative; self-management; working with others.

These emphases impact on how the whole curriculum is taught. They require a strong focus on active, often enquiry-based, learning, together with skills development and connections within and across learning areas. There is flexibility for teachers to devise learning experiences that are both current and relevant to children. To give teachers flexibility, CCEA guidance material exemplifies a 'topic' or 'thematic' approach that emphasises connections within *The world around us*, where appropriate, and links to other learning areas (see *Websites*). Discrete subject teaching thus remains an option.

The national and international context

Scotland

In the late 1980s, the same factors that created national curricula in other countries of the UK gave rise to the 5–14 Development Programme in Scotland. This programme, managed by the Scottish Consultative Council in the Curriculum (SCCC), reviewed the curriculum in the seven years of primary and the first two years of secondary education. National guidelines were developed in five areas:

- language
- mathematics
- environment studies
- expressive arts
- religious and moral education.

Environmental studies included technology, health education and information technology, as well as social subjects and science. Attainment Targets in three areas of science (*Understanding living things and processes of life*, *Understanding energy and forces*, and *Understanding Earth and space*) were defined at five levels (A–E) in terms of knowledge, understanding, skills, and attitudes. Later, a level F was added for all subjects. Unlike the national curricula in other parts of the UK, national guidelines are not mandatory although most schools in Scotland follow the advice offered in them.

Although the *Environmental studies* Guidelines helped primary schools develop a progressive series of topics, some of which were integrated across a number of subject areas and some of which focused mainly on science, many schools found them to be too complex and cumbersome to teach. In 2000, a revision of *Environmental studies* Guidelines was published by Learning and Teaching Scotland (which took over the duties of the SCCC). Revised and separate guidelines in science and the other areas included in *Environmental studies* were produced, simplifying the structure of what was to be taught and the progression across the six levels A to F.

For a few years the teaching of science in primary schools was carried out with only minor modifications. Teachers became more confident in the subject matter and in using Assessment is for Learning (AiFL) techniques in their classrooms. However, consultation on the state of school education conducted by the Scottish Executive (redesignated as the Scottish Government from 2009) led to the publication of *A Curriculum for Excellence* in 2004, identifying the values, purposes and principles that should underpin the curriculum 3–18. Whereas earlier curriculum developments had focused on specific stages (ages 5–14, 14–16, 16–18), *Curriculum for Excellence* sets out to provide a progressive learning experience for all children and young people from the time they enter pre-school until they leave secondary school. In addition, it aims to provide 'more freedom for teachers and greater choice and opportunity for pupils' (see Websites).

After several years of consultation and development, new curriculum guidelines were published in spring 2009 to be implemented in 2011. Guidance is set out for eight curriculum areas:

- expressive arts
- languages

- health and wellbeing
- mathematics
- sciences
- religious and moral education
- social studies
- technologies.

In addition, teachers have the responsibility to promote literacy, numeracy and health and well-being across learning. In science, there are five areas to be taught:

- planet Earth
- biological systems
- forces, electricity and waves
- materials
- topical science.

The guidelines are expressed in terms of 'experiences and outcomes', statements in which the learning process and skill, knowledge and understanding outcomes are combined. Box 2 gives examples of these statements for the Early, First and Second levels in relation to 'biodiversity and interdependence', a sub-area of *Planet Earth*. The rationale for science, in the publication *Curriculum for Excellence: Science. Principles and Practice* (Scottish Government, 2009), sets out how the new curriculum aims for deeper understanding through exploration, interdisciplinary planning and greater engagement in outdoor learning.

Box 2 Examples of experiences and outcomes for science in Scotland's Curriculum for Excellence

---

Planet Earth: biodiversity and interdependence

Early stage (pre-school and P1)
- I have observed living things in the environment over time and am becoming aware of how they depend on each other.

First stage (P2 to P4)
- I can distinguish between living and non-living things. I can sort living things into groups and explain my decisions.
- I can explore examples of food chains and show an appreciation of how animals and plants depend on each other for food.

Second stage (P5 to P7)
- I can identify and classify examples of living things, past and present, to help me appreciate their diversity. I can relate physical and behavioural characteristics to their survival or extinction.
- I can use my knowledge of the interactions and energy flow between plants and animals in ecosystems, food chains and webs. I have contributed to the design or conservation of a wildlife area.

The national and international context

Wales

Until the establishment of the Welsh Assembly Government (WAG) in 1999 the National Curriculum in Wales was the same as in England apart from the inclusion of Welsh language as an additional subject in the core and English not being required until the age of 7. This link was ended in 2002 when all matters concerned with the curriculum and assessment were devolved to the WAG. A review of the curriculum led to the development of the National Curriculum for Wales, in which the primary curriculum is set out in two parts: a Foundation Phase (nursery, reception and Years 1 and 2, ages 3–7) and Key Stage 2 (Years 3–6, ages 7–11). For each part, the Programme of Study sets out what pupils should be taught in terms of skills to be developed and range of topics to be investigated.

Foundation Phase

For the Foundation Phase, the statutory 'Framework for Children's Learning for 3 to 7-year-olds in Wales' (fully implemented in 2010) sets out the curriculum and outcomes under seven areas of learning, science being included in *Knowledge and understanding of the world*. Under this heading, various skills of finding out are to be used across a range of activities relating to:

- places and people
- time and people
- myself and other living things
- myself and non-living things.

Learning from these activities is identified in terms of six Foundation Phase Outcomes, as in Box 3.

Box 3 Foundation Phase Outcomes for 3- to 7-year-olds in the National Curriculum for Wales

'Outcome 1
Children explore objects and materials within immediate and familiar environments. They often ask the question 'why?' and use words, signs or symbols to communicate their observations. They recognise themselves and familiar people in pictures/stories and show knowledge of daily routines. Through adult encouragement children are beginning to communicate about their creations, such as models and pictures.

Part of Outcome 6
They use their everyday experiences to explain differences between, and changes to, living things, materials and physical phenomena. They link the learning, with support, to familiar situations. They talk about their ideas and using their everyday experience they make simple predictions. They plan, with support, the approach to be used for their enquiries. When appropriate, they agree on some simple success criteria. They ask and answer a range of questions, observe, collect and record information in a variety of ways and find answers to their investigations. They express their views supported with reasons and recognise that people have different views. They give a simple explanation, based upon their everyday

> *experiences, for their findings and suggest what they could have done differently to improve their findings. They identify what worked, made sense, what did not work, did not make sense and why.'*
>
> (DCELLS, 2008a)

Key Stage 2

The National Curriculum for Wales at KS2 retains a structure of 11 subjects, with science separate from design and technology. The Programme of Study for science identifies the skills under two main headings (DCELLS, 2008b):

- **communication** – pupils should be given the opportunity to search for relevant information, communicate clearly and use standard measures
- **enquiry** – pupils should be given the opportunities to carry out different types of enquiry, e.g. pattern-seeking, exploring, classifying and identifying, making things, fair testing, using and applying models by planning their work, developing their methods and reflecting on what they have done/learned.

The range is identified under three headings:

- **Interdependence of organisms** – pupils should use and develop their skills, knowledge and understanding by investigating how animals and plants are independent yet rely on each other for survival.
- **The sustainable Earth** – pupils should use and develop their skills, knowledge and understanding by comparing the Earth with other planets, investigating materials around them and considering the importance of recycling.
- **How things work** – pupils should use and develop their skills, knowledge and understanding by investigating the science behind everyday things, e.g. toys, musical instruments and electrical devices, the way they are constructed and work.

Level descriptions describe the types and range of performance that pupils working at a particular level should characteristically demonstrate. As well as levels 1 to 8, there are some non-statutory National Curriculum Outcomes that help in identifying attainment below level 1 and which can be seen to have equivalents in the Foundation Phase Outcomes.

A skills-focused curriculum

A key feature of the curriculum is the focus on skills, and a non-statutory framework – *Skills Framework for 3 to 19-year-olds in Wales* (DCELLS, 2008c) – has been developed. It provides guidance about continuity and progression for learners from 3 to 19 and beyond in thinking, communication, ICT and number – these skills are:

> *'... fundamental for learners of any age to become successful, whether in school, the workplace, at home or elsewhere, and they need to be firmly embedded into the experience of learners across all their learning.'*
>
> DCELLS (2008c, p4)

The national and international context

The framework is organised into four sections – *The development of thinking, Communication, ICT* and *Number across the curriculum*. Progression in these skills is laid out across six stages, notionally linked to broad expectations at the beginning and the end of the Foundation Phase, the end of Key Stages 2, 3 and 4, and Post-16. Although it is recognised that learning and skills development may not happen in a neat linear way, the framework is still presented in a six-column continuum for the sake of clarity.

In conclusion

The twenty-first century has seen radical reviews of the curricula of the four countries of the UK. The new curricula in Northern Ireland and Wales and the Curriculum for Excellence in Scotland diverge from one another – and from the unchanged National Curriculum in England – to a greater extent than for the curricula introduced in the 1990s. One area of difference is how science is separated or integrated with other subjects, particularly technology. In Wales and Scotland science is distinguished from technology, while they are within the same area of learning in Northern Ireland. Scotland's new curriculum stands out from the others in combining skills with knowledge and understanding in statements of 'experiences and outcomes'. The trend towards identifying 'areas of learning', rather than subjects, while intended to make science more meaningful and linked to everyday life, may have unintended consequences for the attention it receives in broad topics. It will be important to monitor this as the new curricula become embedded. However, there are common themes, particularly in identifying skills, such as numeracy, communication and ICT, to be developed across the curriculum.

References

Alexander, R. (ed) (2010) *Children, their World, their Education*. London: Routledge.

CCEA (2007) *Northern Ireland Primary Curriculum*. Belfast: Council for the Curriculum, Examinations and Assessment.

DCELLS (2008a) *Foundation Phase Framework for Children's Learning for 3 to 7-year-olds in Wales*. Cardiff: DCELLS.

DCELLS (2008b) *Science in the National Curriculum for Wales*. Cardiff: DCELLS.

DCELLS (2008c) *Skills Framework for 3 to 19-year-olds in Wales*. Cardiff: DCELLS.

DfEE and QCA (1999) *The National Curriculum for England. Science*. London: Department for Education and Employment.

Scottish Government, Learning and Teaching Scotland, HMIe and SQA (2009) *Curriculum for Excellence: Science. Principles and Practice*. Edinburgh: Scottish Government. Available online at: www.ltscotland.org.uk/curriculumforexcellence/sciences/principlesandpractice/index.asp

Websites

ASE (Association for Science Education): www.ase.org.uk

Cambridge Primary Review: www.primaryreview.org.uk

Curriculum for Excellence (Scotland):
www.ltscotland.org.uk/curriculumforexcellence/index.asp

National Curriculum for England:
http://curriculum.qcda.gov.uk/key-stages-1-and-2/index.aspx

National curriculum for Wales:
http://wales.gov.uk/topics/educationandskills/curriculumassessment/arevisedcurriculumforwales/skillsdevelopment/?lang=en

National Curriculum for Northern Ireland, including 'Ideas for connected learning' documents: www.nicurriculum.org.uk

Chapter 22

How good is our science teaching?

Wynne Harlen

This chapter is about how a primary school can evaluate its provision and performance in science. For many years, the ways in which schools are inspected has increasingly depended on self-evaluation but this is now a regular part of the work of class teachers and school management, independent of whether it is required for an external inspection. After a brief discussion of the meaning and purposes of evaluation, this chapter deals with self-evaluation at two levels – the classroom and the school. For both, it suggests some standards or criteria against which performance can be compared in order to identify where action may be needed, and gives some ideas for sources of relevant evidence. In several places, this chapter draws on the writing of Lynne Wright, author of the chapter on this topic in the last edition of this ASE Guide.

Evaluating provision for science

Evaluation in this context means gathering and using information to help in deciding what action needs to be taken to improve a school's provision for science and its children's learning. Whether or not there is a problem to be addressed, finding out more about what is happening and deepening understanding of the complex processes of teaching and learning can only enhance the experience of both teachers and pupils.

Evaluation requires that there is some basis for making decisions, a standard against which relevant evidence is judged. Here the word 'standard' means the quality or level of some service or performance that is considered to be desirable; examples are the professional standards for teachers published by the Training and Development Agency for Schools (TDA, 2007). This use of the word 'standard' differs from its use as a statement of what has been attained, as in statements about whether standards of behaviour or attainment have risen or fallen.

In evaluation, then, it is necessary to establish and make explicit the standards to be used as criteria in judging whether the practice under review requires attention and, if so, what kind of action is needed. But it is clear that deciding standards (used in the first sense above, of quality standards) involves value judgements. For example, it would be quite possible for a science lesson, delivered as a lecture to silent children sat in rows, to be judged as 'very good' if the criteria were that *'accurate information should be provided to children to learn in silence'*. The judgement would be very different, of course, if the criteria were that *'children should question, discuss and take an active part in their learning'*.

The purposes of evaluation

As in the case of assessment of pupils, the evaluation of teaching and schools' provision can be used for formative or summative purposes. Also as in pupil assessment, the differences between these purposes are becoming more blurred. Standards expected in primary classrooms are embodied in the criteria used by Ofsted, whose evaluations are essentially summative and aimed at categorising schools as 'outstanding', 'good', 'satisfactory' or 'inadequate', but these criteria are being shared with teachers and used in school self-evaluation. They have also been broadened to include far more than pupil attainment. Further extension is identified in the Chief Inspector's Annual Report for 2008/9 among priorities for the future:

> *'First, inspection must engage with users and stakeholders at all levels; we need to ensure that the experiences of children, young people and adult learners are at the centre of everything we do. Second, we must do more to disseminate effective practice and what might be learned from it. Third, we must focus our work on what is happening on the ground, continuing to take performance data into account, but spending more time, for example, talking to social workers and observing teaching in classrooms.'*
>
> Ofsted (2009, p11)

External inspections in all parts of the UK begin with the school's self-evaluation. For many years schools in Scotland have had access to a set of indicators provided by HMIe (2007). Similarly, Estyn provides guidance on inspections for primary and nursery schools (Estyn, 2004). But that is not the only, or even the main, reason for self-evaluation. The purpose we have in mind here is not to prepare for an inspectorial visit but rather to ensure that the school management and staff are regularly evaluating and improving provision. As Wright (2006) points out:

> *'Even without this external pressure, it is in the school's best interest that its own analysis is ruthlessly honest and accurate. School self-assessment at any level and for any aspect or subject, relies upon evidence collected by the school in a measured and planned way, rather than on assertions, expectations or hope!'*
>
> Wright (2006, p74)

Evaluating classroom practice

Quality standards not only provide the basis for judgements, but they also indicate the kind of information to be collected as evidence in the evaluation. Thus they have to be identified at the start of the evaluation. Box 1 gives an example of a set of quality standards for classroom practice in primary school science. They are derived from statements of what is regarded as 'good' practice in many countries and many of the statements are supported

The national and international context

by research evidence of their effect. Nevertheless, as with any standards, those in this list depend on value judgements that some practices (such as giving certain kinds of feedback) are better than alternative ways of doing things. In Box 1 the items are statements of quality standards to be aimed for, but they could easily be expressed as questions – for example, *'Does the teacher use a range of methods suited to the achievement of the various goals of learning science?'*

Box 1   Standards for classroom practice

> *'Teachers should:*
> - *use a range of methods suited to the achievement of the various goals of learning science*
> - *provide simple materials and equipment for children to use in first-hand exploration and enquiry of scientific phenomena in their environment*
> - *regularly ask questions which invite children to express their ideas*
> - *know where children are in the development of ideas and enquiry skills and use this information to provide opportunities and support (scaffolding) for progress*
> - *include in lesson plans what children are intended to learn as well as what they will do*
> - *provide comments that help progress in oral or written feedback on children's work*
> - *ensure that children regularly have chances to raise questions and that these are addressed*
> - *ensure that children always know the purpose of their investigations and other science activities*
> - *provide opportunities for children to discuss observations, plans, findings and conclusions in small groups and as a whole class*
> - *provide opportunities for children to obtain information from books, the internet, visits out of school and visiting experts*
> - *discuss with children the qualities of good work so that they can assess and improve their own and each others' work*
> - *provide time and encouragement for children to reflect on how and what they have learned*
> - *keep records of children's progress based on questioning, observation, discussion and study of products relevant to the learning goals.'*
>
> Harlen and Qualter (2009, p300)

The first step in self-evaluation is for those involved to agree on the standards to be applied. Examples such as those in Box 1 might be taken as starting points. The important outcome is that everyone signs up to what they are aiming for; otherwise the evaluation may not be taken seriously.

The second step is to collect evidence relating to the agreed standards. This will concern a range of aspects of teaching, the main ones being:

How good is our science teaching?

- curriculum documents and teachers' medium-term plans
- teachers' short-term lesson plans
- teachers' records of activities and pupil performance
- teacher actions and talk
- pupil actions and interactions
- pupil–teacher interactions
- pupils' written records and other products.

Methods of collecting evidence about these aspects include:

- classroom observation
- interviews or discussion with the teacher, teaching assistants and pupils
- analysis of documents
- scrutiny of pupils' written work.

The evidence is collected with the help of the science subject leader or other peer, by the teachers themselves or by teachers and helpers working together. Classroom observations always seem to be the most valid way of collecting evidence – and so they are in many respects, particularly in relation to pupil–teacher interactions, teacher actions such as allowing 'wait' time after asking a question and a general impression of pupils' activity and enjoyment. However, even if it is possible for the science subject leader or another teacher to observe in other teachers' classrooms, as may be feasible in a large primary school, at most one or two lessons can be observed and these are hardly likely to be entirely typical of all lessons. For the older primary classes, the pupils' written work provides an easily accessible source of evidence, as pointed out by Wright (2003) in Box 2.

Box 2 The evidence from children's work in science

'Looking through a collection of work also gives a good idea as to whether the pace of lessons is appropriate. A lot of unfinished work may indicate a mismatch between tasks and the pupils' interest and abilities, particularly for the lower attaining pupils. Are the children putting enough effort into it so that it reflects care and pride in their work? In some science activities, such as observing seeds, drawings are probably more important than words. Are drawings and diagrams large enough, neat enough and correctly labelled? Do they show what they are supposed to show?

… Without scrutinising work, it can be quite difficult to get an accurate idea of the balance of recording methods used across the school. There is nothing wrong with worksheets, but if every lesson is recorded on them, have the children enough opportunity to express their own thoughts and ideas fully? Sometimes older children record science as dictation, copying from the board or as a cloze procedure. Again, is there enough chance for the children to describe and explain their own developing science ideas? The scrutiny will provide a check that in each class children have the maximum opportunity to learn by using an increasingly wide range of appropriate recording techniques. These should reflect not only what they know and understand, but also how their science skills are developing. Is there clear evidence of investigative activities?'

Wright (2003, p9)

The national and international context

The third step of using the criteria involves considering the evidence, which may come from several sources, that relates to each standard, scanning across the evidence to see to what extent there is a match and where action is indicated. This procedure may seem rather rough and subjective, as indeed it is, but it is usually the case that in the areas where there is a gap between what we would like to be happening (as represented by the standard) and what *is* happening (evident in the information gathered) it is likely to be large and obvious. Evaluation in this context is not intended to produce judgements of the extent of success, but to make the classroom work more effective. The process of gathering information and sifting it systematically is likely to be of more value in bringing shortcomings to the attention and in suggesting ways of improvement than in deciding how 'good' particular lessons are.

Focused evaluations

It is not necessary for all aspects of classroom practice to be reviewed at one time. It may well be that there are some aspects where a teacher feels uncertain about how to improve things such as the response of lower-achieving pupils, or wants to investigate the reason for the differences in attitude to science of girls and boys, or has new ideas about involving pupils in self-assessment that she or he wants to test. In these cases the overall question is set out in more detail, indicating what should be the focus of gathering evidence. For example, in relation to lower-achieving children:

- What particular aspects of their engagement and performance are giving concern?
- Do these apply to all lower-achieving children?
- Are these children working effectively with others or are they working in isolation even though within mixed groups?
- Are their language skills inhibiting their expression of understanding?
- What activities appear to motivate and interest them?

And so on.

Teachers undertaking evaluation individually

Ideally teachers will have the help of the science subject leader in undertaking evaluation of their teaching. Both benefit from the process, which contributes to the review of science provision in the school. However, this is clearly time-consuming and depends upon the subject leader having the necessary time and skills. Without help, teachers will need to gather information during lessons, which can be reviewed later. Ways of doing this include making brief notes at the time, holding discussions with groups of children about their preferences and how they feel about certain activities, and sometimes tape-recording discussion among children during their group activities. At the stage of reviewing the evidence, however, every effort should be made to involve another teacher, particularly the subject leader, to give an alternative view and advise on change that may improve the quality of the children's learning experiences.

School self-evaluation

The general principles and steps involved in evaluating classroom practice apply also to evaluation provision and performance at the whole-school level. Box 3 suggests some standards as a starting point for agreeing statements of what schools see as important to aim for. They refer to the responsibilities of the school management.

Box 3   Standards for school provision for science

> **The school should:**
>
> - have a school policy for science that reflects the standards for classroom work (such as in Box 1) consistently across the school
> - regularly enable teachers to discuss the policy and update it as necessary
> - expect teachers to use the agreed standards in their lesson planning, teaching and self-evaluation
> - provide regular opportunity for teachers to plan and, where possible, to teach science lessons collaboratively
> - have effective procedures for the provision and maintenance of equipment and materials to support enquiry-based activities, and sources of information for children and teachers
> - keep records of individual children's progress in science based on annual or biannual summaries of teachers' records
> - use records of pupils' achievement and progress to review the progress of different groups
> - ensure that parents and carers are aware of the school science policy and of how they may be able to support their children's learning in science
> - enable teachers to upgrade their science teaching skills and knowledge through regular professional development.
>
> based on Harlen and Qualter (2009, p301)

The wide compass of the statements in Box 3 indicates that the range of information needed extends considerably beyond that required for classroom evaluation. Teachers are clearly a major source. Their plans and records need to be collected and reviewed systematically. In addition, their views on the adequacy of support, equipment, professional development, and so on, can be sought by questionnaire (in a large school), interview or focus group. Documents provide a second source of information; school programmes and procedures and national or regional curriculum standards and assessment requirements or guidelines have to be analysed and compared. Then there are the perceptions of pupils, parents and others, such as school governors or board members, local inspectors or advisers, all of which can be elicited by questionnaire or interview. Where time allows, semi-structured interviews held with a well-selected sample are of great benefit, providing opportunity to probe reasons for satisfaction or dissatisfaction and so suggesting action to be considered. The science subject leader has a key part in collecting these data and in evaluating how well the standards are met.

The national and international context

Analysing the performance of various groups of pupils enables schools to be aware, for example, of how the performance of boys and girls compares at different ages, how children in minority ethnic groups are making progress, how children with special needs are performing compared with special needs performance criteria, where the gap is greatest between high and low achievers. Schools in England have access to RAISEonline (see *Websites*). This resource provides reports based on end-of-key-stage data that enable comparison with schools nationally, and is:

> 'an online tool for use by schools, LAs, inspectors and school improvement partners. By providing a common set of analyses, it supports school improvement and the school inspection process. Schools are able to use a variety of methods to analyse their performance data as part of their self-evaluation process.'
>
> RAISEonline

Analyses are only as useful as the data analysed; so it is necessary to look beyond tests to identify aspects of pupils' performance that may indicate areas of strength and weakness in teaching. Wright (2006) suggests keeping and analysing records that enable questions such as these to be answered:

- How well are children applying their science knowledge and understanding to learning in new contexts?
- Do children use an increasing range of science terms correctly and with understanding?
- Do they conduct investigations in an increasingly well-organised and logical way and choose the most appropriate method of recording and displaying results, using increasingly precise measurements?
- How well do they make predictions based on their science knowledge and explain their findings in relation to their initial hypothesis?

In conclusion

Teachers and other school staff are in the best position to give an account of, and reasons for, what they do and are able to achieve. Giving this account requires the collection and analysis of a range of different kinds of information about teachers' and pupils' actions, interactions, learning materials and pupils' achievements and reactions. Both the collection and analysis of information depends on having a clear view of what standards are to be aimed for – that is, what is understood as good-quality provision and performance. The discussion of standards is in itself a key aspect of improvement through self-evaluation for, like pupils, teachers and schools need a shared idea of the goals of their work.

References

Estyn (2004) *Guidance on the Inspection of Primary and Nursery Schools.* Cardiff: Estyn.

Harlen, W. and Qualter, A. (2009) *The Teaching of Science in Primary Schools.* London: David Fulton.

HMIe (2007) *How Good is Our School? The Journey to Excellence*, part 3. Edinburgh: HMIe. Available online at: www.hmie.gov.uk/documents/publication/hgiosjte3.pdf

Ofsted (2009) *The Annual Report of Her Majesty's Chief Inspector of Education, Children's Services and Skills 2008/09.* London: HMSO.

TDA (2007) *Professional Standards for Teachers.* London: Training and Development Agency for Schools. Available online at: http://www.tda.gov.uk/upload/resources/pdf/t/tda0313%20-%20professional%20standards%20for%20teachers.pdf

Wright, L. (2003) Science under scrutiny. *Primary Science Review*, **79**, 8–10.

Wright, L. (2006) School self-evaluation of teaching and learning science. In Harlen, W. (ed) *ASE Guide to Primary Science Education* (second edition) pp73–79. Hatfield: Association for Science Education.

Websites

RAISEonline: www.teachernet.gov.uk/teachingandlearning/afl/raiseonline

Chapter 23

What are children achieving?

Wynne Harlen

This chapter is about the general picture of children's achievement in the UK rather than the performance of individual children. It is important for all of us – not just policy makers – to know about levels of achievement and whether and in what respects there are changes taking place. This general picture, which is necessarily built on the achievement of individual pupils, has relevance to teaching for it can prompt reflection on possible areas of strength and weakness. Thus the aim here is to draw out these implications by considering information about children's achievement from various sources.

The question addressed in the chapter title seems straightforward enough, but providing an answer is not straightforward. What we want children to achieve as a result of their science education is considerably more wide-ranging than the information most readily available about their achievement. The full range of goals includes skills, concepts, knowledge, attitudes of science such as curiosity and respect for evidence, attitudes towards science, understanding and enjoyment of scientific activity and desire to continue learning science. Yet the most common response to the question in the title is to quote scores in tests mostly concerned with knowledge of content and procedures. This is where we begin, with the national assessment in England, but we then consider other sources, including some from other countries, which help to fill out the picture.

The picture from national assessment in England

In England, the Government reports overall levels of achievement at the end of Key Stage 1 (age 7) and Key Stage 2 (age 11) in English, mathematics and science. National assessment data are reported to the public as the percentages of children reaching level 2 or above at the end of Key Stage 1 and of those reaching level 4 or above in the tests at the end of Key Stage 2. Even though the basis of the assessment data will change after the ending of national tests (known as SATs) in science at Key Stage 2, it is understood that levels will still be reported and targets set in science.

At Key Stage 1, although testing began in 1992, so many changes were made to the tests until they were abandoned in science that it is only teachers' assessment results that can usefully be used to identify trends in performance. These showed a steady rise each year from 84% reaching or exceeding level 2 in 1995 to 88% in 2000, followed by only small fluctuations up to 2008.

Similar patterns of change were found for Key Stage 2 – a steep rise from 1996 to 2000, with only small changes thereafter. 85% achieved level 4 or above in 2000 and this figure rose more slowly to 88% in 2007 and 2008. Science is the only subject where the Government's target of 85% has been reached. This target level, of course, reflects a judgement of what the expected standard ought to be. Although not entirely arbitrary, it is a value judgement, being based on what is found in the most favourable circumstances and is judged to be within the reach of all schools.

However, the accuracy of the results has been challenged on a number of counts. Schools have been under pressure to raise the level of national test scores because these have been used to evaluate the effectiveness of the school and to create league tables that are assumed to indicate how good is the education they provide compared with other schools. Failure to meet their targets for test score improvement has led to sanctions, schools being put under 'special measures' and even to closure. Not surprisingly, some schools saw matching teaching closely to what was tested as a route to ensuring that as many pupils as possible succeeded at level 4 in the test. This may not be the same as achieving level 4, which encompasses far more skills and abilities than were included in the tests. Thus narrowing the curriculum to what is tested was one of many adverse effects of tests widely recognised. Others included giving special attention to pupils just below the target level to the neglect of those well below or already above, and giving multiple practice tests, which is stressful to pupils and harmful to motivation for learning (Harlen and Deakin Crick, 2003).

Further, there is inherent inaccuracy in short tests that are taken by all pupils. A test can only sample the curriculum and a different sample would inevitably be found easier by some pupils and more difficult by others. Calculations based on the KS2 SATs indicate that this effect could result in at least a third of pupils being given the wrong level (Wiliam, 2001). This could be reduced by having a longer test, providing a larger sample of the possible questions, but the gain is not in proportion to the test length, which would need to be about 30 hours to reduce the misclassification to 10%. Moreover, to keep other errors, such as from marking, to a minimum, the sample of items in the tests favours those that are easily marked 'correct' or 'incorrect', tending to exclude items assessing problem-solving and higher-level skills. It was this lack of validity in relation to the aims of primary science that was accepted as a reason for ending tests in science after 2009. However, if all the arguments were taken into account, it would be hard to justify retaining testing in mathematics and English.

Alternative sources of information

The various sources of inaccuracy in SATs results mean that we cannot be sure that the levels of performance at Key Stage 2 have changed in the way the tests results suggest. A more valid picture would emerge from assessing the full range of skills and understanding of the science curriculum, which is possible by using teachers' assessment. The objection to doing this is based on the assumption of low reliability of teachers' judgements. Indeed, there *is* evidence of low reliability, but this is found where no attempt has been made to reduce it by providing training and procedures for moderation. When these are in place, teachers' judgements can be as reliable as test scores. Comparing results of SATs and teacher assessment in national testing has shown a close correspondence between the two (not surprising given the procedures imposed) but the teachers' judgements of pupils reaching the target levels were lower than indicated by the tests (Richards, 2005).

A different way of providing a more valid picture of national achievement is to use sample surveys such as those conducted by the Assessment of Performance Unit (APU) in England, Wales and Northern Ireland in the 1980s and recently by the Scottish Survey of Achievement (SSA). In such surveys, small but representative samples of the age group take different tests created from a large bank of items, resulting in the overall picture when combined. Each of the five annual surveys from 1980 to 1985 involved about 2.5% of the age group. Sampling of this kind, where only a small proportion of pupils are selected and each takes a small sample of items, means that the curriculum domain is covered more adequately than by a single test that is taken by all pupils. In the science surveys large banks of items were created for each of six main categories of science performance including three involving children using equipment and manipulating real objects. Moreover, since in any class few pupils are involved, and there will be many different tests, any 'teaching to the test' must be to the whole range of items and so becomes closer to 'teaching to the curriculum'.

The APU surveys were terminated when the government decided to use the national test results to monitor trends. However, in their brief existence the APU surveys provided rich information not just about whether overall attainment was changing, but about levels of performance in different aspects of the subjects, and of different sub-groups of pupils in relation to conditions of learning. Box 1 shows some examples from the results for age 11.

Box 1 Some results from APU science surveys of pupils aged 11 (1980–84)

There were high levels of performance in observing similarities and difference and using these to classify objects, in reading information from charts, graphs and tables and in setting about practical investigations in a relevant manner. There were lower levels for controlling variables in actual investigations, planning investigations and explaining how they arrived at predictions. Gender differences were particularly illuminating and informative for classroom practice. Difference for individual items related to content and form (girls being more willing to write extended answers) but were found at the main category level only for 'Applying science concepts' (boys higher) and 'Planning investigations' (girls higher). Boys were also rated at a higher level for willingness to undertake investigations.

The picture in Scotland

There is no central collection of individual pupil achievements in Scotland. To provide the overall picture of achievement, sample surveys are conducted by the Scottish Survey of Achievement (SSA) programme, focusing on a different subject area in a four-year cycle. The 2007 survey assessed science, science literacy and core skills. Science was assessed in 2003 by the Assessment of Achievement Programme, which preceded the SSA, and the results for items that were used in both surveys indicate no change in achievement between 2003 and 2007. Samples of pupils in P3 (aged 7–8), P5 (aged 9–10), P7 (aged 11–12) and S2 (aged 13–14) took part in the survey in 2007. Results were reported in terms of proportions of pupils reaching or exceeding expected levels of performance for their age group.

What are children achieving?

The assessment of scientific literacy was included for the first time and based on a small number of tasks and so the findings are tentative. The results showed a high proportion of P3 pupils reaching the expected level but less than half at P5 and under a third at P7 doing so. For science knowledge and understanding, the pattern was similar but the achievement at all levels was lower than for science literacy. At all ages, those pupils from deprived areas achieved at lower levels than those from less deprived areas. Gender differences changed from girls being ahead of boys at P3 to boys being ahead at P7, with no significant difference at P5.

In addition to the tests, some pupils were interviewed about awareness of scientific issues, by a visiting field worker. A further sub-group carried out a scientific investigation during class time and recorded what they had done and were later interviewed by a field worker who judged their work in relation to the expected level. A high proportion of P3 and P5 pupils reached the expected level and just over half of those at P7.

Both pupils and teachers involved in the survey completed questionnaires. The pupils' responses were revealing.

- High proportions rated themselves as being at the highest category of 'being good at science' but this self-assessment was in conflict with their actual level of performance. The proportions rating themselves above average in science fell from P3, to P5, to P7. Boys rated themselves more highly than girls and those from more deprived areas more highly than those from less deprived areas.
- High proportions of pupils at all stages wanted to do well in science and thought it would be useful to other subjects and for employment later.
- Interest in school science topics declined with age.
- Although children were aware of science topics in the news (boys more so than girls), it was reported that '*even for topical issues like diet and exercise, climate change and pollution, only around a third of pupils felt they were relevant to them personally*' (Scottish Government, 2008).

How do UK pupils compare with others?

Whether we are pleased with or dismayed by results expressed in terms of proportions reaching certain levels depends on what the 'expected levels' are. Had the levels expected at P3, P5 and P7 in Scotland, or at level 4 in the National Curriculum in England, been set higher or lower, then the results would have been interpreted differently. In other words, how we judge how well our pupils are doing depends on the standard (in the sense of a standard to aim for) that is set. One way of deciding whether this is a reasonable standard is to compare pupils' performance with that of children in other countries. This is one purpose of international surveys, which have been carried out at various intervals since 1964.

International studies are designed to describe overall achievement, using sample surveys, as in the case of the APU and the SSA. What is assessed by the bank of items is the same for all participating countries and so does not match the particular curriculum of each one. On account of the need for translation and the standardisation of procedures, there are many sources of inaccuracy in these studies and the results need to be treated with caution, especially those before 1990 (Whetton *et al.*, 2008). With this in mind, the main results can only be stated at a very general level. For science, prior to 1995, the only evidence placed England in the middle group of countries. But from 1995, performance of pupils in the age

The national and international context

group tested (Years 4 and 5) increased significantly, placing England in a group with only Singapore and Chinese Taipei scoring at a higher level. The evidence also indicated considerable progress for this age group from 1995 to 2003. The trend suggests some improvement in attainment since 1995, just as did the SATs results, and supports the general high level achieved by about the year 2000.

A finding of some importance from international studies concerns the spread of scores for English pupils compared with other countries. In language, mathematics and science the range of attainment from the lowest 5% to the highest 5% of pupils in England was among the very largest of all countries. The results show that the highest scoring pupils scored more highly than the highest scorers in any other country. Indeed the scores of the higher scoring 50% of pupils were above those of some other countries with a similar overall score. But the lowest 5% scored lower than many other countries including France, The Netherlands and Sweden. There is evidence from the PISA surveys (which assess only 15-year-olds) that the difference increases as pupils get older. In the 2006 PISA survey, the spread of 15-year-olds' scores for England was the largest among 29 OECD countries. The wide range in attainment was found in pre-1980 studies, but its persistence suggests that the introduction of the National Curriculum and SATs-based targets has done little to reduce it and may well have increased it (Box 2).

Box 2 Testing and the achievement gap

> The possibility that pressure of testing has widened the achievement gap receives some support from international comparisons in reading. For lower-attaining children, frequent testing equals frequent failure, inevitably reducing their liking for the subject. England had a high level of pupils with negative attitudes to reading, as did other countries, such as the United States, where testing was prevalent. In Sweden, with no external testing in the primary years, negative attitudes to reading were less common and there was a much smaller gap between the higher and lower-achieving children.

Beyond skills and knowledge

As noted at the start, the goals of science education extend beyond the development of knowledge and skills, to attitudes, interest and engagement in science-based activities. Indeed there is a view that all that is required of primary school science is to make science enjoyable and create the desire for further study in secondary and tertiary education. But we need not go as far as this to agree that the affective as well as cognitive outcomes need to be considered when we are looking at achievement.

It has been known for some time that pupils become less positive towards school science as they get older. This decline as pupils enter the secondary school is part of a general pattern for all subjects but for science it begins rather early. A survey of pupils in the UK in 2002 found that:

> 'most of the older pupils (10–11 years) had significantly less positive attitudes than the younger ones (8–9 years) towards science enjoyment even though the older pupils were more confident about their ability to do science.'
>
> Murphy and Beggs (2005, p46)

What are children achieving?

International studies show that enjoyment of science of 9–10-year-olds generally declined over the period 1995 to 2003, although the data collected in the PIPS project suggest no change from 1999 to 2007 in 11-year-old English pupils' attitudes to science. The picture is, therefore, rather confused partly because attitudes, enjoyment and interest are hard to define and measure and it is not always clear whether the focus is 'science' or 'school science'.

Contrary to what might be expected, there is only a weak relationship, if any, between attitudes to science and achievement in science. Tymms et al. (2008) reported no relationship but the most recent international study of science and mathematics, TIMSS 2007, shows that for 9–10-year-olds those with more positive attitudes to science had higher average achievement than those with less positive attitudes. However, any interpretation has to take into account that attitudes, measured by how much pupils like various activities and find them important, are clearly influenced by the experiences they have had (Chapter 1). The science curriculum in England has been criticised for constraining children's experience of investigative science (Murphy and Beggs, 2003) and it may well be that the image of science given to many children is that it is a body of facts.

Implications

The picture of children's achievement emerging from the various sources considered is somewhat blurred. Some findings recur while others arise from the particular design of a survey, as in the case of the SSA where the involvement of several age groups enables changes with age to be reported. However, the results across all sources are likely to be widely relevant and suggest areas for reflection on current classroom practice. In particular, they suggest giving some attention to the following.

The decline in interest in science across the primary years

Although measured performance in science appears high in England, is the price to be paid for more children reaching the target level, the fact that more children dislike science? Children's interests become wider and more diverse as they get older, so it is not easy to interest all of them all the time, but the methods of teaching can make a difference. A Europe-wide report (the Rocard report) on a range of initiatives in science teaching at the primary level concluded that:

> 'A reversal of school science teaching pedagogy from mainly deductive to enquiry-based methods provides the means to increase interest in science.'
>
> European Commission (2007, p2)

The better performance of younger than older pupils

Is it likely that this, too, is linked to teaching methods. Active exploration and enquiry is characteristic of teaching in early years. There is a good deal of evidence and theoretical argument that this leads to better understanding (Box 3).

Box 3   Findings from the Rocard report

> 'Using enquiry-based methods has been shown to have a positive impact on students' attainments, with an even stronger impact on students with lower levels of self-confidence and those from disadvantaged backgrounds. This allows

The national and international context

> *science education to be inclusive, which is of utmost importance in a knowledge society where being scientifically illiterate is of such a high cost for both the individual and the society in general.'*
>
> European Commission (2007, p12)

The wide gap in achievement between higher and lower-achieving pupils

Teachers can help to reduce this through the practice of Assessment for Learning (AfL). It has been shown that AfL *'helps the (so-called) low attainers more than the rest and so reduces the spread of attainment while also raising it overall'* (Black and Wiliam, 1998). Other chapters in this book deal with the practice of some key aspects of using assessment to help learning but it is relevant to point out here the close relationship with learning through enquiry:

> *'Both serve to develop learning with understanding and to enable pupils to take responsibility for identifying what they need to do to achieve the goals of their activities.'*
>
> Harlen and Qualter (2009, p179)

Linking current science topics to the children's lives

Lack of relevance has been a common criticism of science since the introduction of the National Curriculum. In this respect, the proposal for organising the curriculum in themes and teaching through cross-curricular topics offers an opportunity for science to be seen as linked to everyday life. However, there is concern that cross-curricular topics may mean a return to the pre-National Curriculum topic-based teaching in which science had only a token presence. Thus the position of discrete subjects in the primary curriculum remains a disputed area (Alexander, 2009). There is no lack of contemporary issues – such as pollution, obesity, the need to recycle materials and so on – that are linked to the children's own experience and lives. Thus there is no need to force artificial links between subjects but rather to start from topics where there is a clear core of science understanding that can be developed through enquiry.

The view of science that is conveyed in the classroom

What pupils experience as 'science' in the classroom is central to the attitudes they develop. Attitudes show in people's behaviour; they are 'caught' rather than 'taught' (Harlen, 2006, p25–128). So it is as important for a teacher to show an example of scientific behaviour as it is for pupils to have opportunity for enquiry-based activities. What this means in practice is, for instance, teachers:

- sharing the interest and curiosity about new observations
- providing evidence for their statements and not expecting pupils to accept reasons without evidence
- being prepared to say they do not know an answer to a question and suggesting how to find it out
- discussing different ideas that could explain something
- talking about how ideas change when there is new evidence
- using different sources including books and the internet to find information to help understanding.

In conclusion

As noted in the introduction to this chapter, information about what children are achieving at the national level is useful for everyone from school level to government department in order to identify areas of strength and those needing attention. Information is only useful for this purpose if it is sufficiently detailed and extensive to guide decisions about the whole range of goals of science education. Overall subject levels, based on testing individual pupils, give only limited and uncertain information about attainment and trends over time and are misused for evaluating the effectiveness of schools. More useful, valid and reliable information is produced by regular sample surveys, where large numbers of items can be used while only a sample of pupils need to be tested. However, these need to be supplemented by moderated teachers' assessment of children's enquiry skills, understanding of scientific activity, and their interests in and affective responses to science. This information will provide the basis for evidence-based policy in education not only at the national level, but also at the school level.

References

Alexander, R.J. (2009) *Towards a new Primary Curriculum: a Report from the Cambridge Primary Review. Part 2: The Future.* Cambridge: University of Cambridge Faculty of Education. Available online at:
www.primaryreview.org.uk/Downloads/Curriculum_report/CPR_Curric_rep_Pt2_Future.pdf

Black, P. and Wiliam, D. (1998) *Inside the Black Box.* London: School of Education, King's College London. Available online at:
www.collegenet.co.uk/admin/download/inside%20the%20black%20box_23_doc.pdf

European Commission (2007) *Science Education Now: a Renewed Pedagogy for the Future of Europe* (Rocard report). Brussels: Directorate General for Research, Science, Economy and Society. Available online at: http://ec.europa.eu/research/science-society/document_library/pdf_06/report-rocard-on-science-education_en.pdf

Harlen, W. (2006) *Teaching, Learning and Assessing Science 5–12* (fourth edition). London: Sage.

Harlen, W. and Deakin Crick, R. (2003) Testing and motivation for learning. *Assessment in Education,* **10**(2), 169–207.

Harlen, W. and Qualter, A. (2009) *The Teaching of Science in Primary Schools* (fifth edition). London: David Fulton.

Murphy, C. and Beggs, J. (2003) Children's perceptions of school science. *School Science Review,* **84**(308). 109–116.

Murphy, C. and Beggs, J. (2005) *Primary Science in the UK: a Scoping Study. Final Report to the Wellcome Trust.* Belfast: Queen's University Belfast School of Education and St. Mary's University College. Available online at:
www.wellcome.ac.uk/stellent/groups/corporatesite/@msh_peda/documents/web_document/wtx026636.pdf

Richards, C. (2005) *Standards in English Primary Schools: Are They Rising?* London: ATL.

Scottish Government (2008) *2007 Scottish Survey of Achievement (SSA) Science, Science Literacy and Core Skills.* Available online at:
www.scotland.gov.uk/Publications/2008/06/05104931/1

The national and international context

Tymms, P., Bolden, D. and Merrell, C. (2008) Science in English primary schools: trends in attainment, attitudes and approaches. *Perspectives on Education* 1 (Primary Science) 19–42. www.wellcome.ac.uk/perspectives

Whetton, C., Ruddock, G. and Twist, L. (2008) *Standards in English Primary Education: the International Evidence* (Primary Review Research Survey 4/2). Cambridge: University of Cambridge Faculty of Education. Available online at: www.primaryreview.org.uk/Downloads/Int_Reps/2.Standards_quality_assessment/Primary_Review_WhettonRuddockTwist_4-2_briefing_Standards_-_International_evidence_071102.pdf

Wiliam, D. (2001) Reliability, validity and all that jazz. *Education* 3–13, **29**(3), 17–21.

Chapter 24

What happens in other countries?

Wynne Harlen and Tina Jarvis

In countries as far apart as Chile and China, Argentina and Australia, Iran and India, Senegal and Sweden, science at the primary level has been a priority area for funding and development in the 2000s. Many are countries that are still in the process of economic development, yet despite limited resources – both human and financial – they consider early science education as a worthwhile investment. Such is the important role that science education is seen to have, not only for the scientific and technological development that is essential in the context of globalisation, but also for supporting democracy, quality of life, and an equitable society.

This chapter is concerned with the teaching programmes and approaches in other countries, rather than the aspirations and goals set out in formal curriculum documents and syllabi. It begins by noting some common features of primary science programmes developed in the twenty-first century, followed by some examples of how these features appear in practice in three countries. International cooperation is increasingly being promoted and we describe a particular example of this in Europe: the Pollen Project. Finally, we draw out from what others do some points for reflection on our practices in the UK.

Some common features of primary science initiatives outside the UK

A key feature of developments in science education in a high proportion of countries outside the UK is the involvement of practising scientists, usually through the participation of the country's academy of science. In many cases members of the academy of science have taken the initiative to introduce or to reform science education, usually beginning with the primary school. Involvement of scientists at the academy level means that the reforms have status with potential funding bodies, potential support in universities, and persuasive power when it comes to negotiating with ministries of education.

The national and international context

Some other features shared by many programmes in other countries are:

- determination to change from textbook-based to enquiry-based teaching
- the dual aims of scientific literacy and the development of literacy through science
- building on good practice in other countries
- provision of all materials for teachers, including equipment
- provision of help in the classroom from experienced teachers
- use of the internet for information, ideas and advice
- evaluation of trials and a controlled spread of new practice through professional development
- community involvement
- collaboration with the ministry and district education authorities, to ensure embedding in the system.

What these features mean in practice is best seen through examples. Not all appear in every programme, but many do in the programmes in Chile, France and Australia, which we now briefly describe.

Introducing enquiry-based primary science in Chile

The development of an enquiry-based programme in Chile was an initiative of the Chilean Academy of Sciences. The Academy negotiated the support of the National Sciences Resources Centre in the USA, which had developed an enquiry-based programme known as Science and Technology for Children (STC). A trial of some of the STC units was carried out involving 1000 children in a district of Chile of particularly high deprivation. This was extended to more low socio-economic districts with support of the Ministry of Education. In 2005, the positive results of a pilot evaluation led to it being adopted as a national programme, known by the acronym ECBI.

The ECBI programme comprises a series of units, initially translated from STC units, but later supplemented by home-grown units as local expertise was developed. The units provide structured experiences for children, requiring them to think about a problem, raise questions, share ideas, make observations using equipment, record results and consider how these compare with predictions. There is an emphasis on using notebooks for recording and reflection. At the end of each unit, parents and other members of the community are invited to a presentation of their work by the children. In this way the aims of ECBI become known to parents and community involvement in the work of the school is encouraged.

All equipment and materials for a unit are provided in a kit, which is returned to the local resources centre at the end of the unit, refurbished and sent to another school. Though requiring considerable organisation, the provision of equipment is strongly defended on the grounds that it is unrealistic, even in the absence of economic restrictions, to expect teachers to collect resources needed for lessons. This view is not unique to developing countries, for this is also the practice in Sweden, where teachers are in a much more favourable position to collect resources than those in Chile.

What happens in other countries?

A further feature of the Chilean programme is the provision of help for teachers by the attachment to the school of an experienced teacher, trained in the programme, to work with the teachers in planning and reviewing lessons and in the classroom during science lessons. This form of professional development is in addition to workshops of 40 hours provided by university staff for teachers and school principals starting out in the programme. There are also follow-up workshops for teachers who have been in the programme for two to four years. This intensity of professional development is justified by the great changes in pedagogy that were required. It is, of course, expensive and there is a question over how to sustain it, and particularly the provision of in-school support, as the programme expands to schools across the country. One of the main challenges for reform in science education in Chile, shared by other countries of Latin America, is the shortage of university staff to provide continued professional development.

Using the internet in France

The French programme, *La main à la pâte*, founded and developed by the French Academy of Sciences, has had a particular influence on innovations in countries outside Europe as well as in Europe (see below). It began in 1996 with trials supported by the Ministry of National Education and in 2000 was embodied in a national plan to foster science and technology teaching in schools. It was thus well established and in a good position to provide advice and support to other countries when they began to design reforms in the 2000s. This support, formalised by memoranda of understanding and international agreements, is provided to Argentina, Belgium, Brazil, Cambodia, Cameroon, Chile, China, Colombia, Egypt, Germany, Morocco, Senegal, Serbia, Slovakia and Vietnam. Links with other countries including Iran, Afghanistan and Mexico are in the process of being created.

La main à la pâte (Lamap) is based on ten principles, summarised in Box 1, and it uses the internet to make resources freely available to teachers (see *Websites*). Over 300 units covering all topics and years of the primary school are accessible in this way and the website also provides a service for answering teachers' questions and for information about useful resources. Many of the countries making use of Lamap resources have set up websites based on the Lamap site – for example, the Latin American website *Indágala*.

Box 1   The ten principles underpinning the Lamap project developed in France

---

The ten principles of *La main à la pâte* were established by the French Academy of Sciences and approved by the Ministry of National Education in 1998.

Teaching

1 Children observe an object or a phenomenon in the real, perceptible world around them and investigate it.
2 During their investigations, pupils debate and reason, pooling and discussing their ideas and results, and building their knowledge, since physical activity alone is insufficient.
3 The activities suggested by the teacher are organised in sequence of learning stages, drawing on schemes of work and leaving pupils a large measure of autonomy.

> 4 A minimum schedule of two hours per week is devoted to a particular theme for several weeks. Continuity of activities and teaching methods is ensured throughout the entire period of schooling.
> 5 Each child keeps a notebook, to record their experiences in their own words.
> 6 The prime objective is the gradual acquisition by pupils of scientific concepts and enquiry skills accompanied by consolidation of written and oral expression.
>
> **Partnership**
> 7 Members of families and the community are invited to support work in class.
> 8 At the local level, scientific partners (universities, etc.) support classwork by making their science skills and knowledge available to teachers.
> 9 Local institutions for teacher training also give teachers the benefit of their experience in teaching methods.
> 10 Through the internet site teachers are able to obtain teaching modules, ideas for activities and answers to queries. They can also use the internet to communicate with colleagues, trainers and scientists.

Emphasis on literacy in Australia

The development of literacy through science activities, in addition to the development of scientific literacy, is an explicit aim of several programmes. A good example is the Australian programme *Primary Connections* (see *Websites*). Initiated by the Australian Academy of Science and developed in partnership with the Australian Government, it is designed to link the teaching of science with the teaching of literacy:

> *'Primary Connections supports teachers to improve students' scientific literacy, as well as their learning outcomes in both science and literacy. Linking science with literacy enriches the learning experience for students.'*

The programme provides an integrated approach built into units supported by online resources. The units are based on:

> *'... the theory that students learn best when they are allowed to work out explanations for themselves over time through a variety of learning experiences structured by the teacher. Students use their prior knowledge to make sense of these experiences and then make connections between new information and their prior knowledge.'*

The units are structured by a 5Es model of teaching and learning: Engage, Explore, Explain, Elaborate and Evaluate (Primary Connections, 2008).

International cooperation

Building on development in other countries has been a feature of most of the more innovative and successful recent developments. In many cases, this began with less-developed countries benefiting from years of development, research and the expertise built up in more developed countries. So Egypt has benefited from experience in Japan, China from professional development conducted in Canada, Mexico from materials developed in the USA. As more countries have begun to implement enquiry-based approaches, the emphasis has changed to regional cooperation, where countries with similar histories and challenges are helping each other. Latin America is a good example of this, with experience being shared in workshops for teams from Chile, Colombia, Argentina, Brazil, Bolivia, Peru and Venezuela. South East Asia is another region where materials and training are exchanged.

Collaboration in Europe

International collaboration in developing methods and resources in primary science is actively encouraged by the European Commission. A three-year project that was completed in 2009 brought together science educators from 12 European countries: Belgium, England, Estonia, France, Germany, Hungary, Italy, The Netherlands, Portugal, Slovenia, Spain and Sweden. Set in motion by the French Academy of Sciences, the Pollen Project was described as:

> '... a network, not only on a community level, but also at European level, bringing science closer to society through schooling.'
>
> Pollen (2006)

The challenge for developing close collaboration among so many countries is that they did not start with the same curriculum or teaching approach. For example, at the beginning of the Pollen Project, France, England, Sweden and Slovenia had very directed centrally defined science curricula. In other countries there was a lighter touch where national guidelines for science were mediated by states, local authorities or school management. For example, in Italy, while there were national guidelines, the school decided its own syllabus and curriculum under the guidance of a school governors' committee of which the president had to be a parent. In a few countries, there was little central control, as in the case of Hungary where this considerable freedom was said to be a reaction to the previous centralised control of the communist era. There were also national variations with regard to the content of the science curricula. Biology was the most common science subject taught. However, in the case of some countries, such as Belgium, this was often at the level of vocabulary, such as naming of parts, whereas others set out to teach complex concepts such as photosynthesis. Most countries included physics but little chemistry.

In order to work collaboratively with other countries, it is important to take account of the fact that all curricula change over time and in different ways. Yet while it recognised the different starting points of each country, the Pollen Project aimed to develop an agreed common approach, which could be customised to fit each country's unique situation. The common approach was to develop hands-on Inquiry-Based Science Education (IBSE), which combines: '*global research, scientific learning, experimentation and evidence-based reasoning, language and debating skills*' (Pollen Science Education Charter, see *Websites*). Teacher education was the key focus and the project provided many hours of professional development for teachers in the participant cities led by a local trainer. Leicester was the city in the case of England. The Pollen Project additionally set out to provide meaningful contexts for IBSE by making links with the local community where parents, scientists and industrialists could be involved. A local coordinator for community involvement was identified in each city. To give consistency, online advice and materials were developed and

The national and international context

shared by coordinators from all the countries. All trainers and coordinators met once a year and also had at least one visit to another country.

Once the basic model was agreed, it was expanded and individualised by each country. Teachers in the project were given training lasting 20–40 hours and mentors visited them in their schools. Some countries developed kits similar to the Chilean ones with all the equipment needed for a class to carry out the activities. The kit approach, already developed in Sweden, was taken up by Germany, Slovenia and Estonia. The boxes proved to be an excellent support for inexperienced teachers in countries where there had been little science taught in their primary schools previously. They were less successful with experienced and able teachers who wanted more creative freedom.

The range of science ideas covered during the in-service varied quite considerably between the different countries. Italy and Portugal, for example, had very focused topics. The Italian teachers had one main unit with a particular focus on environmental issues. There were two main topics in Portugal based on the kitchen as a laboratory, and vegetable gardens, with parents and grandparents often involved in activities. In contrast, the English and French in-service covered most aspects of their country's primary school curriculum.

While most of the collaboration was between each country's trainers and coordinators, individual teachers and pupils had the opportunity to share practice. For example, there was a weblink between a primary school in Leicester with the Pollen Science Centre in Portugal to share science activities. The English pupils showed the results of their experiments into conditions necessary to grow yeast while the Portuguese demonstrated their investigation on what would happen if you put chestnuts in a microwave with and without cuts.

The in-service programme did increase teachers' confidence to teach science in most countries and attitudes to specific Pollen objectives showed significant improvements.

> 'The methods used by Pollen have proven to raise primary teachers' interest, self-confidence and skills in science teaching and therefore the quality and quantity of science teaching sessions. Pollen also increases children's interest in science learning activities.'
>
> European Commission (2007)

However, the amount of change varied in the different countries. It was clear that change takes many years. Inexperienced 'new' teachers and those with initial low science knowledge require two or more years to develop their science knowledge and IBSE skills. Once this is achieved, able experienced teachers need to be challenged as a way of keeping up their enthusiasm for science (and thus that of their pupils) by using strategies such as making greater use of the environment, involving the local community and links with other curricular subjects. Greater change was also seen where there was a wide range of topics, as this allowed new skills to be practised in many situations. Related to this was that greater success was seen where activities matched national and local needs as teachers were more likely to be able to apply their new skills and be supported by the school management to do so.

This project generally managed to provide an opportunity for countries in Europe to share expertise and experience to develop a pedagogical approach without stifling local needs and interests, alongside providing a wealth of examples to share. However, this collaboration is still in its infancy. Time is needed for teachers to establish practice in IBSE and for experiences to be disseminated beyond the project schools. Educationalists also need more time to understand more about each country's similarities and differences so that they can share more effectively.

So what can we learn from other countries?

One of the awkward questions asked by colleagues in other countries is about 'the enquiry-based programme in the UK'. Even if the question referred only to England, it would still be impossible to answer. To say there isn't such a thing would be to deny that there is an enquiry approach to primary science, yet the difficulty of answering draws attention to the similarities and differences between approaches within and outside the UK.

As implied in the brief accounts of programmes above, we share across country boundaries many of the goals of enquiry-based science education and the ways of putting it into practice, including taking account of children's initial ideas and using assessment for learning, even if not expressed in these terms. Practice in the UK is so varied, however, that it is not possible to make generalisations about what is and is not part of existing practice. Rather, what we can do is highlight points that may help in reflection on our particular approaches. Six points seem to stand out.

The involvement of the science community

The academies of science have played a key role in many countries' reform of science education. This has been not merely in promoting science in order to increase the body of scientists and technologists, but also in recognition of the importance of ensuring science education for all. Nobel laureates have been prominent in several cases, using their intellectual weight to inspire others and to persuade politicians. In the UK the science professional bodies, including the Royal Society, tend to be more reactive to government initiatives, as well as taking the initiative themselves in relation to primary school science.

The involvement of the local community

Those countries that have had to make large changes in a short time have recognised the potential danger of leaving behind the parents and members of the local community, who may then resist rather than support new goals. The value of involving parents, local industry, agriculture, and service providers is two-way. Children learn about their environment and the relevance to it of what they are learning in science, and the local community understands what the school is trying to do through its science programme.

Cooperation with institutions and policy makers

Developments in teaching methods and ideas for activities often originate in the activities of groups of educators and/or researchers. Sometimes they are supported by funding from trusts or foundations or by a professional association such as the ASE. After publication, dissemination is often dependent on the initiative of publishers. Widespread change, however, requires cooperation between teacher education institutions, science learning centres, inspectors' organisations, local authority personnel and, depending on the extent of central control, the national government. For instance, in the highly centralised system in France, Lamap could only spread when it evolved into a national programme. Although adoption in this way may not be desirable, it is important for the best practice to be reflected in teacher education, inspectors' criteria and government documents. This requires cooperation with these institutions from an early stage and the collection of convincing evidence of the value of reforms.

The provision of teaching sequences, materials and equipment

Teachers with little background knowledge of science, and/or lack of confidence in teaching it, welcome the idea of teachers' guides that tell them exactly what to do. In the short term, it ensures activities for children that they otherwise may not have, but in the long term it restricts their opportunities for exploring their own ideas, which may emanate from their experiences. Some structure to the lesson is necessary, however, otherwise some key aspect, such as time to reflect at the end of an activity on what has been learned, may be overlooked. Thus a loose structure, such as the 5Es of Primary Connections, or the three-part lesson, can be useful as long as it is applied appropriately. Following any pattern or procedure slavishly without understanding why inevitably leads to a dull routine.

The provision of a set of equipment specific to a particular unit of work can have the same restricting effect, although it ensures suitable materials are used. The sustainability of the organisation needed to service equipment kits outside the school must be questioned. A compromise between providing everything or nothing needs to be found, such as schools having a basic set of equipment to which everyday materials that can be added within the school. How feasible this is depends on the help that is available at the classroom level.

The provision of classroom support

It takes a great amount of time and effort to prepare for and conduct a lesson involving first-hand investigation and physical movement of children in the classroom. The help that a classroom assistant (or parent) can provide, as an extra pair of hands, is fine when the teacher is confident and well trained, but help of a different kind is needed by the less confident teacher. In Chile this is provided by external peripatetic advisers, acting in a similar way to the teams of local advisory teachers that were effective in raising standards of practice in England in the 1980s – before they fell victim to changes in the role of local authorities. The idea of each school having a science coordinator is only a suitable substitute if this role is associated with non-teaching time to work with other teachers.

The value of talking and writing

The importance of talking and writing to learning (Chapter 10) is widely recognised and built into many science programmes. Many also emphasise the value of writing to aid reflection and the use of personal notebooks. To be effective this needs to be more than completing worksheets, but enable children to work out their ideas in words and drawings without fear of giving 'a wrong answer'. Such notebooks are not 'marked' but constitute a form of dialogue between teacher and pupils.

In conclusion

Science has been introduced or reformed in the primary school of many countries across the globe in the past decade. The approaches developed, often through collaboration among countries and the initiative of scientists who are members of academies of science, share the aim of changing teaching from traditional to enquiry-based practices. At the same time, projects vary in various respects such as the extent to which they provide detailed guidance for teachers and kits of equipment for schools. Primary science practice in the UK can only benefit from closer international collaboration, opening up alternatives and showing how to support teachers and schools in different contexts.

What happens in other countries?

References

European Commission (2007) *Science Education Now: A Renewed Pedagogy for the Future of Europe* (Rocard report). Brussels: Directorate General for Research, Science, Economy and Society. Available online at: http://ec.europa.eu/research/science-society/document_library/pdf_06/report-rocard-on-science-education_en.pdf

Pollen: Seed cities for science (2006) Information booklet. Available online at: www.pollen-europa.net/?page=y%2BtfLHIZSts%3D

Primary Connections (2008) 5Es model of teaching and learning. Available online at: www.science.org.au/primaryconnections/teaching-and-learning/images/5Es.pdf

Websites

Indágala: www.indagala.org (enter URL into Google Translate (http://translate.google.co.uk/#) for English version)

La main à la pâte: http://lamap.inrp.fr/index.php?Page_Id=1179

Pollen Project: www.pollen-europa.net

Primary Connections: www.science.org.au/primaryconnections

Index

absolutist thinking 21
achievement 186, 193
    alternative sources of information 187–8
    beyond skills and knowledge 190–1
    comparing UK pupils with others 189–90
    implications 191
        better performance of younger than older pupils 191–2
        decline in science interest 191
        gap in achievement 192
        linking current topics to children's lives 192
        view of science conveyed in classroom 192
    national assessment in England 186–7
    national assessment in Scotland 188–9
adolescence, brain development 37
affective domain 94
analogies, use of to aid learning 14
analysis 29
argumentation 21–2
assessing pupil learning 119
    UK practice 119–20
Assessing Pupils' Progress (APP) project 120–1, 124
    map 121–2
    strengthening reliability 123–4
    supporting both formative and summative assessment 122–3
assessment 51
assessment, formative 14, 85, 92
    Assessment for Learning 85–6
        principles 86
        reviewing progress 91–2
        using 86–7
assessment, pupil peer 90–1
assessment, self- 91
Assessment of Achievement Programme 188
Assessment of Performance Unit (APU) 188
Association for Science Education (ASE) 147
asynchronous communication 14
attention deficit hyperactivity disorder (ADHD) 39
attitude development 5–6
    Early Years 30
axons 35

behaviourist view on child learning 11
benefits to society of science education 3
big ideas in science 4–5
brain
    activity and learning 37
    development 36–7
    emotions 38–9
    language 38
    memory 37–8
    structure 34–6

Cambridge Primary Review 2
Chartered Science Teacher (CSciTeach) 147
Chartered Scientist (CSci) 147
childhood, brain development 36
Children Challenging Industry (CCI) programme 159
classroom management 48–9
climate change 116
communication skills 29, 49–50
Communications Manager role 159
concept cartoons 80–1
concept development 39–40
conceptual understanding 19
    progression in 19–20
concrete–symbolic devices 22
context of learning 13
continuing professional development (CPD) 141, 148
    forms 142
    funding 147
    impact 142–3
    maximising impact 144
        collaboration 146
        continuity 146
        embedding 146
        relevance 144–5
        sustainability 145
    necessity 141–2
    opportunities 143
        Science Learning Centres (SLCs) 144
    structure, value and accreditation 147
coordination of subjective with objective elements 21
creativity in teaching 102–3, 109
    definition 103–4
    examples 106–8
        creative communication 109
        cross-curricular links 108
        lesson endings 109
        real-world problems 108
        urban myths 108
    importance 104–5
    methods 105
CREST Award 108
Criminal Records Bureau (CRB) check 160

Index

critical thinking 48
cross-curricular contributions to science
    progression 18, 53, 60
        benefits 54
        science and language 54–5
        science and mathematics 55–6
        topic or topic web 56
        topic, integrated 57
        topic, personalised 57–8
        definition 53–4
        professional dialogue 59
cross-curricular links 108
cross-sectional data 20
Curriculum for Excellence 119–20, 127–8, 172, 173
curriculum for science, planning
    long-term 126–9
    medium-term 129–30

data gathering 47
dendrites 35
dialogue, promoting understanding through 77, 84
    contentious topics 83–4
    development 79
        big fat questions 81–2
        creating environment 79
        paired discussions 81
        puppets 83
        using concept cartoons 80–1
        using 'wow' events 79–80
    purpose 77–8
differentiation 50
Discovery Dog 151
discussion in class 13–14, 49
Discussions in Primary Science 158
distributing subject expertise 138

Early Years 25, 33
    approaches 31–2
    contributions to science progression 18
    issues 32–3
    supported experiential learning 25–6
        early attitudes 30
        early skills 26–9
        early understandings 29–30
        language development 30
Eco Schools 145
education versus entertainment debate 95–6
emotional engagement with science 94, 101
    education versus entertainment debate 95–6

    importance in education 96–7
    increasing interest 97–100
    neglect of affective domain 94
emotions 38–9
energy saving 117
England
    curriculum 166–7
        level descriptions 167
        review of primary curriculum 168–9
    national assessment 186–7
Enquiring Minds 58
enquiry skills 5, 15
environment, serving 115
    climate change 116
    energy saving 117
    waste and decay 116–17
environment, using 111, 117
    Earth in space 114–15
    exploring habitats 114
    helping children develop ideas 112
    investigating life and living things 112–14
        essential equipment 113
    reason for 111–12
Environmental studies 172
ESA Kids 61
evaluativist stage of learning 21
evidence-based thinking 5
exemplification 47
exploration 47
exploration and enquiry 15
exploring skills 26

feedback 87–8
    communicating success criteria 89–90
    goals and success criteria 88
    nature of 88–9
formative assessment *see* assessment, formative
fun aspect of education 4

governors, school 161–2
graphs, charts and tables preparation 27
Guskey's five levels of CPD impact 143

Higher Level Teaching Assistant (HLTA) 157–8
home activities supporting classroom learning 51
'hooks' to increase interest in science 97–100
human resources 157, 164
    older science/engineering students 162–3
    school governors, parents and other adults 161–2

Index

scientists, technicians and engineers 159–61
teaching assistants 157–8
hypothesis development 5, 13–14
hypothesis formation 27

ICT 61, 67
  supporting pupil learning 64
    case studies 65–6
    examples 66–7
  teachers as users
    accessing information 62
    best use of information 63
    communicating with others 63
    expanding teachers' knowledge and skills 63–4
    modelling effect use 62
    preparing teaching 63
  teacher's role 61–2
ideas and evidence in science 19, 20–1
importance of science education 2, 8
  experiences for science learning 7
  obstacles to science learning 7–8
  primary school starting point 4
    developing attitudes 5–6
    developing enquiry skills 5
    developing scientific ideas 4–5
    learning how to learn 6–7
  value of science knowledge 2–3
increasing interest in science 97–100
intelligence, social 48
interactive displays 151
interactive whiteboard (IWB) 64
international experiences 195, 202
  common features of initiatives outside the UK 195–6
  emphasis on literacy in Australia 198
  enquiry-based science in Chile 196–7
  European collaboration 199–200
  international collaboration 198–9
  internet use in France 197–8
  lessons to be learnt 201
    cooperation with institutions and policy makers 201
    local community involvement 201
    provision of classroom support 202
    provision of teaching sequences, materials and equipment 202
    science community involvement 201
    value of talking and writing 202
interpreting skills 29
investigation 47

joint learning 12

Key Stages 166
  Key Stage 1 (KS1) 186–7
  Key Stage 2 (KS2) 186, 187

Lamap project 197–8
language 38
language development 30
Learning and teaching Scotland 172–3
learning how to learn 6–7
learning in children 10, 15
  helpful experiences 12
    analogies 14
    assessment, formative 14
    context 13
    discussion 13–14
    encouraging questions 13
  ideas about 11–12
  implications for teaching 14–15
  teachers' need to understand 10–11
Learning in Depth Project 58
Leonardo Effect 58
life-long learning skills 3, 17–18
Local Authority Primary Science advisors 147

Masters Qualification in Teaching and Learning 147
measuring 27
meetings to smooth transfer between primary to secondary school 154
memory 37–8
metacognition 21
mixed ability group learning 12
motivation 48
motivational attitudes 30

National Assessment Resource 120
National Curriculum, dissatisfaction with 168
National Science Learning Centre 158
neuron structure 35
neuroscience and learning 34, 41
  brain 34–6
    activity and learning 37
    changes over lifetime 36–7
  emotions 38–9
  health and wellbeing 39
  implications for primary school science 40–1
  language 38
  memory 37–8
  physical action and concept development 39–40

Index

Northern Ireland
   curriculum 138, 169
      The world around us 169–71

observation 26, 28–9, 47
obstacles to science learning 7–8
Ofsted 179
open and closed questions 71
open days 154
Open Learn 63
oracy 18
outcomes of science education 3, 46–7

pace of lessons 49
parents 161–2
pedagogical factors in science education 150
personal capabilities 48
picture and diagram drawing 28
planning effectively 44, 51
   creativity 45–6
   key elements 46
      activities 47
      adult support 50–1
      assessment 51
      classroom management 48–9
      differentiation 50
      discussions 49
      effective questions 47
      home activities 51
      learning outcomes 46–7
      pace and timing 49
      personal capabilities 48
      recording and communication 49–50
      starting points 47
      vocabulary 48
   levels 44
      long-term 44–5
      medium-term 45
      short-term 45
planning posters 82
planning skills 27
planning, school-level see school-level planning
Pollen Project 195, 199–200
positive self-image 48
practical/behavioural attitudes 30
prediction 27
Primary Science Enhancement Programme (PSEP) 159
Primary Science Quality Mark 139, 145
'Primary Upd8' 55
procedural understanding 19, 21–4
progression in science learning 17, 24
   conceptual understanding 19–20
   cross-curricular and Early Years contributions 18
   ideas and evidence 20–1
   life-long learning 17–18
   procedural understanding 21–4
   science-specific 19
pupil passports 155
pupils' experiences of learning science 7
puppets 83, 151

quality of science teaching 178, 184
   evaluating classroom practice 179–82
      evidence of children's work 181
      focused evaluations 182
      individual teacher evaluation 182
      methods of collecting evidence 181
      standards 180
   evaluating provision 178–9
   purposes of evaluation 179
   school self-evaluation 183–4
      standards 183
question-generating spinners 74
questioning 26
questions, effective 69, 75
   children's questions 73–5
   dealing with difficult children's questions 75
   teachers' questions 69–70
      based upon childrens' ideas 72
      developing children's ideas 70–1
      open and closed questions 71
      promoting collaboration and encouragement 70
      setting classroom climate 73
questions in class, encouraging 13

real-world problems 108
recording skills 27–8, 49–50
reflective attitudes 30
report writing 27
research 47
Resources Manager role 159
Rocard report 191–2

SATs 122–3
SAW project 57
school self-evaluation 183–4
   standards 183
school-level planning 126, 132
   policy 130–2
      document outline 131–2

Index

science curriculum
   long-term 126–9
   medium-term 129–30
science curricula in the UK 166, 176
   England 166–7
     level descriptions 167
     review of primary curriculum 168–9
   Northern Ireland 169
     The World Around Us 169–71
   Scotland 172–3
   Wales 174
     Foundation Phase 174–5
     Key Stage 2 (KS2) 175
     skill-focused curriculum 175–6
Science Learning Centres (SLCs) 144, 157, 158
science subject leader 133, 139
   changing models 137–8
   importance 133–4
     performing the role 135–7
     analysing information and making judgements 136
     engaging wider school community 137
     establishing learning community 136
     good practice 136
     monitoring 136
     motivating colleagues 137
     setting priorities 136
     tracking pupil progress 136
   responsibilities 134–5
   strengthening leadership 139
scientific literacy 3
scientific skills, Early Years development 26–8
scientific thinking 4, 29–30
Scotland
   curriculum 172–3
   national assessment 188–9
   Scottish Survey of Achievement (SSA) 188
self-image, positive 48
self-motivation 48
self-regulated learners 18
Smart Science 57
social attitudes 30
social factors in science education 150
social intelligence 48
Sphere Science 162
SPLATS 162
Standards Files 123
STEMNET ambassadors 160
success criteria 88
   communicating 89–90
Sustainable Schools Framework 115

Teachers TV 63
teaching assistants 157–8
tenacity 48
theory of mind (ToM) 20
thinking skills 22
thinking tools 22
thinking, critical 48
timing learning 49
topic approaches 56
   integrated 57
   personalised 57–8
Training and Development Agency for Schools (TDA) 178
transfer points 149, 155–6
   problems 150
   early learning to infant class 151
   infant to junior classes 152–3
     aspects of progression 152
   primary to secondary school 153
     jointly planned teaching projects 154–5
     meetings and open days 154
     sharing practice 155
   transitions and transfers in science 149–50

urban myths 108

value of science knowledge 2–3
variable handling 27
Virtual Learning Environment (VLE) 63
visas to mark achievements 155
vocabulary 48

Wales
   curriculum 174
     Foundation Phase 174–5
     Key Stage 2 (KS2) 175
     skill-focused curriculum 175–6
waste and decay 116–17
'wow' events 79–80

zone of proximal development 12